The International Boundaries of Nigeria

IBADAN HISTORY SERIES
Editor K. O. Dike Ph.D.

Other titles will follow

IBADAN HISTORY SERIES

The International Boundaries of Nigeria 1885-1960

The Framework of an Emergent African Nation

J. C. Anene
Lately Professor of History in the University, Nsukka

NEW YORK

THE HUMANITIES PRESS

*First published
in the United States of America 1970
by Humanities Press Inc.
303 Park Avenue South
New York, N.Y. 10010*

Library of Congress Catalog Card No. 67–16972

Printed in Great Britain

Acknowledgements

We are indebted to the following for permission to reproduce
copyright material:
The Clarendon Press, Oxford, for material from *Southern
Nigeria*, Vol. IV, by P. A. Talbot, and the Proprietors of The
Daily Times of Nigeria Ltd. for material from *The Daily
Times*, 6 February 1959.

Abbreviations

Calprof.	Calabar Province.
C.M.S.	Church Missionary Society.
C.O.	Colonial Office (London).
Conf.	Confidential.
C.S.O.	Chief Secretary's Office (Lagos).
D.D.F.	Documents Diplomatiques Français.
F.O.	Foreign Office (London).
F.O.C.P.	Foreign Office Confidential Print.
J.H.S.N.	Journal of the Historical Society of Nigeria.
P.R.O.	Public Record Office (London).
Parl. Pap.	Parliamentary Papers.
R.G.S.	Royal Geographical Society (Journal and Proceedings).
R.N.C.	Royal Niger Company.
W.O.	War Office (London).

To Obiajulu, Nnonyem and Chuma

Publishers' note

Events in Nigeria, the difficulty and, later, impossibility of communicating with the author, even before the news of his untimely death, or with the General Editor of the Series, have delayed the publication of this work. We have brought it to completion in the belief that Professor Anene would have made no substantial alterations after his own revisions to the original thesis, and in the hope that we have faithfully reflected his intentions in matters of detail. We are indebted to his former colleagues at Ibadan for advice and assistance, in particular to Professor J. F. A. Ajayi, who has contributed the memorial notice which follows.

Professor J. C. Anene: a tribute

The publication of this his most important work provides an opportunity for us in the History Department at Ibadan to pay tribute to the memory of Joseph Christopher Okwudi Anene as a colleague and former Head of the Department. He was essentially an individualist, considerate and charitable, generally reserved but warm-hearted to those close to him, strangely innocent and non-combative in a highly competitive society. At the age of forty-seven he was hurried to the grave by a fragile constitution that could not sustain the anxieties and disillusionments of the current conflicts in Nigeria.

Joe Anene was born at Onitsha in 1921 and educated at Roman Catholic Schools there. Having shown great promise, he became a teacher at his *alma mater*, Christ the King College, and it seemed as if his future career lay in close relationship with the Roman Catholic Church. However, he began to study for the External degree in History of the University of London and by 1948 when a local trader was persuaded to sponsor him to the University College of Cork, he was already far advanced in his studies. Within a year at Cork, having passed the B.A. of London in the Upper Division of the Second Class he decided to move to London. Gradually, the dogmas and formalities of religion lost their hold on him, but the humanism of his early Catholic upbringing always remained an unmistakable part of his character.

He did postgraduate work in London from 1949 to 1952 when he was awarded the M.A. for a thesis on 'The Establishment of British Rule in Southern Nigeria 1885–1906'. Following a Diploma in Education, he went to teach at the Ibadan branch of the Nigerian College of Arts, Science and Technology from 1954 to 1956 before moving to the University of Ibadan. His basic training was in Imperial history and for most of his teaching career he taught courses in British Colonial History and the Growth of the British Commonwealth which, under the scheme of special relationship with London, constituted a third of the History Honours Courses at Ibadan until 1962. The way in which, in his later research, he gradually made

ix

the transition from Imperial to African history is a significant part of the history of historiography in West Africa. This is best illustrated by the M.A. thesis of 1952 which in 1966 became the book *Southern Nigeria in Transition 1885–1906*, essentially a history of the peoples of South Eastern Nigeria, following on Dr. K. O. Dike's *Trade and Politics in the Niger Delta*. His work in the Eastern Nigerian Research Scheme focussing attention on the traditional history of Nri and a biography of Jaja of Opobo remain uncompleted.

This work on the *International Boundaries of Nigeria*, based on his Ph.D. thesis approved by London in 1960, shows essential characteristics of the transition he had made as well as his scholarship at its best. He is no longer concerned only with the foreign acts of partition, but with the impact of colonial boundaries on the peoples in whose history the acts of partition were a major intervention. This necessitated a multi-disciplinary inquiry into the ethnic situation at the time the boundaries were made, the history of the different peoples, particularly the almost untouched question of the history of political and economic inter-group relationships, the knowledge of these available to the treaty makers, and the consequences of their decisions. It is to be hoped that the political and historical problems highlighted by this pioneering and original study will receive further attention from scholars.

Joe Anene's contribution to historical scholarship went beyond his own research and publications. He was a stimulating and methodical teacher who meticulously revised his notes every year, and is remembered with affection by a wide range of former students. He actively encouraged the better teaching in schools of history in general and African history in particular. Above all, as a senior member and later Head of the Department of History, he was an important architect of the new Ibadan B.A. degree structure and of the postgraduate School in History which has produced so many of Nigeria's teachers of history.

University of Ibadan June 1969   J. F. Ade Ajayi

Bibliography

ARTICLES

1. The Protectorate Government of Southern Nigeria and the Aros, 1900–1902 (*Journal of the Historical Society of Nigeria*, vol 1, 1956, pp. 20–26)

2. The Foundations of British Rule in Southern Nigeria 1885–1891 (*JHSN* vol. 1 No. 4, 1959, pp. 253–262)

3. Jaja of Opobo (*Eminent Nigerians of the Nineteenth Century*, London 1960, pp. 17–25)

4. The Nigeria-West Cameroons Boundary (*JHSN* vol. 2, No. 2, 1961, pp. 186–195)

5. The Nigeria-Dahomey Boundary (*JHSN* vol. 2, No. 4, 1963, pp. 479–485)

6. Towards a National History (*Ibadan* No. 16, 1963, pp. 3–10)

7. The Eclipse of the Borgawa (*JHSN* vol. 3 No. 2, 1965, pp. 211–220)

8. Liaison and Competition between Sea and Land Routes in International Trade from the 15th Century—The Central Sudan and North Africa (*Les Grandes Voies Maritimes Dans le Monde*, Paris, 1966)

BOOKS

1. *Africa in the Nineteenth and Twentieth Centuries* (Edited with G. N. Brown) (Nelson and Ibadan University Press, 1965) to which he also contributed four chapters.

2. *Southern Nigeria in Transition* (Cambridge University Press, 1966)

3. *The International Boundaries of Nigeria* (Longman, 1969)

General Editor's Note

THIS book breaks new ground on the issue of African international boundaries. There are indeed numerous references to colonial boundaries in existing works on the European partition of Africa, but these references have invariably tended to ignore the realities of the conditions which existed before the Partition of Africa. The author has avoided this one-sided treatment of an increasingly important and explosive subject. The result is an interesting study of European diplomacy against the background of indigenous African political organization and activities, with emphasis on the African side of the story. In other words the diplomacy of the boundary arrangements of the European Powers are analyzed in a predominantly African context. The book makes an important contribution to African history and to an understanding of the diplomacy of European imperialism in the period under review.

This book has come at a time when the international agreements of the era of the 'Scramble for Africa' are becoming a source of conflict among emergent African states, themselves, ironically, the creation of these boundaries. As this study has attempted to show, historical research may enable African statesmen to borrow a leaf from their pre-colonial ancestors, whose attitude to 'international' frontiers between one ethnic group and the other was much less emotional, much less rigid and much more pragmatic than that which many African leaders are adopting today. After all, as Professor Anene has contended, 'international' boundaries were for our ancestors not a barrier to movement of peoples and cultural diffusion. A survey of the European boundary arrangements for the African continent, along the lines essayed by this book, would be of tremendous aid to statesmen and persuade them to adopt a more objective and 'pan-Africanist' attitude to their frontier problems.

K. O. DIKE

Ibadan, 1966

Preface

It will probably come as a shock to the reading public to be confronted with what seems to amount to a defence of the European-imposed colonial boundaries. It should not however take the reader long to discover that all this book seeks to do is to examine objectively the validity of the fashionable and generalized claims that the international boundary arrangements for Nigeria were 'mortally injurious' to the pre-existing political order. The early maps indicating the progress of the European partition of the Guinea Coast and the Niger Sudan are full of blanks and short straight lines suggestive of precipitate and arbitrary boundary decisions. These straight lines do not tell the whole story. The advance made in recent years in African studies and historiography shows conclusively that African societies were not the amorphous mass which academic prejudice hitherto adjudged them. African ethnic and political groups were, within the limits of their environment, making their own history. Being dynamic societies, they were subject to internal and external upheavals, with the consequent periodic expansion and contraction of the territorial framework within which they were organized.

With the transformation of Africa from an imperialist preserve of Europe into independent states, emotive phrases in denunciation of the existing international boundaries are not only unhistorical but are indeed dangerous. It is for this reason that I came to the conclusion that a useful purpose may be served in undertaking a historically objective study of the evolution of Nigeria's international boundaries. One hears only too often unqualified assertions that the international boundaries disrupted the Yoruba empire, the Efik empire, the Fulani empire and so forth. These assertions are made without the slightest reference to the political fortunes of these indigenous states in the period immediately antecedent to the boundary negotiations.

The study falls into two parts. First, the boundary zones and their people are examined in order to discover the character of ethnic distribution and the posture of local politics. This investigation naturally throws abundant light on the fluctuations of indigenous frontiers brought about by the pressures of war and migration. This aspect of the study is therefore primarily a study in African history. The remarkable state systems evolved by Nigerian peoples—for instance, the Yoruba, the Borgawa, the Kanuri and others—are examined fully. Decentralized societies which dominated the Cross River basin and the central highlands of Adamawa are not left out. The political activities of neighbouring indigenous states—for instance, Dahomey, Maradi and Zinder—also come in for close scrutiny, because the boundary decisions made by Europeans involved these states as much as they did the states within Nigeria. Second, against the background of the indigenous political order, the European boundary negotiations are traced with a view to assessing the extent to which extraneous considerations rather than the special circumstances of the indigenous frontiers influenced the outcome of the boundary negotiations. It seems to me that only by a synthesis of the two parts of the study can a rational basis be provided for revisions of the international boundaries, if revisions should become necessary.

There are inevitably conditions of fluidity along most of the boundary zones of Nigeria and her neighbours, which are potential sources of boundary disputes. As is well known, several boundary disputes have broken out between African states and, so far, nobody has put forward the criteria which may afford the best guide to a settlement of an 'unhappy legacy of colonialism'. It is therefore hoped that this study of the evolution of Nigeria's boundaries will be followed by similar studies with regard to other African states.

The book concludes with a brief reference to the hopes of Pan-Africanists. The emergence of the Organization of African Unity is a partial realization of these hopes. Yet, in spite of this happy development, it is evident that the contemporary African scene displays two conflicting tendencies: (a) balkanization and (b) federation or union. All sane Africans certainly wish all good luck to the latter tendency. But if the former should prevail, Africa may well enter a phase of frontier wars, primarily because the boundaries have acquired a sanctity alien to African traditional frontiers.

The material which forms the basis for this book comes primarily from three sources. The documentary material on the diplomatic negotiations can be found in its most accessible form in the British Foreign Office Confidential Prints and their French and German counterparts, Documents Diplomatiques Français and Die Grosse Politik. Secondary sources deal with African ethnography and general accounts of the European partition of the region involved. It has also been found indispensable to use oral traditions, partly recorded and partly gathered during field work. Interviews held with representative groups in the boundary zones throw abundant light on the prevailing sentiments in regard to the functioning of the international boundaries.

My thanks are due to Dr K. O. Dike, who, in spite of his burdensome duties, found time to direct my Ph.D. research. Professors G. S. Graham and A. F. C. Ryder, Drs I. M. Cumpston, J. E. Flint and E. A. Ayandele helped enormously with suggestions during my research work. Messrs J. Ramsaran and W. Stevenson undertook the task of a final scrutiny of the manuscript and made useful literary corrections. I should like lastly to express my appreciation of the generous assistance given me by the officers and attendants of the British Foreign Office Research Library, the Colonial Office Library, the Public Record Office, the University of Ibadan Library, and the National Archives of Nigeria.

J. C. ANENE

Nsukka, Nigeria

Contents

Contents

List of Maps

I

Introduction

THE African territories which have attained independence and national sovereignty cannot, in a strict sense, be regarded as national states; they do not embrace one people with a common language, a common past, and a common culture; they are, indeed, the arbitrary creations of alien diplomats. The manner in which European nations descended on Africa during the closing years of the nineteenth century in their scramble for territory was bound to leave a heritage of artificially contrived borderlines which now demarcate the emergent African states. Within each state there is a multitude of ethnic and linguistic groups, some of which are separated from their kith and kin by the international boundaries. In some of these states there is no greater unity among the component groups than that deriving from the common experience of alien rule. African leaders are fully aware of this disability, and it is reasonable to assume that they will give priority to the task of preserving and consolidating what unity there already exists within the individual states, talks of pan-African unity notwithstanding. The use of a common, if alien, language by the educated sections of the community, the improvement of facilities for travel and communication, and the determination of the diverse groups to stick together, are all serving to transform the new African states into nations. The process of coherence is only just beginning. Yet, this very process of national consolidation will increasingly outrage communities which the boundaries have sundered. Herein lies a cruel dilemma.

I

Reflecting on the emergence of many new sovereign states in contemporary Africa, Basil Davidson observed:

> Their history begins anew. They reappear today in the sad evening of the world of nation-states; yet their own tradition, one may note, was seldom one of narrow nationality. Their genius was for integration—integration by conquest as the times prescribed, but also by an ever fruitful mingling and migration. They were never patient of exclusive frontiers. . . . Nineteenth-century imperialism cut across boundaries and peoples and left, for a later Africa, the problem of redrawing frontiers on a rational plan. As independence widens across these coming years, will this plan stop short with the making of nation-states, aping European example? . . . It remains to be seen.[1]

The contemporary African scene does not leave room for optimism and complacency. People who had assumed that, in view of the arbitrariness of the boundaries, the preservation of the frontiers would arouse no patriotism have been proved wrong. Morocco and Algeria resorted to war in order to maintain the integrity of the boundaries which national honour appeared to demand. In many other African areas there is an uneasy stirring of irredentist claims kept alive by the clamour of groups whose traditional frontiers have apparently been outraged by the international boundaries. Somalia, for instance, makes territorial claims against Ethiopia and Kenya. Togo, the home of the Ewe groups, insists that Ghana should return to her the portion of Ewe country incorporated into Ghana. There are therefore many potential sources of trouble arising from dissatisfaction with the international boundaries.[2]

It is perhaps necessary to observe that all political boundaries are artificial because they are demarcations by man. The accidents of history, the vagaries of geography and the exigencies of economics have all played a part in determining even European boundaries. The special circumstances which operated in Africa make her international boundaries doubly

---

[1] Davidson, *Old Africa Rediscovered*, 1959, pp. 267–8.
[2] See *Morning Post* (Lagos), 4 May 1963 and *Daily Times* (Lagos), 25 January 1962.

artificial in the sense that they are not, like European boundaries, 'the visible expression of the age-long efforts of [the
indigenous] peoples to achieve political adjustment between
themselves and the physical conditions in which they live.'[1] In
the successive phases of the European partitioning of Africa,
the lines demarcating spheres of interest were often haphazard
and precipitately arranged. The European agents and diplomats were primarily interested in grabbing as much African
territory as possible, and were not unduly concerned about the
consequences of disrupting ethnic groups and undermining the
indigenous political order. This criticism obviously represents
only a very generalized picture of the attitude of the European
agents involved in the drawing of Africa's boundaries.

The manner in which these boundaries were made was often
a subject for after-dinner jokes among European statesmen. An
example may be quoted from a speech made by the British
Prime Minister, Lord Salisbury, at a Mansion House dinner,
after the signing of the Anglo-French Convention of 1890 which
foreshadowed the international boundaries between Nigeria,
Dahomey, the Niger and the Chad Republics. In what was
supposed to be a humorous reference to the boundary mentioned here, Lord Salisbury observed that

> We have been engaged in drawing lines upon maps where no
> white man's foot ever trod; we have been giving away mountains
> and rivers and lakes to each other, only hindered by the small
> impediment that we never knew exactly where the mountains
> and rivers and lakes were.

Another example is provided by a former Commissioner and
Consul-General who played an active part in the drawing
of the boundary between Nigeria and what is today Western
Cameroun. He had this to say in a speech to the Royal Empire
Society:

> In those days we just took a blue pencil and a rule, and we put it
> down at Old Calabar, and drew that blue line to Yola . . . I

---

[1] East and Moodie, *The Changing World*, 1956, pp. 54–5; also Boggs,
International Boundaries, 1940, p. 25.

recollect thinking when I was sitting having an audience with the Emir [of Yola], surrounded by his tribe, that it was a very good thing that he did not know that I, with a blue pencil, had drawn a line through his territory.[1]

Serious writers on African affairs have added their own strictures on the manner in which African boundaries were made by European soldiers and diplomats. Two examples will suffice to illustrate the general condemnation to which the reckless drawing of African boundaries has been subjected. Oliver asserts that

> The imagination of statesmen and diplomats were still bounded by concepts of 'coast' and 'sphere' and 'hinterland', which tapered towards the centre into the vagueness of ignorance. . . .[2]

The Hilton Young Commission on Closer Union in Eastern and Central Africa came to the conclusion that

> [The boundaries separating the territories] are the effect of historical accident and not of any reasoned plan. They have grown up piecemeal as a result of the labours of the early travellers, who wandered at large, and of international diplomacy in search of rough-and-ready compromises . . . and with little knowledge of geographical conditions and less of ethnographical.[3]

It is of course so much easier to condemn the boundaries than to devise a basis for remedying their inadequacies.

Boundary disputes in Europe are said 'to arise in many instances because too much history is remembered by both parties concerned.'[4] Too much true history is certainly safer than fictitious history based on generalizations or on popular traditions of conquest, greatness and unity in the past which had ceased to have political significance long before the Euro-

---

[1] *The Geographical Journal*, vol. xxviii, Proceedings, 9 March 1914.
[2] Oliver, *Sir Harry Johnston and the Scramble for Africa*, 1957, pp. 99–100.
[3] Report of the Commission on Closer Union in Eastern and Central Africa, 1929 (Cmd. 3234). See p. 298.
[4] Boggs, op. cit., p. 17.

4

peans appeared on the African scene. It is extremely dangerous to declare glibly that the international boundaries imposed on Africa by aliens were little adapted to indigenous historical antecedents. What were these antecedents? A few questions ought to be considered objectively in preference to making vague and over-simplified generalizations about the boundaries, especially since boundary disputes are already beginning to bedevil relations between some African states. In the first place we cannot talk of discrepancies between the international boundaries and traditional frontiers without first examining the character of the indigenous frontiers which the international boundaries are assumed to have outraged. In the second place, the ethnic and other groups affected by the imposed boundaries were not indeed living in a political vacuum. Therefore, what is the relevance of the assumption that African tribes and groups traditionally enjoyed coherence, only to find themselves and the territories disrupted by the colonial boundaries?

Between most African traditional communities boundaries, as lines separating states, did not exist. There were frontiers in the form of zones of varying width. Three types of frontier can be identified in Africa during the nineteenth century. The first is best described as a frontier of contact. This existed in situations where distinct cultural and political groups lived and operated side by side. Politically active African groups were likely to have this type of frontier. The Yoruba states and Dahomey, in West Africa, Buganda and her neighbours, in East Africa, afford excellent examples. The second type of traditional frontier was the frontier of separation. Here communities were separated by a buffer zone over which neither side claimed or exercised any authority. Unhealthy forests and deserts usually provided the frontiers of separation found in Africa. The states of the Central Sudan, including Bornu, Maradi, Air and the Fulani empire had frontiers of separation. The third type of traditional frontier can be identified in regions of considerable overlapping of diverse groups, where indeed it is easy to talk more intelligibly in terms of enclaves rather than of frontiers. When too we consider the migratory tendencies of the Masai, the Tuareg and similar nomadic

5

groups, the idea of any type of frontier between these groups and their neighbours seems inconceivable. Moreover the types of frontier described above were not static, and no assessment of the discrepancies between the international boundaries and indigenous frontiers should leave out of account the fluctuations which indigenous frontiers underwent in the period immediately antecedent to the imposition of the European-made boundaries. Aggressive Dahomey and Buganda invaded their neighbours and attempted to extend their political boundaries during the nineteenth century. Where then lay the indigenous frontier when Dahomey and Buganda were annexing territory which traditionally was not their own?

An analysis of African political systems is also indispensable to an objective study of the precise extent to which the international boundaries disrupted the indigenous groups. The problem here is how to define a homogeneous African group. The usual reference to collective terms like 'tribe', 'clan' and so forth does not solve the problem. The term 'tribe' is not necessarily equivalent to the European concept of state which postulates an in-group sentiment, a shared political tradition, possibly a common language and the assumption of an ascertainable territorial framework. The idea of a tribe as an isolated and closed group is certainly a myth for many parts of Africa. There were many instances of overlapping and inter-locking of diverse tribes. The migration of segments of one tribe and their mingling with or absorption by other ethnic groups produced considerable complexity. New communities and new languages were often the result.

In the study of African communities the tendency has been to demarcate groups in terms of political organization. Social anthropologists make a two-fold division.[1] There were the communities which had evolved centralized authority and an administrative organization. The others which lacked a comprehensive political structure are described as stateless societies. This kind of classification is arbitrary and in any case it cannot throw much light on the problem of identifying homogeneous African groups. There is of course no doubt that

---

[1] Fortes and Evans-Pritchard, eds., *African Political Systems*, 1940.

politically centralized African communities were more easily recognized by Europeans during the nineteenth century. On the other hand, the existence of a state structure did not necessarily imply ethnic, cultural or linguistic homogeneity. Nor too did the absence of political focus rule out close affinities in respect of culture, religion and language. The Fulani imperial framework which lay astride the central Sudan included within its boundaries peoples as diverse as the Hausa, the Songhay, the Yoruba and innumerable 'pagan' groups. On the other hand, the Ibo of West Africa and the Kikuyu of East Africa evolved no visible comprehensive political organization and no central administration, yet they were each a single community territorially unbroken. They possessed a common culture and a feeling of exclusiveness.

Group demarcation is therefore an extremely complex exercise. There were many African groups organized in a manner that approximated to the European concept of a state. There were, too, many areas where a group must be defined in terms of consciousness of unity and interdependence, and not in terms of submission to a central authority. Even then, there were many parts of Africa where these generalized criteria of group demarcation collapse, and the human pattern recalls the following description:

> Tribes roll one upon another like the waves of the sea, and these human currents intermingle to form fresh combinations, the characteristics of whose various elements are barely discernible.[1]

Where it is possible to identify centrally organized states or linguistically homogeneous communities, it still has to be borne in mind that during the nineteenth century there were hardly any neighbouring groups which did not indulge in large scale or small scale warfare.

Wars of conquest were important in Africa, as elsewhere. The result of a successful war was to establish one people as conquerors over others, who were reduced to the status of subjects and were wholly or partly incorporated into the

---

[1] Orr, *The Making of Nigeria*, 1911, p. 67.

political and maybe, too, the cultural complex or framework of the conquering group. Sometimes there were wars of conquest which were not followed by attempts at assimilating the conquered groups. The relations between the Masai and their East African neighbours during the nineteenth century exemplify the latter situation.[1] The overriding passion of Masai young men was warfare. The region between Lake Victoria and the sea was the Masai domain in which they raided in all directions. These activities were motivated by a desire to capture other people's cattle, but were never directed to the conquest of territory or subjects. Masai enemies withdrew, when they could, into highland or forest shelter, to reappear when the Masai were gone. What constituted Matai country at any given time depended on the whereabouts of Masai warriors. In West Africa, Dahomian armies periodically invaded outlying Yoruba states for slaves and not for permanent occupation.

Apart from the many wars which tended to alter traditional frontiers in Africa as well as the indigenous political landscape, there were also revolutionary movements of almost continental dimensions. The effects of the Nfecane—a movement which began in Natal in 1820 and engulfed the area stretching from Natal to the Central African lakes—cannot be ignored. In terms of conquest and the disruption of tribes, the movement certainly reduces to absurdity any view of Africa during the nineteenth century as a continent neatly demarcated by distinct tribes. The same observation can be made in respect of the effects of the revolutionary jihads inaugurated by Fulani clerics in many parts of West Africa during the nineteenth century.[2] It should be obvious then, that Africa did not present a tidily uniform political, linguistic and cultural pattern. It was if anything a continent of constantly changing variety, and it is therefore useless and misleading to generalize when one is discussing the effects of the international boundaries on African frontiers and communities.

The complexities of African traditional frontiers and human

---

[1] Oliver and Mathew, eds., *History of East Africa*, vol. i, 1963, pp. 301–2.
[2] Trimingham, *A History of Islam in West Africa*, 1962, pp. 165–207.

patterns have been emphasized in order to underline the argument that each boundary zone should be separately subjected to close scrutiny in any study which attempts to assess the discrepancies between indigenous frontiers and the international boundaries, and the effects of the latter on what Professor Westermann called 'the backbone of the indigenous political order'. The present study is therefore confined to the boundaries which today separate Nigeria from her neighbours. In other words, when African boundaries are described as being so little adapted to indigenous historical antecedents, with what degree of historical objectivity can this criticism be applied to the international boundaries of Nigeria? And if there are indeed traditionally homogeneous groups which the boundaries disrupted, is there a basis for a rational revision of the boundaries? The first task must be an attempt to reconstruct ethno-political conditions prevailing in the boundary zones up to the period immediately antecedent to the drawing of the international boundaries. The second task involves a scrutiny of the diplomatic negotiations out of which the boundaries emerged, with a view to ascertaining the extent to which the peculiarities of the local political conditions at the end of the nineteenth century influenced the decisions of the boundary negotiators.

Nigeria, as a modern politico-territorial unit, emerged in stages. So too did the international boundaries which demarcate her territory. The ethnic, linguistic and political complexity of her peoples is hardly a matter for argument. The Hon. W. G. A. Ormsby-Gore rightly observed that

> The peoples inhabiting this vast tract of territory are of many and varied races with many different systems of government, from the village communities of the pagan tribes to the highly-organized States.[1]

This picture of heterogeneity may be briefly elaborated. Along the Nigerian coast are to be found diverse Ewe, Yoruba, Edo, Ijaw and Ibibio groups. These had made their way to the coast and established city-states which figured prominently in the

---

[1] *Report on a Visit to West Africa*, Cmd. 2744, 1926.

history of that region for many centuries. In the hinterland, east of the Niger River, there are the Ibo, the Ibibio, the Ekoi and many others living in independent, unconsolidated and usually small groups, subject to no central authority. To the west of the Niger are found large Edo and Yoruba-speaking groups which had successfully evolved state systems which remained more or less effective to the end of the nineteenth century. The northern region of Nigeria is the home of diverse peoples including the Hausa, the Fulani, the Nupe and innumerable 'pagan' groups. The religious upheaval precipitated by Othman dan Fodio, however, had culminated in the welding together of many of the last-mentioned groups. In addition there were other peoples grouped in vague but different political entities. Examples of these are to be found in the northern region of Nigeria. It is therefore hardly surprising that the claim has been made that the very name 'Nigeria' is the invention of Lady Lugard's imagination.[1]

A rough classification of the indigenous political systems prevailing in the boundary zones suggests four types. Foremost in importance and size was the Fulani empire of the central Sudan traversed by two sections of the international boundary. The empire was a state of a broadly feudal type, in which the provinces under Emirs enjoyed considerable autonomy, and revolted from time to time against the central powers of Sokoto and Gwandu. The Islamic religion did, however, provide an ideological substructure which tended to reinforce the secular authority of the Sarkin Musulmi, the leader of the faithful. In the zone of the western boundary, the Yoruba and the Borgawa had evolved two different state systems. The Yoruba states were united under Oyo hegemony into a loose empire which began to disintegrate during the middle years of the nineteenth century. The Borgawa state system contained within itself elements of political instability and incoherence. Incursions from outside substantially added to the confusion which progressively engulfed the Yoruba and the Borgawa state systems.[2] The third category of indigenous political organization would

---

[1] *The Times* (London), 8 January 1897.
[2] Dowd, *The Negro Races*, 1907, pp. 198–303.

conveniently cover the region of the first section of the eastern boundary and also the coast. The groups which occupied this region lacked the cohesiveness which perhaps centralized authority could alone provide. Nowhere had political organization gone beyond the bounds of the town or the village, and political authority was in the hands either of a trading aristocracy (as along the coast) or of village elders and rain-maker chiefs. Lastly, to the north-east of Nigeria, was the shadow of the Bornu empire. There certainly had been an effective Bornu empire, but the situation prevailing in the nineteenth century has quite rightly been described as follows:

> [The princes] lived on the memories of ancient glories, blinded by the flattery of courtiers, absorbed in state ceremonial and the infinite quarrels of Kaigamas, Mestremas, Chiromas, Galadimas, of generals without armies and governors without provinces.[1]

None of the categories of political organization described above was without difficulties during the nineteenth century. The Fulani empire had to face the increasingly energetic efforts of insubordinate Habe rulers from the north, north-west and west to recapture the land of their fathers. The Yoruba states were fighting one another, and their peripheral areas were exposed to Dahomian militarism. The Borgawa states were at no time politically and linguistically united. The uncoordinated groups of Eastern Nigeria lent themselves to the harsh description of 'a mere sterile and stagnating conglomeration of humanity'. As for the trading 'republics' and 'kingdoms' of the Nigerian coast, the Europeans did not disguise their contempt for them. If the views of one of these Europeans are anything to go by, then the question of preserving the coast states did not arise.

> The disappearance of their [the rulers'] barbaric sway is hardly a fit subject for even sentimental regrets. Most of them would have sold the kingdoms and their subjects for a few bottles of bad gin, and have thrown their own souls in to clinch the bargain.[2]

---

[1] Urvoy, *Histoire de l'Empire du Bornou*, 1949, p. 86.
[2] Tilby, *Britain in the Tropics (1527–1910)*, 1912. See footnote p. 174.

The political upheavals and wars which chequered the history of the indigenous empires and states undoubtedly left their frontiers in a state of fluctuation, and it was bound to be extremely difficult during the nineteenth century to demarcate a precise political community. In the areas where there were segmented communities and where probably no dramatic wars of conquest occurred, the extreme intermingling of splinter groups created intractable problems in the matter of demarcating a homogeneous community. No study of the effects of the international boundaries on the local inhabitants should ignore the historically objective posture of affairs outlined here.

In view of what has been said about the haphazardness of African boundary making at the beginning of this chapter, it may seem preposterous to observe that no one who goes through the documentary material of the boundary negotiations for Nigeria will fail to be impressed by the extent to which data on treaties with native rulers including the extensiveness of their states figured in the negotiations. The data available were not necessarily accurate, full or decisive. Nevertheless, it should be pointed out that the diplomatic agreements based on longitudes and latitudes were for the most part provisional, and Delimitation Commissioners were in some cases authorized by their governments to ascertain on the spot the exact disposition of indigenous 'boundaries' and recommend rectifications of the provisional lines. It was not for nothing that Sir George Goldie, the 'founder' of Nigeria, warned the British negotiators of the boundaries of Nigeria not to

> trust too implicitly to meridians of longitude. They move about in Africa like mountains. . . . An error of a degree or even half a degree might otherwise cost England Kuka, and therefore all Bornu.[1]

Dame Margery Perham certainly exaggerates the situation when she writes with reference to the negotiations for one of the sections of the boundary that the procedure was

---

[1] F.O.C.P. Africa no. 35, Confidential 6471, Royal Niger Company to F.O., 8 September 1893.

a game in which the players on each side changed the rules to suit their position at any given time in the field and, as there was no umpire, confusion and bad temper, with the possibility of something worse, were the inevitable results.[1]

Two examples will suffice to show that, in the negotiations for practically all sections of the boundaries of Nigeria, the existence of native states and the inclusiveness of their territorial dominion afforded a sort of 'umpire', though not necessarily always an effective one. The famous Anglo-French Convention of 1890 which foreshadowed the northern boundary of Nigeria began by producing a straight line—the Say–Barrua Line. Yet, Article II of the same Convention took cognizance of the Fulani empire when it declared that the Say–Barrua line should be drawn 'in such a manner as to comprise in the sphere of action of the Niger Company all that fairly belongs to the kingdom of Sokoto'.[2] With regard to the second section of the western boundary, the negotiations for which produced a dangerous crisis in Anglo-French relations, the controversy for a long time centred on the extent and nature of the 'kingdom' of Borgu. The British view was that 'in treating with a suzerain, the rights conferred . . . extended to the whole of the territory under his dominion'.[3] The principle enunciated here was not disputed by France, but the Anglo-French negotiations almost broke down when each side sought its own data on the character of indigenous political structure, or interpreted available data in a manner that suited its overall interests. At that stage of the negotiations the scathing comment by Perham, already quoted, might seem justified.

To insist on the thesis that the peculiarities of indigenous political conditions played a part not generally acknowledged in the evolution of Nigeria's international boundaries is not to ignore the indisputable fact that colonial questions were not completely isolated from the exigencies of general European

---

[1] Perham, *Lugard, Part I: The Years of Adventure 1858–1898*, 1956, p. 627.
[2] Hertslet, *The Map of Africa by Treaty*, vol. ii, no. 229.
[3] F.O.C.P. Africa 35, Confidential 6837, Inclosure 1 in no. 66, Dufferin to Salisbury, April 1896.

diplomacy. It is also obvious that the first duty of the aliens who argued about Nigerian frontiers was to the honour and interest of their own country. Full and reliable data on local conditions were not always available to the boundary negotiators. How they interpreted what they had, and the consequences, are better judged in our own day than in their own. The diplomats in London, Paris and Berlin sought to have before them (a) treaties with native states, (b) the accounts of European travellers, and (c) the personal reports of local European agents or (in colonial parlance) the men on the spot. These sources of information produced their own difficulties.

The treaties considered in this study are examined not from the standpoint of the old question of whether or not they constituted a legitimate basis for the imposition of European authority, but with a view to ascertaining how far they revealed estimates of indigenous frontiers and the often baffling question of the precise relationship of suzerain and vassal. Treaties with native states did all sorts of things. They provided a basis for territorial claims and for demarcations of spheres of influence. The establishment of spheres of influence and African boundary evolution were often parallel activities. To what extent did the treaties accurately describe traditional frontiers and indigenous political relations? Certainly the European agents were interested parties. They were not dispassionate scholars seeking material for genuine research. The documents provide ample evidence that the European treaty-seekers often prompted the descriptions of their frontiers given by the local rulers. Nor were native kings averse to asserting their sovereignty over territory lost in war by their forefathers. A few examples will help to illustrate the manner in which treaties could themselves become a source of confusion in the boundary negotiations. The Sultan of Gwandu, in confirming an old treaty with the Royal Niger Company, claimed, as he was no doubt instigated to do, that 'the country of Gurma [is] included in my dominions—the latter extending to Libtako'.[1] Then the chiefs of Bussa spoke to the Royal Niger Company about 'our country, its dependencies, and tributaries on both

---

[1] Vandeleur, *Campaigning on the Upper Nile and Niger*, 1898, pp. 247–52.

banks of the River Niger and as far back as our dominion extends, in accordance with our laws and customs . . .' In the face of this vagueness, it is little wonder that the French at the conference table not only questioned the validity of the Bussa treaty, but also asserted that they had 'discovered' that Bussa was actually a vassal of another state in Borgu. The British were constrained to agree that 'experience shows that it is not safe to place reliance on the statements of the Suzerain'.[1] The tendency to give fanciful interpretation to the extent of native political frontiers was also indulged in by the European agents themselves. During the Anglo-German negotiations for the second section of the eastern boundary, the German agent, Lieut. von Stettin, produced a 'treaty' with 'the Ruler of Adamawa, whose recognized and uncontested dominions extend as far as N'gaundere and Gaza'. This 'treaty' turned out on translation at the Oriental Seminary of Berlin to be 'chiefly a letter of thanks for the presents given'.[2] Another German agent, Dr Gruner, claimed that his treaty with Gwandu had clearly indicated the extent of the Gwandu empire. The dependencies enumerated by Dr Gruner included Karamama, a place yet to be identified anywhere in West Africa.

The European treaty-makers were often very contemptuous of the status of the chiefs whose 'X' marks they so fanatically collected. This contempt was not of course revealed at the conference table, but helps to explain the ease with which some of the treaties were relegated to the background of the boundary negotiations. For instance, when Lugard set out to find the ruler of the country he probably felt that 'no one could force his way through the unknown [interior] of such a country as Borgu unless he were buoyed up by the sense of nobility and high importance of his mission'. Yet Lugard's personal diary reveals that after he had 'accomplished' his mission his view was that the 'king of all the Bussas' was 'a specially dirty and mean-looking savage seated on a filthy and greasy carpet . . . the

---

[1] F.O.C.P. Africa 35, Confidential 7144. See observations on African Treaties.

[2] *Nord-deutsche Allgemeine Zeitung*, 25 October 1893.

doorways were blocked with gazing crowds of naked girls'. The visits to such and other kings were to Lugard no more than 'abasement before these petty African chieflets'.[1] Captain Decoeur, the French agent, who traversed almost the same ground as Lugard, publicly questioned the accuracy of Lugard's claim to have found the suzerain of Borgu. The king of Nikki was not blind, as Lugard claimed. He, Decoeur, therefore had secured the valid treaty to decide the Anglo-French boundary negotiations. Privately, Decoeur does not seem to have thought much of what he saw. Whatever Nikki was in the past, Decoeur could see only a collection of small and miserable villages. He came to the conclusion that the ruler of Nikki could not conceivably have the comprehensive authority over the whole of Borgu as was being claimed for the prince.[2]

The use of treaties for the interpretation of indigenous frontiers was in some cases abandoned. The statesmen, the boundary negotiators and even the European agents themselves began to accept the view later expressed by Lord Lansdowne that tribal limits were of the most elastic and uncertain description. A tribe belonged to one petty ruler at one moment, and to another petty ruler at another. He therefore concluded that 'we cannot . . . attribute to such boundaries the sanctity of well-established limits'. The same view was echoed in the French newspapers to the effect that the negotiators should have 'no faith in treaties with native chiefs'.[3] Even then the negotiators agreed that their agents should endeavour to obtain the exact limits of the dominions of local kings and those of his vassals. The kings and their vassals should be visited. Finally, 'officers should also endeavour to obtain full information respecting the antecedents of the kings, their families and predecessors, their relations with neighbouring states, and the history of their countries . . .'.[4] All this admonition came

---

[1] Perham, op. cit., quoted p. 501. See also p. 540.

[2] *Politique Coloniale*, 17 and 20 August 1895.

[3] Gooch and Temperley, *British Documents on the Origins of the War*, vol. i, no. 397, Lansdowne to Cambon, 5 March 1904. See also *Le Figaro*, 12 April 1898: Conversation between M. Ballot and M. Jean Hess.

[4] F.O.C.P. Confidential 7144, see Observations by Gosselin and Everett, Inclosure in no. 119 Africa, Monson to Salisbury, 26 March 1898.

very late, and it is extremely doubtful whether 'the men on the spot' would have been willing to lose their country a tract of territory by forwarding objectively assessed data on local political conditions.

When the boundary negotiators were tired of haggling over treaties with the native rulers, they usually turned their attention to the accounts produced by European travellers who claimed to have visited various parts of the country. The travellers may be divided into two categories: those who collected information and recorded personal observations in the interest of ethnographical and geographical knowledge, and those who were directly or indirectly committed to the boundary controversies and therefore tended to interpret their facts backwards. The latter did much to contribute to the confusion which surrounded the boundary disputes. The interested, and therefore unreliable, travellers included Mizon, Gruner, von Stettin, Wallace and Uechtritz, to name but a few. The diplomats in London, Paris and Berlin did not discriminate between the two types of traveller indicated above. It is however not to be assumed that the boundary controversies might have been easier if the diplomats had appealed only to the reasonably honest data collected by men like Barth, Monteil, Zintgraff, Macdonald and Flegel. For instance, Barth and his observations on the conditions of the Central Sudan were to add substantially to the controversy over the effective political limits of the empire of Sokoto. Both sides to the boundary did often on suitable occasions appeal to the same authority. Thus when the British commissioner quoted Barth to show that the northern extension of the Sokoto empire embraced Asben in the Sahara, the French could also refer to paragraphs in which Barth more or less concluded that Sokoto political control over vast areas was nebulous.[1] In any case, when the evidence of Barth would seem to be conclusive, the party to the dispute whom the verdict did not favour would not fail to point out that Barth wrote on the conditions which prevailed between 1851 and 1855. The half century that

---

[1] See Barth, *Travels and Discoveries in North and Central Africa*, 1857; also Monteil, *De Saint-Louis a Tripoli par le Lac Tchad*, 1895.

followed was time enough for revolutionary changes to have completely altered the local political landscape. As a matter of fact, the French produced Monteil's account of 1891 to 'correct' Barth.

A study of the documentary sources reveals also that in negotiations concerning the boundaries of the areas in and near Nigeria where European administration was fairly well established, the local knowledge of the European administrators was sought on the issue of the boundary. Some of these administrators were appointed to sit with the Boundary Commissions in the European capitals. An administrator who possessed the intellectual curiosity of a man like Sir Harry Johnston of the Oil Rivers Protectorate was invariably an indefatigable traveller. There were many who were at best unashamed empire builders and at worst armchair historians and ethnographers. The latter were likely to mislead the Boundary Commissioners by their contributions on local conditions or on the political antecedents of indigenous groups. Lord Salisbury must have had Sir Harry Johnston in mind when, writing to the British Ambassador in Berlin on the impending negotiations with Germany for the first section of the eastern boundary, he observed that

> When the geography of the country and the position of the various tribes are more accurately ascertained, it may be found practicable to settle a fresh [boundary] line in accordance with their requirements.[1]

Johnston in due course forwarded his findings, which accurately confirmed that the region was one of extreme linguistic and ethnic complexity.

Administrators who were either empire builders or armchair historians approached the task of collecting data on local peoples differently. A later Commissioner and Consul-General of the Oil Rivers Protectorate, Sir Ralph Moor, undertook to summarize, for the benefits of the boundary negotiators, the evidence assembled by his predecessors, by missionaries, and

---

[1] F.O.C.P. Confidential 5753, no. 13, Africa, Salisbury to Malet, 25 January 1888.

by himself on the peoples of the boundary zone. His conclusion was quite simple, the evidence of Sir Harry Johnston notwithstanding. The Efik, already included in the British sphere of influence, had an empire which embraced Efik, Ekoi and innumerable other groups of Bantu stock. The inhabitants, claimed Sir Ralph, regarded themselves as under British rule, and many of the towns 'up to a late date, paid tribute to Efik kings and chiefs as subjects'.[1] The German governor of the Cameroons, von Soden, was not slow in collecting his own data which contradicted Sir Ralph's in almost every particular. Another illuminating instance of the unsatisfactory nature of the reports by administrators, for the purposes of the Nigerian boundary negotiations, is seen in the controversy over the first section of the western boundary. In one and the same document, a governor of Lagos said that

> The four corners of [the Oyo empire] are and have been from time immemorial known as Egba, Ketu, Jebu, and Oyo, embracing within its area that inhabited by all Yoruba-speaking peoples . . .,

and that the kingdom of Ketu 'is perfectly independent, and pays tribute to no other Power . . .'.[2] At the time when these claims were being forwarded to London, the governor must have been aware that for at least half a century the political power of Dahomey had absorbed the western portion of the disintegrating empire of Oyo, particularly Ketu. The conflict of claims revealed in the governor's document was not lost on the French who, having conquered Dahomey, forthwith assumed that the area politically dominated by Dahomey belonged to her.

It is not to be expected that the French and the Germans would accept the reliability of data on indigenous groups forwarded by the officials of the Royal Niger Company, the legality of whose political activities they questioned. The officials of this Company were preoccupied with furthering the profit-making potential of the region under their control. The

---

[1] F.O.C.P. Confidential 6837, no. 50, Moor to F.O., 21 December 1895.
[2] Hertslet, op. cit., vol. ii, pp. 647–52.

acquisition of as much useful territory as possible was essential. Thus, when the frontiers of the empire of Gwandu, with which the Company claimed it had a treaty, were under consideration by the Boundary Commission, the officials of the Niger Company maintained, in 1889, that Borgu lay within that empire. Two years later, when Borgu became the centre of another boundary controversy, the same officials of the Niger Company categorically asserted that

> It will be remembered that the latter [the native ruler of Borgu] is a powerful Ruler, who has proved himself more than a match for the Sokoto Empire, so far as the defence of his own territories is concerned.[1]

It is therefore easy to see how useless the information provided by the 'men on the spot' was bound to be to the Boundary Commissioners, especially when the information contained glaring contradictions or when the nationals of the disputing countries produced diametrically opposed data on the structure and political fortunes of the same indigenous peoples.

The nature and the source of the data available to the makers of the boundaries of Nigeria have been briefly discussed to show why, although the nature and extent of indigenous frontiers figured prominently in the negotiations, they could not have had more than marginal influence on the outcome of the boundary negotiations. There was certainly one area—the region south of Lake Chad—in which the Anglo-German Boundary Commission did not bother themselves with the indigenous political or cultural landscape. It may therefore be misleading to give the impression that but for the difficulties which the data on the local peoples presented, the boundary negotiators would have acted as honest men. The documentary sources which support the view that extraneous factors played a decisive role in the evolution of Nigeria's boundaries are indeed substantial. From a study of the negotiations it is not difficult to identify these extraneous factors which tended to neutralize the importance which might have been attached to the preservation of indigenous frontiers as the latter were

---

[1] F.O.C.P. Confidential 6164, R.N.C. to F.O., no. 8, 9 February 1891.

understood by the European negotiators. These factors may be reduced to the following: the mood of the European Powers, the 'hinterland' theory, the theory of 'effective occupation', fiscal considerations. A final and constantly recurring factor was the fact that negotiations for the boundary in one part of Africa invariably sparked off controversy about other areas of conflicting territorial claims. Only a very cursory illustration of these factors is appropriate to this introductory chapter.

The first factor is impressively stated in a memorandum forwarded to the British Foreign Secretary, Lord Rosebery, by the British Ambassador to Paris, Lord Dufferin, even before the controversy over the Borgu boundary had assumed alarming proportions.

> I am afraid that I can only describe the sentiments of French people of all classes towards us as that of unmitigated and bitter dislike. . . . These causes of hatred [colonial conflicts] are envenomed and intensified by the press of Paris. Denunciations of England are therefore pretty sure to command a large and lucrative circulation.[1]

Rosebery's successor, Lord Salisbury, unwittingly contributed to French exasperation by his scathing comments on what the French were to expect from the partition of the central Sudan. For instance, he said in the British Parliament that the Say–Barrua Line of 1890 which safeguarded the empire of Sokoto 'left nothing for the Gallic cock to do but scratch the sand'.[2] The national mood of bellicosity or timidity was often reflected in the attitude of the European leaders to the boundary controversies and the territorial claims they involved. Lord Salisbury might make scoffing comments but he was not prepared to fight the French over what he once described as 'the malodorous African desert'. It required a man of Joseph Chamberlain's calibre, and a measure of insensibility to the sentiments of the French people which Dufferin had written

---

[1] Gooch and Temperley, *British Documents on the Origins of the War*, vol. ii, France 3121, no. 450, Confidential, Dufferin to Rosebery, 3 November 1893.

[2] Hourst, *French Enterprise in Africa* (translated by Bell), 1898, p. 414.

about, to be prepared to confront the French in Borgu with the West African Frontier Force. In the end both Powers preferred to continue the boundary controversy at the conference table rather than on the field of battle. They then invariably sought what they described as a *modus vivendi* which involved a loss neither of face nor of national honour. In the Anglo-German negotiations for the eastern boundary of Nigeria, Bismarck assumed an aggressive front, and the British Foreign Secretary, Granville, was only too happy to initiate what was called the Anglo-German colonial 'honeymoon'. This meant no more than concessions to German claims, the structure of indigenous communities notwithstanding.

With regard to 'the hinterland theory', it must be remembered that European occupation of Africa, north, south, east and west, usually began on the coast. Each European Power was thereafter anxious to secure the hinterland, without the exploitation of which the coast possessions were not profitable. The Berlin West African Conference of 1884–5, which established conditions for the European occupation of the African coast, failed to agree on the criteria for usurping the hinterland. During the boundary negotiations, a European Power could appeal to 'the hinterland theory' when it suited her, although the meaning of this theory was not precisely defined by any of the Powers until the boundary controversies began to get out of hand. Thus, for instance, after the French conquest of Dahomey, the French Foreign Minister, Hanotaux, declared that

> The sacrifices we have made for the war, and the arrangements we shall have to make at its conclusion, will probably force us to insist on more territory in the rear of that territory.[1]

The British Boundary Commissioners not only accepted Hanotaux's proposition but proceeded to formulate a definition of 'hinterland'. According to this definition, any Power was at liberty to acquire new possessions beyond the Treaty Hinterland. They concluded that,

---

[1] Gooch and Temperley, op. cit., vol. ii, no. 450 Confidential, Dufferin to Rosebery, 3 November 1893.

If then we have failed to shut out Togoland and the French Colony of Dahomey from access to the hinterland of the continent, it is certainly not because we were hindered by scruples as to the morality of such a proceeding.[1]

The issue of fiscal considerations was not one that often came into the open. Naturally the parties disputing the boundary liked to pretend that they were safeguarding the well-being of some native ruler, not their own material gain. The British determination to secure the Lower Niger and the hinterland arose out of the apprehension entertained by British traders that the exclusive tariff policy of France would undermine British commercial enterprise. Successive British Governments had held on to the hope that if free trade could be adopted by the Powers of Europe, the hinterland of Africa might indeed be a 'free-for-all', without European spheres of influence and without European-made boundaries.[2] This was however not to be. Thus, in the subsequent negotiations, access to navigable portions of the River Niger became a serious factor. The British were willing to allow the French a place on the Niger, by means of a corridor through Borgu, if only they could be sure the French would liberalize their colonial trade policy. The Germans for their part emphasized 'river systems' in their negotiations for the eastern boundary. They argued that 'river systems' were mutually beneficial, and certainly more important than considerations of ethnology and indigenous frontiers.

The recurring factor already mentioned concerns a situation in which the negotiation for any colonial boundary was often inextricably involved in the general European diplomatic landscape.[3] There is ample evidence, for instance, that throughout the Anglo-French controversy over the structure of Borgu and the extent of the Sokoto Empire, Lord Salisbury was in fact thinking primarily of the security of the British position

---

[1] Ibid., vol. i, France 3410, Monson to Salisbury, Memorandum by the British Commissioners.

[2] Flint, *Sir George Goldie*, 1960, p. 35.

[3] Dugdale, *German Diplomatic Documents, 1871–1914*, 1928, vol. i, pp. 375–82.

in the Nile Valley. Even the aggressive Chamberlain expressed his willingness to make concessions to France on the Niger if France renounced all pretensions to the Nile region. Similarly, the Anglo-German negotiations for the second section of Nigeria's eastern boundary were certainly influenced firstly by Britain's fear of Franco-German collusion, and secondly by a genuine desire for Anglo-German amity in the face of the increasing discomfiture of British policy in the Nile Valley. In the final analysis, no European Power was really prepared to upset the peace of Europe in order to preserve the territorial integrity or the political structure of an African state. No objective study of the 'shortcomings' of the boundary arrangements should ignore either the factors discussed here or the fluidity which characterized indigenous frontiers.

The Atlantic Littoral and Problems of the Hinterland

Students of European activities in West Africa are familiar with the fact that the history of the acquisition of a colony or a protectorate has been the story of the occupation of the coast and a gradual linking up with the interior. The coastline was therefore the foundation of most of the 'states' which emerged during the closing years of the nineteenth century. Nigeria, for instance, came into existence because Britain first secured a continuous stretch of coastline, negotiating with other Powers in order to establish a right to the end-points, or termini, of the sea-frontage, and subsequently engaged in controversies with France and Germany out of which emerged the hinterland boundaries which today define Nigeria. It is therefore necessary to examine the conditions which prevailed on the coast as a background to European action in the hinterland. The establishment of the Atlantic termini decisively determined the points on the coast from which Nigeria's international boundaries originated. Presumably the history of the evolution of the boundaries might have been a different one if Britain had not secured an uninterrupted coastline between two defined points. These points were in fact defined in 1885.

Apart from the coast problem, the control of the Lower Niger and the Benue was destined to affect materially the history of the boundaries of Nigeria. The success achieved by Britain in this respect, thanks largely to the founder and the agents of the Royal Niger Company, guaranteed for Britain a territorially strategic position from which to deal with hinterland boundary problems when they arose. There is abundant evidence to

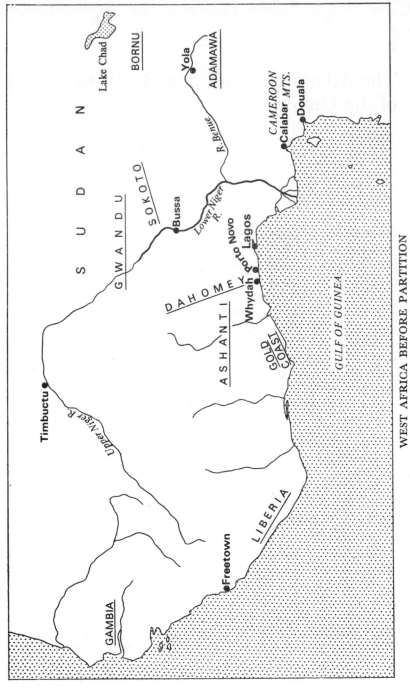

WEST AFRICA BEFORE PARTITION
Prior to 1885

demonstrate that without British exclusive control of the Lower Niger, a compact territory which was to become Nigeria might never have emerged.[1] The British struggle at the Berlin West African Conference 1884–5 for international recognition of the British position on the Niger deserves study. In other respects, too, the conference provided the background to European political and other activities in the hinterland of this portion of West Africa.[2] The nature of the exclusive control of the Niger which Britain managed with great dexterity to secure from her European rivals and the inability of the conference members to lay down generally accepted principles for the partition of the African hinterland were to provoke controversies intimately connected with boundary demarcations.

Looking at the present-day political map of West Africa, with the French-speaking African countries dominating the scene, it is not easy to imagine that between 1807 and 1880 Britain was the only colonial Power exercising almost unquestioned control along the West Coast, from Freetown to the Cameroons. The British Navy was supreme along this section of the Atlantic littoral. Although there were small trading stations and forts belonging to the Dutch, the Danes and others, most of these were in the course of the century either abandoned or sold out by their owners. The measures undertaken by the British government to exterminate the slave trade across the Atlantic had the result of bringing Britain into close relations with many West African coastal peoples and chiefs. At any time between the dates mentioned above Britain could conceivably have acquired a continuous coastline from Freetown to the Cameroons. If there was any interruption along this coastline, it might be at points in what is today Liberia, where American philanthropic societies had decided to land Negroes from the United States, though in any case there was no reason why the British government could not have bought over the precarious 'American' bases. In spite of these possibilities, it was as much as Britain could do to secure in 1885 the

---

[1] Incidentally, the part played by the River Niger in determining the outcome of the demarcations of the hinterland justifies the name which today designates the territory.

[2] Cook, *British Enterprise in Nigeria*, 1943, pp. 132 f.

inclusion of the short coastlines of Sierra Leone and the Gold Coast, and the Nigerian seaboard within her internationally recognized sphere.[1]

The reasons for the remarkable transformation in the British position are too well known to require elaboration here. It is perhaps enough to call attention to the 'apathy' which characterized the attitude of successive British governments before 1885 towards the acquisition of territorial and political responsibilities in West Africa. This apathy, often amounting to antagonism, was accurately reflected in the Report of the Adderley Parliamentary Committee of 1865.[2] For the purposes of the present study, what is important is to ascertain why it was that the boundaries of Nigeria had to begin somewhere near Lagos, in the west, and in the neighbourhood of Rio del Rey, in the east. Then Britain had to secure a continuous stretch of coastline between the two termini in order to have the coast foundation of what became Nigeria. Any two other termini would have produced a different boundary history. The dreams later entertained by Goldie and Johnston for a massive British territory embracing the whole of West Africa was by 1880 a forlorn hope.

Before 1880 the British government did not really anticipate an international scramble for the West African coastline, although the French had apparently innocuously established themselves at one or two points. In 1851 Britain bombarded Lagos, and acquired it ten years later 'to disinfect a disreputable haunt of slavers'. For the same reasons, and also in the interest of peaceful commercial development, British consuls were appointed to advise the rulers of the coast city-states between Lagos and the Cameroons. Even then the British Colonial Secretary, Lord John Russell, appeared to regret the British acquisition of Lagos. Writing to Consul Foote in 1861, he observed that

> It is not without some reluctance that Her Majesty's Government have determined, by the occupation of Lagos, to extend the

---

[1] Oliver, *Sir Harry Johnston and the Scramble for Africa*, London, 1957, pp. 23 and 91.

[2] Parl. Pap., 1865, vol. i, Proceedings on Col. Ord's Report on the Condition of the West African Settlements.

number of British Dependencies on the West Coast . . . the permanent occupation of this important point in the Bight of Benin is indispensable to the complete suppression of the Slave Trade...[1]

From the Lagos vantage point, the most dynamic of the early governors of Lagos, Sir John Glover, attempted to initiate an expansionist policy by offering British protection to 'mushroom' states to the west and north-west of Lagos. The treaties with Appa, Katanu, Ipokia, Addo and so forth were, however, not ratified by the British government, in spite of Glover's allegation that

> I found that the French authorities at Porto Novo were seeking to absorb all the surrounding country to their flag.[2]

The only permanent addition of territory west of Lagos during the period of Glover's administration was Badagri, acquired by cession in 1863. In spite of the self-effacing proceedings described above, Britain did between 1870 and 1876 engage in intermittent negotiations with France for the purpose of ceding Gambia to France as the price for a continuous coastline under British control from Sierra Leone to the Niger. The negotiations fell through because of the British Parliament's 'sentimental attachment' to Gambia.[3] When the imaginative project collapsed, the governor of the Gold Coast pressed in 1879 for a more modest scheme. He argued that taking into account the close proximity of the British possessions of Lagos and the Gold Coast, it seemed only natural that the two colonies and the intervening territory should be amalgamated into a new consular jurisdiction to be exercised by the colonial authorities. All these aspirations were, however, neutralized when the French revived their short-lived protectorate of Porto Novo, a place which, according to a belated lament of the

---

[1] Hertslet, *The Map of Africa by Treaty*, vol. i. See Notes on Lagos, p. 91.

[2] Lady Glover, *Life of Sir John Glover*, 1897, quoted pp. 91–7.

[3] Parl. Pap., 92, C. 6701, Salisbury to the British Ambassador in Paris, 30 March 1892; Hargreaves, *Prelude to the Partition of West Africa*, 1963, pp. 151–65, and 179–95.

British Colonial Office, 'cannot be otherwise than an object of special solicitude to the Government of Lagos'.[1]

The acquisition of a continuous coastline between Lagos and the Gold Coast was also advocated by the British chambers of commerce. For instance, the London Chamber of Commerce passed resolutions which urged the British government to secure an uninterrupted coast between Lagos and the Gold Coast by some exchange of territory with France. The French were however not willing to surrender their hold on Porto Novo. Within two years the position was further complicated by the arrival of the Germans at Togo. The new situation developing between the Gold Coast and Lagos was accurately summarized by the intelligence division of the British War Office as follows:

> Until 1879 the strip of coast belonging to the kingdom of Dahomey formed the only serious obstacle to this scheme [of extending British control of the coast from Lagos to the Gold Coast], and consequently the establishment of the French Protectorate [of Porto Novo] appeared to be especially vexatious. Now we have two French Protectorates, a German Protectorate, and a part of Dahomey to deal with, and it is impossible that we shall be able to clear them all in order to get our continuous coastline. . . .[2]

By 1885 the western boundary of the Nigerian coast had become confined to the neighbourhood of Badagri. The slight extension westward achieved through British negotiations was insignificant, being merely an addition of a part of the derelict state of Appa. The British government of Lagos had in the meantime became involved, largely because of the problem of defining the Lagos limit of the Atlantic littoral, in the tangled politics of Dahomey, Abeokuta, Porto Novo, Ipokia, and a multitude of Egbado 'town' states. The political vicissitudes of these states and their relationship with Britain and France

---

[1] F.O. 27/2417, no. 127, Ussher to Hicks-Beach, 26 July 1879; also C.O. 806/242, C.O. to F.O., 15 June 1885.

[2] C.O. 806/242, W.O. to C.O., 1 July 1887. See Memorandum by the Intelligence Branch on the territorial differences with France in the neighbourhood of Porto Novo.

played a decisive part in the definition of the first section of the western boundary of Nigeria. In 1885 the British Colonial Office observed that 'the present condition of affairs is not only inconvenient but dangerous'.[1] This was a reference to a situation in which British and French agents made claims and counter-claims in regard to treaty relations with the indigenous states and the relationship of the latter with one another. The British proposed tentatively in March 1885 that the Addo River might be mutually accepted as the boundary, because that river was assumed to separate the sphere of Dahomey and her 'sister' states from that of the Yoruba. The suggestion was a futile one because the French were not prepared to accept the British interpretation of the local situation as a basis for negotiations.

As regards the stretch of coastline east of Lagos, Britain had up to 1883 remained complacent. British merchants, however, were very active and fully endorsed the imperialist designs of the local British consul. The latter had, in furtherance of his plans, reported to the British government that 'kings' of Duala, Bell and Akwa had willingly ceded their country to Britain. The plea was in vain. In the same year the consul, Hewett, wrote what he believed was an alarming report to the effect that 'this year a French gunboat went to Bonny with a view to making a treaty'. The British Foreign Office was inundated with protests against the inactivity and spinelessness of the British government. The various British firms trading along the Oil Rivers coast, the chambers of commerce, and the African Association of Liverpool, all wrote profusely on the danger to British interests on the coast east of Lagos.[2] The British Foreign Secretary, Lord Granville, observed with criminal lack of foresight that

> [Great Britain] was indeed well pleased to see that other Powers were ready to undertake the charge of protecting the natives of the continent, and preventing the anarchy and lawlessness which

---

[1] Ibid. C.O. to F.O., 31 March 1885.
[2] Parl. Pap., no. 1, 1885, C. 4279, The African Association to F.O. 1 October 1885. See also F.O. 84/1880—mostly letters of complaint.

must have resulted from the influx of traders of all nations into countries under no recognized form of government.[1]

There were, however, two officials at the British Foreign Office who fully appreciated the advantages of a British controlled and uninterrupted coastline from Lagos to the Cameroons. T. V. Lister and H. P. Anderson, Assistant Under-Secretary and Senior Clerk in the African Department respectively, put pressure on their chief, who was in the end constrained to present for Cabinet approval what came to be called Granville's 'Nigerian policy'. The Foreign Secretary submitted that the time had come for Her Majesty's Government to decide on how best to secure those parts of the West Coast of Africa 'which lie between Capes St Paul and St John, in the Bights of Benin and Biafra, and which comprise the healthy regions around the Cameroons . . .'. Consul Hewett was then instructed to return to the Oil Rivers and unostentatiously conclude the necessary treaties to secure the whole coast.[2] If the British plan had materialized, the coastline of what became Nigeria might have stretched from Lagos to Duala. The Germans had, however, decided to enter the 'colonial game'.

With the diabolical expedition of a genius, the German visiting Consul-General, Dr Nachtigal, anticipated Consul Hewett at Duala. German flags were unfurled not only at Bageida in Togoland but also at King Bell's town in the Cameroons on 14 July 1884. All Hewett could do in the circumstances was to annex a mushroom Baptist missionary settlement at Victoria. Even then the German agent moved up to the east of Victoria and planted the German flag in the town of Bimbia. It is easy to imagine the fury and frustration of the officials of the British Foreign Office, who described the German action as an 'anti-English raid'.[3] Protests flooded the British Foreign Office from all and sundry—the Steamship Company, the Bristol Chamber of Commerce, the African Association, the Congo District Association, the Liverpool,

---

[1] Parl. Pap., no. 2, vol. iv, C. 4284.
[2] F.O. 84/1681, Anderson to Sanderson, 15 January 1884.
[3] F.O. 84/1688, Minute by Lister on Admiralty to F.O., 26 August 1884.

London and Glasgow Chambers of Commerce. These protests spoke of 'blindness, procrastination, and indifference to British interests'. For reasons difficult to appreciate, the British government still hoped to persuade the German government to withdraw from the Cameroons. Duala was in the end lost as the prospective starting point of Nigeria's eastern boundary. There is indeed ample evidence to show that the British government had not intended that the Cameroons should be other than part of Nigeria.

The officials of the British Foreign Office were apparently determined to secure what was left—the coast west of Bimbia and the Cameroon Mountains. Victoria, which had grown up round the Baptist Mission on Ambas Bay after the expulsion of Alfred Saker and his followers from Fernando Po in 1858, might then become the eastern terminus of the Nigerian coast. British plans for the highlands behind Victoria included the following: (i) a sanatorium for British officials in Nigeria, (ii) a convict station and (iii) a colony for Negroes 'who instead of loafing about Canada . . . might here do valuable work in lumber cutting, cacao growing, exporting the fibre and meal of the plantain, and expressing cocoa-nut and palm oil'.[1] Hewett and his assistant, White, set about their work of empire building with great energy. In fact, White, on his own authority commissioned two Polish nationals, Rogozinski and Janikowski, to make treaties for Britain behind the 'Cameroons' coast. Both knew the area very well, and between November 1884 and January 1885, accomplished their assignment. In spite of the jubilation of the *Pall Mall Gazette* on 21 January 1885, the British Foreign Secretary, Granville, peremptorily ordered the dismissal of the Poles and repudiated their treaties.

British plans for a continuous coastline from Lagos to Victoria received an unexpected set-back. The German trader G. L. Gaiser successfully made a treaty with the 'king' of Mahin between Lagos and the Niger Delta. The Lagos Administration had indeed attempted to frustrate the inconvenient German action here. The Deputy Governor of

---

[1] F.O. 84/1655 and F.O. 84/1681. See Drafts and Exchanges between the F.O. and the C.O. re the Cameroons.

Lagos, Barrow, had sent two Africans from Lagos, Alex Thomas and Isaac Macaulay, to Mahin Town. They accomplished nothing in spite of the fact that they carried with them presents for the 'king' of Mahin. Gaiser succeeded where the Lagos agents had failed, and the nucleus of a German 'enclave' on the Nigerian coast was established at Mahin Beach.[1] The Governor of Lagos confirmed that, with the acquisition of the protectorate of the Mahin Beach territory, the Germans 'contemplated working thence a trade with the interior from which they anticipated great results . . .'.[2] Thus, up to about the middle of 1885, it was still not clear where the western and eastern boundaries might start. There was even the possibility that a compact territory controlled by Britain might never materialize if the Germans held on tenaciously to their Mahin acquisition and developed its hinterland. The Berlin West African Conference prepared the ground for the negotiations which in the end removed the anomalies and uncertainties along the Nigerian coast. In order to eliminate the German Mahin enclave, Britain agreed to compensate Gaiser for the loss sustained. The latter estimated his expenses on Mahin Beach as follows:

Cash payment to Amapetu . .		£20
5 pieces of silk ⎫		
5 puncheons of rum ⎬ . . .		£100
100 cases of gin ⎭		
Presents from Hamburg . . .		£6
Other presents in sundry goods, including one musical clock, to various chiefs		£229 15s
	Total =	£355 15s

Even the German government itself would not accept the figure produced by Gaiser as other than fantastic. The claims eventually lapsed. The British for their part virtually sold out

---

[1] C.O. 806/242, no. 36, Young to Derby, 31 January 1885.
[2] Ibid. F.O. to C.O., 7 April 1885.

the Baptist Mission in respect of Victoria.[1] Nigeria's Atlantic littoral thus emerged.

The Atlantic littoral was only part of the struggle for a compact territory. A glance at any map of Nigeria will show the strategic position occupied by the Rivers Niger and Benue. The exclusive British control of the navigable portions of these rivers was destined to play as decisive a role in the evolution of Nigeria's international boundaries as the termini of the Atlantic littoral. It was not British agents alone who appreciated the potentialities of the rivers in question. A French Minister admirably summarized the aspirations of his country in regard to the rivers:

> On the Niger from the Delta up to its confluence with the Benue, our only aim must be to make sure of the freedom of our trade . . . But on the Benue we can win a more privileged position by signing political or commercial conventions . . . . Such a policy, if it is skilfully pursued, would give our traders a route to Lake Chad and to the rich markets of Adamawa and Bornu.[2]

Frenchmen who possessed skill, foresight and tenacity were not lacking. French activities in this region began with the appearance of the Comte de Semelle in 1878 in Nupe, with whose ruler he successfully negotiated a commercial treaty. In a short time a French company was formed and trading stations were established along the Niger at Abo and Onitsha and, on the Benue, at Loko. Through the good offices of the French government, the company secured the services of Commandant Mattei, who attempted to strengthen the French political and commercial hold on the Lower Niger. The year 1883 saw not only the emergence of the imperialist-minded French Premier, Jules Ferry, and the virtual encirclement by France of Gambia and Sierra Leone, but also the presence on the Niger of an *agent consulaire* who knew how to use the capital provided freely by the French government.

A chain of fortuitous circumstances produced a champion

---

[1] C.O. 806/262, see Inclosure in no. 9, F.O. to C.O., 12 January 1886; *London Gazette*, May 1885.

[2] Robinson and Gallagher, *Africa and the Victorians*, 1961, quoted p. 166.

for the British cause on the Niger. Taubman Goldie, who had an interest in one of the four struggling British firms trading on the Lower Niger, was to prove more than a match for Commandant Mattei. In 1882 he accomplished the amalgamation of the British firms, preparatory to a commercial war with the French company. His ultimate aim was to buy out the rival company and thus guarantee British predominance in the Lower Niger and the Benue. Goldie accomplished this task on the eve of the Berlin Conference.[1] He was able to report that 'the Union Jack alone flew on the Lower Niger'. This was however not the end of the controversy over the control of the Nigerian rivers. As a matter of fact, the French and the German governments had already agreed to include the question of the Niger in the agenda for the Berlin West African Conference, 1884–5. A system of international control might yet nullify the dominant position of the British company.

The British government was indeed prepared to press with remarkable tenacity their claim on the Lower Niger. A special memorandum was prepared by Anderson of the Foreign Office. This document reminded the delegates of the great expenditure of men and money which had accompanied British efforts to explore the Niger. That work was now being completed by the enterprise of British traders. It concluded that the whole basin of the Lower Niger was in British hands. At the conference, Britain managed with great skill to nullify the original Franco-German project which stipulated a joint system of international control of the Niger similar to that arranged for the Congo.[2] British rights were upheld, and the British government was given the responsibility of supervising the navigation of the Niger. The history of the evolution of Nigeria's boundaries might have been different if the control of the Niger and the Benue had been assigned by the Berlin Conference to an international commission. The manner in which the Royal Niger Company exploited the exclusive supervision of the Lower Niger and the Benue to establish what may be described

---

[1] F.O. 84/1814, Goldie to Anderson, private, 1 November 1884. See also Flint, *Sir George Goldie*, London, 1960, pp. 67–8.

[2] See General Act, chapter v, articles xxx, xxxi and xxxii.

as Nigeria's 'anchorages' was of fundamental importance in the subsequent struggle for the definition of the international boundaries of Nigeria. Three illustrations will suffice to justify this contention.

In the first place, the agents of the Royal Niger Company had secured innumerable treaties with petty chiefs along the course of the Lower Niger and the Benue. The company's agents could therefore travel up and down the rivers without much interference from the hostility of the local rulers. The company's agent Joseph Thomson no doubt exploited this facility to beat his German rival in the race for a treaty with the Sultan of Sokoto in 1885. Thomson indicated the importance he attached to his mission in a private letter:

> At the expense of a few pounds and a demoralised stomach, I bring back to the English nation a present of incalculable value...[1]

Other agents of the Royal Niger Company were also successful in obtaining vital treaties with the potentates of Bussa and Yola—treaties which figured prominently in the controversies over Nigeria's boundaries.

Both Germany and France were shortly to subject to severe tests the reality of the British hold on the Niger and the Benue. It dawned rather late on Germany that the easiest access to the hinterland of the region was through the waterways. A German agent, Honigsberg, made his way to Nupe, with the ruler of which he established close amity. This relationship with a local ruler ostensibly under the jurisdiction of the Royal Niger Company occasioned considerable confusion. The British government firmly supported the Niger Company and thus safeguarded the exclusive British control of the Niger. The case of Mizon appeared even more serious. In 1890 and 1892, the French traveller claimed the right of free navigation to push forward French colonial ambitions in the region of the Benue. The Agent-General of the Royal Niger Company had to take drastic action to put a stop to the Frenchman's pretensions. Thus the British government would not permit a possible

---

[1] Thomson (Rev.), *J. Thomson, African Explorer*, 1896, quoted p. 162.

misinterpretation of the importance it attached to the Sokoto and Yola 'anchorages'.

The significance of these British successes is best illustrated by a brief reference to French activities in the Sudan. These activities provoked the preludial controversies of 1890 which foreshadowed the emergence of the northern boundary of Nigeria. Much indeed has been written in praise of the exuberance with which the French approached the question of expansion into the Sudan. By 1870 France had a compact block of territory organized as the colony of Senegal. There were also posts on the West African coast between Grand Bassam and Porto Novo which were indeed *points d'appui* for systematic advance inland:

> The Sudan, Timbuktu, the Niger, all clad in a kind of mysterious uncertainty, entered the orbit of French politics, and appealed the more to Latin temperament by their romance and suggestion of things unknown.[1]

The Berlin West African Conference had, it is true, confined the French to the Upper Niger, but where the Upper Niger ended and the Lower Niger began nobody had yet any conception. The French government approved the plan of a railway from the Mediterranean coast southwards into the Sudan, although the scheme associated with the name of Colonel Flatters was to prove abortive. Between 1880 and 1881 Colonel Gallieni consolidated French imperial authority over the western Sudan as far as Segu. Colonel Frey in 1886 secured a treaty with Samory and, shortly afterwards, the Futa Jallon came under French protection. Two years before the Say–Barrua Anglo-French Convention, Captain Binger had traversed the region of the great bend of the Niger and secured French influence over Kong. Lastly, Monteil, as if to put the finishing touch to the unprecedented activities of France in West Africa, pushed his way to Say and thence to Lake Chad.[2]

---

[1] Roberts, *History of French Colonial Policy*, 1925, vol. i, pp. 302–3.

[2] *Le Figaro*, 23 January 1892; see Supplement, 'Notre Domaine Africain'. Also *Le Temps* quoted by Mockler-Ferryman, *British West Africa*, 1898, p. 420.

In view of the ramifications of French colonial activities in the western and central Sudan, the desirability of forestalling potential French and German 'enclaves' on the Lower Niger and the Benue added considerable militancy to the British insistence that the emerging boundaries should safeguard the Sokoto empire, the region south of the Say–Barrua Line, and Yola.

Just in case the British government might not fully have appreciated the role of the Royal Niger Company, the company undertook to reiterate its achievements, to which the British government had contributed precious little. It was the company's hold on the Lower Niger and its treaty with 'the Empire of Gandu' which had stopped France extending her operations beyond Timbuktu.[1] The Council of the Company therefore prayed that Her Majesty's Protectorate might be extended to include 'these territories'. This was in fact done, and the background was consequently provided for the Say–Barrua Line mentioned above, 'drawn in such a manner as to comprise . . . all that fairly belongs to the kingdom of Sokoto . . .'.

The importance of the Royal Niger Company's treaties with Sokoto, Yola and Bussa, and the political relationships the treaties entailed arose indirectly out of the failure of the Berlin West African Conference to establish specific and internationally accepted conditions for the demarcation of the West African hinterland. Attempts were indeed made during the conference to regulate future acquisitions in Africa. Controversies had followed one another and produced no results. What came to be called 'effective occupation' was confined to the coast. As the coast itself had virtually been carved up, the subsequent application of the principle of 'effective occupation' hardly arose. It is therefore wrong to assume, as many writers on colonial history do, that the Berlin Conference succeeded in laying down a set of principles by which conflicting imperial claims could be adjusted by the colonial Powers.[2] The general

---

[1] F.O.C.P. Confidential 5610, no. 22, R.N.C. to Pauncefote, 11 January 1887.

[2] Crowe, *The Berlin West African Conference 1884–5*, 1942.

principles of European occupation of African territory were indeed discussed, and a Franco-German project on effective occupation was submitted to the conference in January 1885. Germany's attitude was quite understandable. As a new colonial Power, she stood to gain by a rigorous test for the validity of colonial claims. It was for this reason that the German Chancellor, Bismarck, described the British policy of 'informal sway' as 'the shilly-shally proceedings of England'. This policy constituted a serious handicap to the activities of a young and vigorous nation like Germany which lacked 'initial advantages'.

The extraordinary thing was that the British Foreign Secretary, Lord Granville, completely misconstrued the possible effects of rigid principles on Britain's colonial position. His request that the principle of 'effective occupation' should be extended to the whole of the African continent would, as subsequent happenings showed, have meant confining the boundaries of Nigeria close to the Lower Niger and the Benue, with deep thrusts of foreign occupation westward from Rio del Rey and eastward from Porto Novo. In the end, however, Granville's inexplicable request was rejected, and the original Franco-German project was progressively emptied of all meaning, thanks largely to the intervention of the British Lord Chancellor, Lord Selborne.[1] All that emerged from the conference by way of laying down a principle was simply that

> Any Power which henceforth takes possession of a tract of land *on the coasts* of the African continent outside of its present possessions or which, being hitherto without such possessions, shall acquire them . . . shall accompany the respective act with a notification thereof addressed to the other signatory powers of the Act, in order to enable them, if need be, to make good any claims of their own.[2]

When Granville wanted to know what meaning the Germans

---

[1] F.O. 84/1819, Lord Chancellor on the Law Officers' Report; Ibid. Law Officers' Report, 7 January 1885.

[2] F.O. 84/1822, Malet to Granville, 21 February 1885. See also Malet's Final Report on the Conference.

attached to the word 'coast', the German reply was irritatingly simple: 'territories bordering on the sea'.

The British Ambassador in Berlin, Malet, in his final Report to the Foreign Office rather rejoiced that 'dangerous definitions had been avoided'. No other conclusion is tenable from a study of the proceedings of the Berlin Conference on the question of the conditions which should confer international validity to the occupation and demarcation of the African hinterland. This failure to establish a set of principles had important consequences in the subsequent controversies over the definition of Nigeria's international boundaries. All kinds of conditions had been discussed, or had hovered around in the background: the hinterland theory, voluntary consent, treaties with the African rulers, flag planting and so on. With regard to the demarcation of the hinterland of Nigeria, it was not accurate to describe the situation existing at the time as Mockler-Ferryman did:

> The West Coast of Africa resembles a huge estate that has been split up in building lots, with desirable frontages on to the Atlantic, and boundary fences running back on either side of each lot, but in many cases having no fence at the end of the back garden.[1]

It is demonstrably true that the Atlantic littoral of Nigeria and its limits emerged before the controversies over the hinterland boundaries began. Any suggestion, however, that this hinterland was a sort of 'tabula rasa' is far off the mark. The effectiveness of the British position in respect of the Lower Niger and the Benue, the inescapable reality of the existence of politically active indigenous states, for instance, the Sokoto Empire and the Yola Emirate, were important in the definition of Nigeria's boundaries. Hence, the failure of the Berlin Conference to define principles to govern European occupation of the hinterland in effect reinforced the role of treaties with Nigerian rulers and the part which the European 'interpretation' of indigenous political frontiers could play in the boundary controversies. Goldie himself confirmed this view,

---

[1] Mockler-Ferryman, *British West Africa*, London, 1898, p. 411.

and there was certainly no one in those days better qualified to judge. In an article, Goldie argued that

> The existing rights . . . have been entirely based on treaties with native potentates. On this ground . . . [have] . . . relied all the West African arrangements made during the last ten years.[1]

Since the settlement of the termini of the Atlantic littoral preceded arguments for the demarcation of the hinterland, attention must now be turned to a consideration of the local conditions which existed along the coast and the European appreciation of these conditions in defining the Nigerian Atlantic frontage. It is also possible to discern, through a scrutiny of proceedings relative to the coast, a faint fore-shadowing of the future problems which the hinterland boundary controversies ultimately involved. For reasons of convenience, the western terminus of the Atlantic littoral is considered first. Here undoubtedly the coast state of affairs was a picture in miniature of the immediate hinterland.

Badagry, to the west of Lagos, was acquired by Britain in 1863 when the local ruler ceded his state to the Governor of Lagos. Its history and political relations with Porto Novo reveal the extreme difficulties involved in ascertaining the limits of indigenous political frontiers. The portion of the Guinea Coast with which the determination of the western terminus of the Atlantic littoral was concerned is occupied by groups belonging to two great linguistic clusters: the Ewe and the Yoruba (Awori).[2] Particularly along the coast, splinter groups of Ewe and Yoruba fugitives overlapped one another. In many of the city-states which emerged, the two linguistic groups were intermingled. The settlement which grew up at Badagry was the most eastern projection of Ewe migration. Whether the Ewe or the Yoruba arrived first at Badagry is not known, but what is worth noting is that recent census records show that the population of Badagry Division comprises about

---

[1] *The New Review*, June 1897. See also F.O.C.P. Confidential 7000, Memorandum by the Intelligence Division of the War Office.
[2] See Forde, *Ethnographic Survey of Africa*, part iv, 1951: Yoruba Speaking Peoples of South-Western Nigeria.

30,500 Ewe and 14,360 Awori. Appa, another settlement west of Badagry, was founded, according to local tradition, when Ewe fugitives from Old Ardra were granted their present home by the king of Ipokia. Although all these mixed communities to the west and north-west of Lagos were indeed grouped in sparse settlements, any suggestion of a political vacuum would be wrong. As in the states of the Oil Rivers, the slave trade not only provided a basis for prosperity and the emergence of the peculiar political structure typical of the coastal region, but also accelerated the intermingling of Ewe and Yoruba fugitive elements. Whydah, Appa, Porto Novo and Badagry were at the time of the boundary negotiations distinct and easily recognizable political entities. Lander's observations about Badagry convey, however, a rather depressing picture of the political organization of the coast states of the region under consideration.

> There is hardly any knowing who is monarch here, or even what form of government prevails. Besides the King of Kings himself, the redoubtable Adooley, four fellows assume the title of royalty; namely, the Kings of Spanish Town, of Portuguese Town, of English Town, and of French Town—Badagry being divided into four districts, being the names of the European nations just mentioned.[1]

Johnson, the Yoruba local historian, also takes a poor view of the mixed communities of the coast, whom he described as

> scanty in number, ignorant and degraded . . . through their demoralising intercourse with Europeans, and the transactions connected with the oversea slave trade.[2]

Burton claimed that, according to what he heard on the coast, Whydah

> was originally a den of water thieves and pirates. . . . It rose to the rank of a prosperous ivory mart and slave port.[3]

---

[1] Lander, *Narrative of an Expedition*, etc., 1843, vol. i, pp. 16–17.

[2] Johnson, *The History of the Yorubas*, p. 40.

[3] Burton, *A Mission to Gelele, King of Dahomey*, 1864, vol. i, pp. 62–4. Burton's views are not in accord with the account of the foundation of Whydah available in European records. According to the latter, Whydah

However unsavoury their origin, here on the coast were perhaps 'mushroom' states, organized for trade, for war, for government and for foreign relations. For most of the nineteenth century the rise of Dahomian military and political ambitions completely dominated the politics of the area. In due course the presence of European official representatives, either as consular or as naval commanders became a new factor in the political relations of the states. The Europeans were themselves often baffled, and the intelligence division of the British War Office summed up the local situation as follows:

> It is very hard to build up a connected history of any particular State. Wars were frequent and produced constant changes in the political relationship of the various territories.[1]

Dahomian expansion and military predominance produced more far reaching effects on the political landscape of the hinterland. Their impact on the coast states was quite important. Early in the eighteenth century, Whydah was in fact conquered by Dahomey and was ruled through a representative of the Dahomian monarch. The same monarch put forward claims to the other coast states of Katanu, Appa and Badagry, but regarded Porto Novo as a sister-state and ally during this period. On the whole, Dahomian claims included the right to use the coast states for the export of slaves, and this was where the powerful African state was bound to fall foul of Britain. British policy on the West Coast was at this period one largely inspired by her philanthropic resolve to suppress the sea-borne slave traffic. It involved the occasional naval blockade and bombardment of the coast states. It was therefore primarily the effects of British policy which determined the attitude of the coast states towards Britain and, indirectly, towards France. The results may be summarized very briefly. British policy antagonized Dahomey, Porto Novo and Lagos. Lagos opposition was eliminated in 1861 with its outright

---

owed its origin to the decision of English and French factors to obtain in 1685 land near the beach from the Hueda chiefs of Savi. Whydah is a corruption of Hueda. (See Newbury, *The Western Slave Coast and its Rulers*, Oxford, 1961, pp. 19–20.)

[1] C.O. 806/281, W.O. to C.O., 1 July 1887.

44

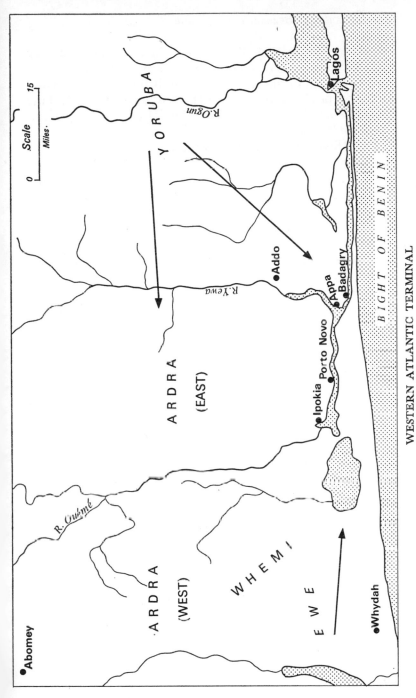

WESTERN ATLANTIC TERMINAL

Map showing movement of Ewe and Yoruba Mixed Groups during the nineteenth and twentieth centuries

acquisition by Britain. Porto Novo, in fear, turned to the French for protection. Badagry itself, still exposed to Dahomian threats, agreed to cede the territory to Britain in 1863 'as also for the purpose of setting aside all pretensions on the part of the King of Porto Novo and others to the right and royalty of this district of Badagry'.[1]

The British and French local representatives attempted at this time to separate their spheres of influence on the 'slave' coast. The idea was that the states which had accepted the protection of Britain should be separated from those which looked towards Dahomey and were therefore friendly to France. This unofficial demarcation of the coast was certainly based on a correct appreciation of the political alignments prevailing on the coast at the time. Although the local boundary arrangement was not approved by the British and French governments, the existing pattern of political relations between the coastal states and the European Powers concerned persisted after 1863. The factors which would influence the later and permanent arrangement of 1889 were clear. The western boundary on the Nigerian seaboard, west of Badagry, partitioned the state of Appa.[2] What needs to be emphasized here is that no boundary on this part of the coast could be ethnologically satisfactory because the inhabitants of the states were mixed and were often bilingual. The states could not be separated in neat linguistic or ethnic compartments. Furthermore, the state frontiers were extremely fluid, and to talk about splitting Appa is euphemistic. Today, Ewe and Yoruba mixed groups are found west and east of the western terminus of Nigeria's sea coast.

In view of the British and German entrenched positions in Calabar and Duala respectively, the eastern end of the Nigerian coast was bound to become a subject of controversy between the two Powers. The neck and neck race for treaties between Hewett and Nachtigal had already created considerable confusion as to the respective spheres of influence of the

---

[1] *Payne's Lagos and West African Almanack and Diary*, 1894, pp. 94–6.

[2] C.S.O. 1/1, no. 90, Moloney to Granville, 27 March 1886; *Etudes Dahoméennes*, ix. pp. 74–6, Letters exchanged between Moloney and Ballot; also pp. 76–8, Convention of 1888.

European Powers involved. The negotiations which took place led to a provisional boundary which remained unaltered as far as the coast was concerned. The details of the negotiations are left for a later chapter. What is therefore attempted here is an assessment of the extent to which the eastern coast boundary (fixed at Rio del Rey) affected the peoples of the coast and their political structure. As on the western side of the Atlantic littoral, the local situation on the eastern coast also foreshadowed the problems which featured in the demarcation of the hinterland. There was no dominant native potentate to consolidate the fortunes of the city-states and those of the innumerable neighbouring groups. Calabar and Duala were settlements founded by splinter groups from the hinterland. Between the two 'states' no settlements of importance appear to have attracted the notice of European merchants and travellers, with the possible exceptions of the small settlements of Victoria and Bimbia. Thus, on the whole, the coast region between Calabar and Duala was regarded as a sort of political no-man's-land.

The Efiks of Calabar, it is true, claimed to be in political control of the region east and north-east of Rio del Rey, but their political pretensions became a serious factor only in the controversies over the extension of the boundary inland. The organization of Efik settlements, as indeed of the settlements along the coast from the Niger Delta to the Cross River mouth, was based on trading associations called 'houses'. A 'house' included freemen and slaves under a leader who could command an impressive number of canoes and could look after the solidarity and welfare of the members of the 'house'. The leading Efik settlements—Old Calabar, Cobham Town, Creek Town, Duke Town, Henshaw Town and Archibong Town— were under 'kings' or 'dukes' who owed their position to direct descent from the original founders of the settlements. Although direct descent was a factor which contributed to the internal stability of the settlements, it must not be over-emphasized. As Simmon has argued, kingship did not confer effective or centralized authority:

This rank [king] is not native, but adopted to regulate the

47

> intercourse of the people of the country with foreigners . . .
> As the office had special relation to European traders they came
> to have something to say in the election of persons to fill it. This
> began with Eyamba (1834) . . .[1]

What was certainly not in doubt was the fact that the Efiks
carried on extensive trading transactions with their neighbours
in all directions.

According to recent, though often conflicting ethnographic
surveys, unattached Semi-Bantu and Bantu groups in their
migrations overlapped one another on both sides of the Rio del
Rey coast region. The Efiks themselves were a splinter from the
Ibibio linguistic group who made their way from the north-
west to the lower courses of the Cross and Calabar Rivers, and,
in due course, partially absorbed the aboriginal inhabitants of
the region, the Akwa. Also located in this region of the Cross
River system near the sea is an Efut group which claims that
the first Efuts migrated from the Cameroons. To add to the
ethnic complexity, there was a cluster of Fish Towns east of Rio
del Rey occupied by Efik fishermen. The classification of these
diverse groups was at first a simplified linguistic one. European
agents spoke of Semi-Bantu and Bantu-speaking peoples.[2] The
Rio del Rey 'estuary' appeared therefore to be a reasonably
correct 'ethnic' frontier. This was the view of the local British
administrators, who recommended it as a dividing coastal
boundary between the British and the German spheres of
interest. The British believed that they had thus secured the
Efik (Semi-Bantu) portion of the Nigerian coast.

It cannot be pretended that the indigenous political situation was studied by the European agents at the time they made
the coast demarcation. The European traders, administrators
and, to some extent, missionaries appear to have taken a very
poor view of the coastal peoples before and after 1885. In the
Calabar 'republics' and in Duala the European observer was
constantly reminded that the creation of 'houses' pre-occupied
with competitive trade was hardly conducive to internal

---

[1] Forde, *Efik Traders of Old Calabar*, 1956, p. 116.
[2] *Journal of the African Society*, no. 24 (1924–5); see Talbot, 'Some Foreign Influences on Nigeria'.

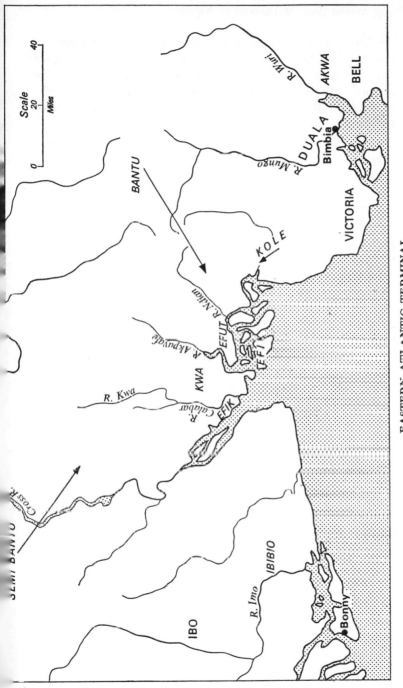

EASTERN ATLANTIC TERMINAL

Indicating Tribal Movements in the nineteenth century

stability, let alone political expansion. There is therefore much reference, in the descriptions of the peoples and their affairs, to domestic turmoil.[1] The European traders were certainly not pleased with the implacable hostility shown by the coast rulers to any attempts at European inland penetration for trade. The missionary Goldie recorded that

> When the Mission entered the country [Calabar] the chiefs, in giving us settlements for our stations, stipulated that we would not go beyond Calabar. Their fear was, that if we went into the upper tribes where the oil markets are, our countrymen would follow, and buying at first hand, deprive native traders of their business as middlemen.[2]

H. H. Johnston, who was the most travelled of the early European administrators, had nothing but contempt for 'the degraded coast tribes who seem to have lost all their ancient culture'.

Nobody believed or had reason to believe in 1885 that the Efiks had effective political influence beyond the bounds of their 'republics'. It is significant that the treaties signed by Hewett with the Efik chiefs in 1884 did not include the coastal territory east of Rio del Rey. The Duala chiefs had also independently solicited British protection in 1882 and subsequently accepted German authority in 1884. Neither the Efik rulers nor the 'kings' of Duala had any say in the affairs of the intervening mushroom settlements of Victoria and Bimbia. As already stated, one conclusion is inescapable. The coast region between Calabar and Duala was a political 'vacuum'. The only unifying factor between the Efik 'republics', Victoria, and Duala seems to have been no more than 'a form of English [which] had become a virtual vernacular'.[3] The choice of Rio del Rey as the terminus of the eastern Atlantic littoral was a 'happy' one both ethnically and politically, the Efuts and the Efiks of Fish Towns notwithstanding.[4] The backbone of the

---

[1] F.O. 84/2020, no. 29, Annesley to F.O., 19 June 1890. Kingsley, *West African Studies*, London, 1899, Appendix 1, p. 536.

[2] Goldie, *Memoir of King Eyo VII of Old Calabar*, 1894, p. 37.

[3] Ardener, *Coastal Bantu of the Cameroons*, part xi, 1956, p. 37.

[4] *Report of H.M. Government to the Council of the League of Nations on the Cameroons*, 1929, p. 11.

indigenous political order was not undermined by the coast boundary demarcation.

The choice of the Atlantic seaboard of what emerged as Nigeria is in retrospect highly fortunate. No major coast groups were arbitrarily disrupted. There is another consideration. A glance at a linguistic map of Nigeria will show that the coast posts, together with the British hold on the Niger, Sokoto and Yola 'anchorages', potentially guaranteed that in the demarcation of the hinterland boundaries, the major Yoruba, Edo, Ibo, Ibibio and Hausa–Fulani groups would not be outrageously disrupted. Those who argued about the coast did not of course foresee this happy eventuality. No study of the international boundaries can properly ignore the preliminary but decisive role of the Atlantic termini,[1] the existence of a continuous coastline, the Lower Niger, and the hinterland 'anchorages'.

---

[1] Hargreaves, *Prelude to the Partition of West Africa*, 1963, p. 348 and pp. 349–50.

3

The Eastern Boundary—I

Technically, the line which emerged as the first section of the eastern international boundary of Nigeria was the Rio del Rey–Yola line described in the Anglo-German agreements of 1885 and 1886. The zone traversed by this line cannot be treated as a unity, and so a great deal of confusion will be avoided if attention is confined to the region below the 7th degree of north latitude, a line which roughly demarcates Eastern and Northern Nigeria. The boundary zone north of this latitude was given its unique cultural landscape by the political and religious activities of the Adamawa Fulani and by the intrusion of the Jukun along the tributaries of the Benue. This region conveniently belongs to the second section of the boundary question to be treated in the next chapter. The boundary zone being discussed in the present chapter is that traversed by the Eastern Nigeria–West Cameroun international boundary. This zone includes the territory watered by the Cross River and its tributaries issuing mostly from the Cameroon mountains and the plateau of Bamenda. A brief description of the geographical environment is essential to an understanding of the complex pattern of human settlement.

The region near the coast is a low-lying plain, swampy and encumbered with mangrove trees. The numerous distributaries which form the delta of the Qua, Akpayafe and Ndian rivers break up this otherwise monotonous coastal stretch between the Cross River mouth and Victoria. Immediately north of the mangrove swamps appear the tropical forests.

52

Here is a vivid description of the forest environment and the trees which dominate it:

> They cover . . . the interior across the whole region of the boundary. In rain forests [where trees often] tower to a height of 200 feet and even more and compete in their struggle to reach the light . . . man feels himself small and mortal, for little light and fresh air penetrate the thickness of the jungle's leafy surface to relieve the hot-house atmosphere and cathedral dome.[1]

Further to the east, the massive bulk of the Cameroons Mountain rises to a height of 13,350 feet, its lower slopes to the west also covered with dense forest. To the north, it falls away into thickly wooded country which gradually gives way to the grasslands of the Bamenda plateau and North Ogoja.

On a broad linguistic basis, the peoples occupying the boundary zone fall into two categories—the Bantu and the Semi-Bantu. The zone is indeed considered to be the borderland of the Bantu and Semi-Bantu speaking peoples, but neat demarcations are impossible. According to Talbot's classification, the Semi-Bantu groups include the Efik–Ibibio, the Ekoi, the Boki and many heterogeneous elements found along the Cross River. North of the Cross River bend, the Iyala, the Yache and small intrusive groups from the Benue valley also belong to the Semi-Bantu. The linguistic classification of the Tikar and Bafumbum groups of the Bamenda plateau is a subject of controversy. Talbot considers them Semi-Bantu, but Murdock, following the conclusions of Greenberg, suggests that the Bamenda groups are a Bantu subdivision.[2] West of the Cameroons Mountain, the Bantu-speaking peoples include the Abaw, the Bakundu, the Balundu and the Balung. The direction of Bantu migration has itself become a matter of controversy. The traditions of the peoples point to a westward movement but modern research is questioning the reliability of these traditions. For instance, Murdock vigorously argues that the uplands of Central Cameroon must have been the original

---

[1] Rudin, *Germans in the Cameroons (1884–1914)*, 1938, p. 103.
[2] Talbot, *The Peoples of Southern Nigeria*, vol. ii, pp. 4 f and Table no. 1. Murdock, *Africa: its Peoples and their Culture History*, 1959, pp. 13–14 and pp. 238 f.

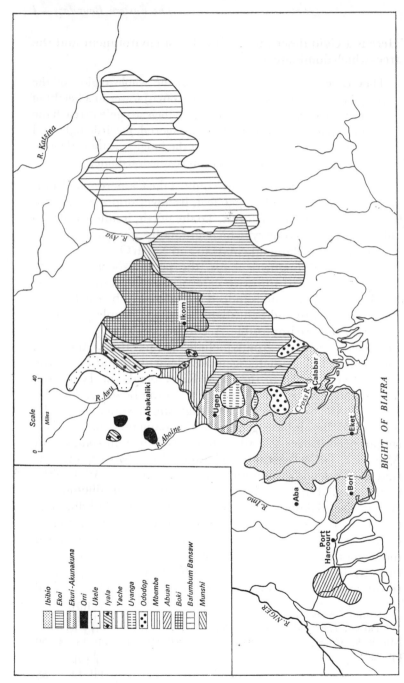

THE ETHNIC CLUSTERS OF THE NIGERIA–SOUTHERN CAMEROONS BOUNDARY ZONE

habitat of the Bantu. This would imply an eastward rather than a westward movement into the boundary zone.

The first question that arises is whether or not the Bantu can be geographically demarcated from the Semi-Bantu in the boundary zone. Johnston, who made a close study of the region and its peoples, admitted that it was not easy to delineate geographically this northern boundary of the Bantu-speaking peoples of Africa. But he oversimplified the problem when he suggested that

> [The boundary] may be said to start on the west coast of Africa in the Bight of Biafra (due north of the island of Fernando Po), at the mouth of the Rio del Rey in the southern portion of the Bakasi peninsula, which flanks the estuary of the Old Calabar river. From the eastern bank of the Rio del Rey the boundary is carried to the Ndian river, and thence with zigzags to the western flanks of the . . . mountains of western Kamerun.[1]

One example may be taken west of Johnston's hypothetical line to demonstrate the extreme difficulty of attempting a neat geographical separation of Bantu and Semi-Bantu speaking peoples in the region. The Bantu speaking Okoyong group occupy the territory between the Cross and the Calabar rivers, in the very centre of a predominantly Semi-Bantu country. The Scottish missionaries in Calabar noted this 'phenomenon', and advanced an explanation which is summarized here. Some time in the dim past, a raiding force had swept down from the mountains to the east of Calabar, entered the triangle of dense forest-land formed by the junction of the Cross and Calabar rivers, fought and defeated the Semi-Bantu Ibibio who dwelt there, and had then taken possession of the territory. The missionaries concluded that Okoyong must be the most westerly Bantu outpost thrust like a wedge into negroland.[2] Many other Bantu 'enclaves' have been identified in the region enclosed in the loop of the Cross River.

The difficulties in analyzing the complex human pattern do

---

[1] Johnston, *A Comparative Study of the Bantu and Semi-Bantu Languages*, 1919, pp. 15–17.

[2] Livingstone, *Mary Slessor of Calabar*, 1916, p. 57.

not end here. Assuming for a moment that the human groups can be labelled Bantu and Semi-Bantu, it may be asked whether the problems of ethnic affinity and common origin are thereby solved. In the Cross River–Cameroons region, the use of collective tribal names is extremely misleading. Some groups, originally Semi-Bantu speaking, have in the course of their migrations adopted Bantu. Others who were Bantu speaking adopted Semi-Bantu languages. It was for this reason that a warning was expressed by the missionaries of Victoria to the effect that in the region of the boundary

> A common speech cannot be taken to imply community of culture, origin, or race, and speakers of Bantu languages exhibit as many differences in these other respects as do speakers of Indo-European languages, who include Hindus as well as Welshmen.[1]

There is a further complication. The Bantu and Semi-Bantu migrations into the region were not massive and ethnically coherent movements. Splinter groups moved in and about when they liked and settled where they could.

The Semi-Bantu peoples encountered in the boundary zone who are numerous enough to deserve the traditional designation of the term 'tribes' include the Ibibio–Efik, the Ekoi and, north of the Cross River bend, the Boki. The bulk of the Ibibio are confined to the west of the Cross River, and so raise no direct problem in the assessment of the international boundary. The Efik 'sub-tribe' which moved into the estuaries of the Cross and Calabar rivers also raises no ethnic problem except in the neighbourhood of Rio del Rey, where Efik fishermen founded Fish Towns. The two Semi-Bantu 'tribal' groups directly affected by the boundary are the Ekoi and the Boki. In regard to these peoples, it is necessary to reiterate that the term 'tribe' is dangerously misleading. The groups not only lack self-consciousness and political focus, they also include a considerable diversity of ancestral stock. Take the Ekoi for instance. The term 'Ekoi' is an Efik word and not Ekoi. Some Ekoi groups call themselves the Ejagham, but the latter word

---

[1] Basel Mission Book Depot, *Victoria, Southern Cameroons 1858–1958*, pp. 11–13.

means nothing to many other Ekoi groups usually described by the collective tribal name, Ekoi. Some ethnographers have attempted to list Ekoi sub-tribes and clans, such as the Akaju, Banyangi, Ejagham, Keaka, Manta, Nde, Nkumm and Obang.[1] These designations do not necessarily indicate coherent groups, and a closer acquaintance with the forest conditions in which the Ekoi lived and formed their small autonomous communities would explain the reason.

Administrators and missionaries who attempted to penetrate the region which the Ekoi call 'our country' left on record their impressions of the Ekoi country and settlements. For instance, Talbot described the sensation he felt on his first visit to the thickly-forested mysterious region as follows:

> As one passes up the [Aqua] river, further and further from Calabar . . . [one] glides backward through the ages up the stream of time to the childhood of the world.

The missionaries who operated from Calabar described the Ekoi communities in the forest as the 'fragments of an earlier world'.[2] Instances of the manner in which Ekoi settlements were formed and of the rapidity with which migrations were accomplished help to explain the considerable intermingling of diverse ethnic groups which took place in the Ekoi country. Oban town is situated in the very heart of this region. The tradition associated with its foundation by an Ekoi group affirms that the land belonged to the Ojuk people who charged the Ekoi newcomers:

> One matchet, one sheep, one piece of iron, one hoe and seven iron hooks for the right to settle; forty pieces of dried meat for the hunting rights; 15 baskets of fish for water rights; one goat, five pieces of dried meat and 500 pieces of ebony for forestry rights; three pots of palm oil, 500 yams, 500 sleeping mats and 10 bundles of corn in final settlement.[3]

---

[1] Talbot, op. cit., vol. ii, see Table no. 1. Murdock, op. cit., p. 243.

[2] R.G.S., vol. xxxvi, December 1910; see Talbot, 'The Land of the Ekoi'. Also Goldie, *Calabar and its Mission*, 1890, p. 282.

[3] Talbot, *In the Shadow of the Bush*, 1913, p. 262.

The Ojuk, having obtained the material compensations listed above, abandoned their land and moved off. This was but one instance of how groups and settlements broke up and scattered for all kinds of reasons, including the ravages of elephants and the scarcity of bachelors to woo the maidens. The missionary Edgerley and his companions, travelling through the Ekoi country, asked the small community in the Awi district why it engaged in apparently endless migrations. In answer the Ekoi spokesman argued that

> We cannot take our farms with us, and food is heavy to carry on a long journey. So we go forward a little, eat all we can there, and go forward a little more.[1]

The circumstances involved in Ekoi settlements and migrations have been outlined above to emphasize the unreliability of applying collective terms like 'sub-tribe' and 'clan' to Ekoi groups which happened to occupy neighbouring districts. These circumstances also explain the ease with which intrusive non-Ekoi peoples founded settlements in an area generally known as Ekoi country. Examples of non-Ekoi intrusive elements include the Uwet, the Umon, the Uyanga, the Akunakuna and the Ekuri. The remarkable Ododop example of a Bantu 'enclave' forming a kind of wedge between the Efik and the Ekoi has been mentioned already.

The Umon, the Uyanga, the Akunakuna and the Ekuri—all Semi-Bantu—have traditions of migration which recall the Akpa (Jukun) invasions. These traditions shared with many Ekoi groups appear to suggest similarities of earlier environment and culture. But however close the affinities of the past, the fugitives from Jukun power, Ekoi and non-Ekoi, arrived in the Ekoi country and then broke up into even smaller groups and scattered into various isolated openings in the forest. The more enterprising moved towards the Cross River to found towns such as Okerike and Ediba. The ethnic complexity all this involved can only be imagined. These communities have been quoted as examples of 'enclaves' within ethnic 'enclaves'.

---

[1] Goldie, op. cit., pp. 271–8.

North of the Cross River bend is the region usually called Boki 'country'. Here also the human pattern is confused beyond description. Every report on or survey of the region speaks of a very heterogeneous collection of peoples speaking a number of different languages and mutually unintelligible dialects.[1] These groups include the following which have been identified: the Akaju, the Nkim, the Boki, the Iyache, the Iyala and the Yakoro. It would be wrong to imagine that these classified groups occupy necessarily homogeneous and distinct territories. They were fugitives from the Benue region and did not arrive in coherent ethnic groups. There were also among them Idoma and Tiv 'splinter' communities. Each community regarded itself as a distinct unit. The Bamenda plateau, to the north of Boki 'country', contains yet another human 'cluster' which includes the Bali, the Bafut, the Mbembe and innumerable Tikar groups. It has been said of this part of the boundary zone that 'so marked is the linguistic heterogeneity that villages only a few rules away from one another often speak languages which are mutually unintelligible'.[2]

In conclusion, the Cross River–Cameroon zone traversed by the first section of the international boundary is one in which we should not talk glibly of tribes and clans. It has been suggested that the use of the terms Ekoi 'cluster', Boki 'cluster', Idoma 'cluster' is a more appropriate description of the peoples occupying the boundary zone. The complexity of linguistic pattern and the diversity of origin are perhaps without parallel in any African territory. In a situation such as this, any question of ethnic demarcation is both difficult and meaningless.

It is perhaps no more than euphemistic to talk about indigenous political organization in an area of small, isolated and autonomous forest communities. These peoples practised what has been described as 'primitive democracy', in which

---

[1] Jones, *Report on the Position, Status, and Influence of Chiefs and Natural Rulers in the Eastern Region of Nigeria*, 1956, p. 49.

[2] Forde, ed., *Ethnographic Survey*, West Africa, part x, *Peoples of the Niger–Benue Confluence*, pp. 91–2; pp. 128–30. Buchanan and Pugh, *Land and People in Nigeria*, 1955, see map no. 3.

sanctions were applied to all in ways which did not become visibly institutionalized. Political integration did not transcend the bounds of an autonomous local community. The region, it must be remembered, was one subjected on two sides to the disintegrating evils of the slave trade. The Jukuns, in the Benue basin, and the Efik, on the estuary of the Cross River, procured the human commodity at the expense of the inhabitants of the boundary zone. In these circumstances, the peoples wedged between the Jukun and the Efik tried, not always successfully, to find security in dispersion and constant mobility especially when they lacked political consolidation. The fragmentary communities lived in a state of perpetual warfare. Usually the slaves for sale northwards or southwards were the victims of constant and unprovoked village wars. The legacy of the slave trade, enmity and strife had certainly left its unmistakable mark. One hinterland community declared that 'Inside or outside, speaking, eating, or sleeping, we must have our guns always ready for use . . . we . . . know not the moment we may be attacked'.[1]

It will however be wrong to leave the impression that within the villages themselves anarchy prevailed. The village communities were under the control of persons designated as chiefs or elders. The functions performed by these elders or chiefs were primarily ritual rather than political. The solidarity and the well-being of the village community were the concern of all, although the elders, as representatives of the ancestors, were specially qualified to perform religious rites and other acts of supplication on behalf of the whole community. The 'chief' of Atam, in the Ekoi country, explained his status as follows: The whole town forced him to become head-chief by hanging the buffalo's horns (regarded as big juju) round his neck. As was the custom, he never left his compound. Here he was expected to look after the village juju and perform appropriate ceremonies to 'bring game to the hunter, cause yam crop to be good, bring fish to the fishermen, and make the rain to fall'.[2] There were other villages in the neighbourhood of Atam, each

---

[1] Goldie, op. cit., p. 271.
[2] Partridge, *Cross River Natives*, 1905, pp. 200–2.

with its own independent 'chief'. Although there were periods of inter-village warfare, no village sought to dominate another or to impose political control over its neighbours. It was for this reason that indigenous political activity in the boundary zone was negligible and, if anything, intensified the isolation in which the communities lived.

The Cross River basin was a notable exception to the picture of isolation sketched above. The Efik of the estuary and the Akunakuna group on the upper reaches of the river exploited the opportunities afforded by their location to achieve extensive economic power. Economic power carried with it considerable political and cultural significance. The situation created by the commercial activities of the Efik and the Akunakuna was one which lent itself to controversy. Was there or was there not an Efik empire during the nineteenth century? Efik proverbs are full of suggestions of extensive political power. Here are a few examples: 'Efik can inflict any injury it pleases on the country around'; 'Efik feeds on all the neighbouring tribes, and therefore has supremacy'.[1] But what was the reality? The Efik, like many of the communities of the coast, formed settlements which developed into city-states primarily because of the prosperity derived from the trade with the hinterland on the one hand and with Europeans from across the seas on the other hand. The organization of the Efik city-states was based on the well-known 'house system'. In Duke Town, for instance, there were Duke 'house', Archibong 'house', Ntiero 'house', Eyamba 'house' and so forth. The head of the 'house', usually hereditary, was responsible for the trading activities of the free and slave members of the 'house'. In the immediate hinterland of the Efik 'republics', there were Efik-owned colonies of slaves who cultivated available farm land to provide food for their Efik masters.

As for Efik relations with the indigenous groups of the real hinterland, it should be borne in mind that the Efik were primarily the chief medium through whom the demands of European trade, first in slaves and then in hinterland products, were met. It was also through the Efik that European goods

---

[1] Calprof 8/2, Macdonald's observations, 26 October 1895.

reached the hinterland peoples. The situation was described as follows:

> The Calabars were rich in goods and wanted people; the Barondos had nothing but brothers and sisters, children, and poor hungry slaves—and they wished to become rich.[1]

There were therefore a large number of Barondo, Ekoi and Efut slaves in the hands of the Efik. Some of the slaves might find their way back to their country, taking back with them the Efik language, Efik culture and fetishes. This sort of cultural infiltration did not amount to Efik political domination. The Efik chiefs gave an annual dash to the 'chiefs' of the hinterland groups with which they traded and received in return what was known as 'utomo', annual gifts of yam, fish and meat. These were exchanges of presents to symbolize amity and friendship. They were not tribute.

As a matter of fact the Efik political system possessed no central organs of government through which to govern the hinterland. The slave colonies in the immediate neighbourhood of the Efik 'republics' became quite a problem during the second half of the nineteenth century. The political history of the Efik during this period is mainly one of the assertion of their political rights by the slave colonies against the Efik factions in the towns which, in turn, were struggling among themselves for political dominance. The slaves in the Efik 'colonies' formed, in 1850, an association known as the Blood Men in order to defend themselves against the arbitrary exactions of their masters and the periodic excesses of the Ekpe society. The latter indeed came to play an increasingly important part in Calabar politics, to the prejudice of the power of the natural rulers of the Efik 'republics'.[2]

The Scottish missionaries left a very clear picture of the character of Efik supremacy over the region north-eastwards to the neighbourhood of the Cameroons Mountain, and northwards in the Cross River basin. In 1877 Rev. A. Ross and his

---

[1] Calprof 6/1, Casement to Macdonald, 18 July 1894.
[2] Jones, op. cit., p. 34. Calprof 4/3, The Memorial of Chief Henshaw to Lord Granville, April 1885.

colleagues visited the Rio del Rey region and beyond. There was indeed much evidence before them that enterprising Efik slave members of the Efik 'houses' had built up for their Efik masters considerable trade stations in the area. The missionaries noted that Efik was widely spoken. But they also observed that the presence of Efik traders depended on the goodwill of the local inhabitants. The former were often expelled from the trade stations for 'strong-handed dealings'.[1] It is difficult, in these circumstances, to claim that the Efik successfully established extensive political authority in the region north-east of Calabar.

The hinterland directly north of Calabar was accessible to Efik traders, who possessed fleets of armed canoes for trade along the Cross and Calabar rivers. Even today, it is interesting to see the way the Efik like to recall the days of 'our naval power'. The trading expeditions of the Efik brought them into contact with the Bantu Ododop people on the Calabar River and with the Semi-Bantu Umon on the Cross River. These hinterland groups north of Calabar were strategically placed to facilitate or make hazardous Efik penetration to the upper reaches of the rivers which were the main arteries of Efik trade. It can therefore be assumed that if the Efik had the will and the power to found a commercial as well as a political empire, the subjugation of the hinterland peoples mentioned above would be a prerequisite. The missionaries in Calabar left very graphic sketches of the manner in which the Efik rulers sought to demonstrate Efik naval power and the consequences.

Waddell was an eye-witness of Efik naval preparations for a showdown with Umon town on the Cross River, the people of which were becoming more uncompromising in their hostility to Efik traders:

All preparations being made, Eyamba [King of Duke Town] left his town with as much of the pomp and circumstance of war as possible. His great canoe was gaily decked out with several ensigns streaming in the wind. Astride . . . sat two men beating drums with might and main. . . . In the bows a large gun pointed forward, and before it stood a man with a bundle of reeds, which

---

[1] Goldie, *Calabar and its Mission*, pp. 297–8.

he kept shaking at arm's-length, to exorcize every obstacle and danger out of the way. A train of smaller canoes . . . were in the wake. . . . Thus they made a grand show, with colours waving, guns firing, drums beating, and men singing and shouting, while the women, crowding the beach, admired and applauded by their peculiar animating cheers with all their might.[1]

The Umon people—the target of the military expedition—were not overawed by the arrival of the Efik war-canoes. They merely lined the bush on either side of the river and defied the Efik to do their worst. Eyamba held a council of war near Umon and decided to return to Calabar without as much as firing a shot. On reaching home, the Efik warriors 'were received by the women . . . as if they had been conquerors'. Subsequently, when peace was restored between the Umon and Calabar, it was the former and not the latter who dictated the terms of peace. The Efik were compelled to make an annual 'dash' to the Umon chiefs and further agreed to lower their flags whenever they arrived at Umon.

The relations between the Efik and the Ododop of the upper Calabar River also afforded the missionaries of Calabar the opportunity to confirm the hollowness of Efik pretensions to political authority in the hinterland. About the year 1870 Archibong, the king of Duke Town, declared war on Okoyong on the ground that the vagaries of Okoyong internal politics prejudiced Efik trade. Archibong was resolved on this occasion to reduce Okoyong to a dependency of Calabar. The details of the military expedition are not available, but the missionary Anderson noted that 'in so far as I have been able to learn, the expedition has been bloodless, except among fowls and goats'.[2] He felt great thankfulness that the result was just as it was. The Efik warmongers found the people of Okoyong ready to defend themselves and their independence, and came to the conclusion that peace with Okoyong, not warfare, was the condition for good trade.

The Akunakuna, who occupied the upper reaches of the

---

[1] Goldie, *Calabar and its Mission*, quoted pp. 100–2. Waddell, *Twenty-Nine Years in the West Indies and Central Africa*, 1863, p. 373.
[2] Goldie, op. cit., quoted pp. 228–9.

Cross River, played a role in this region similar to that of the Efik at the estuary. The commercial activities of the Akunakuna embraced the bend of the Cross River and the Aweyong tributary. In the latter region, they tapped the trade of the territories occupied by Tiv splinter groups 'who have yet to learn that the days of bows and poisoned arrows are numbered . . .'.[1] These peoples who dwelt astride the Aweyong naturally welcomed the arrival of European goods which the Akunakuna bartered with their Efik allies. But just as the Efik had to rely on the goodwill of Umon and Okoyong, the Akunakuna had to accommodate themselves to the vagaries of Akaju and Indem politics. The Efik and the Akunakuna undoubtedly showed great resourcefulness in expanding trade in all directions, but a close study of the prevailing political situation during the nineteenth century reveals nothing remotely resembling what has been called a 'Cross River political area'.

The prevalence of one institution—the Ekpe society—appeared however to give the whole boundary zone a kind of cultural unity. The Efik, the Ekoi and many Bantu groups had some form or other of 'these all-purpose clubs'. The influence of the Ekpe society permeated far and wide throughout the region. But then each town had its own Ekpe, which was independent and controlled the affairs of the separate isolated community. The Efik Ekpe enjoyed superior status, but the Ekoi would be the first to claim that they originated the cult. It can be seen therefore that the Ekpe society, though widespread, did not provide any basis for 'tribal' solidarity.[2]

The above sketch, inevitably bewildering, is none the less the necessary background for judging the manner in which European agents sought and used data on indigenous social and political institutions at the time they argued about the boundary. It is true that the British negotiators claimed that there was an Efik commercial empire because they occupied Calabar and not because they had reliable evidence of the existence of such an empire. The Germans, on the other hand, who had

---

[1] *Annual Report on the Eastern Province,* 1909. C.O. 520/16, Moor to C.O., no. 522, 18 November 1902.
[2] Forde, op. cit., part x, pp. 133–4. Partridge, op. cit., p. 207.

neither the men nor the resources to undertake inland expeditions, merely rejected without proof whatever claims the British made as to the local ethnic landscape. The point, however, is that at least both sides had before them data which purported to represent the local situation. What these data were and how decisive they were in the boundary arrangement are best traced through the diplomatic negotiations.

Because of their comparatively large trade with Europeans, Calabar and Duala appeared, during the hectic months of the 'scramble' for the coast along the Bight of Biafra, to be centres of an enormous Cross River–Cameroons commercial zone. As already recounted, the British consul Hewett secured Calabar for the British, and the German commissioner Nachtigal obtained a protectorate over Duala for his country. These achievements on the coast were but the preliminaries to the extension of European control to the hinterland. It was this situation which made the region between Calabar and Duala a boundary zone, involving problems which neither Britain nor Germany had anticipated. The problem of demarcating their 'spheres of influence' had at first seemed no more difficult than merely separating the Calabar political and commercial sphere from that of Duala. There were, however, two complications: the Baptist Mission settlement at Victoria, and the Cameroons Mountain.[1] The latter was to the Europeans the most remarkable and arresting geographical feature of the region. One European after another had attempted to explore it. Captains Allen and Burton, missionaries Merrick and Saker, botanists Calvo and Mann—all made attempts with varying success to collect information about one of the world's largest volcanoes.

To make intelligible the initial ups and downs of Anglo-German negotiations for a boundary here, it is perhaps necessary to recall the British plan for colonizing the Cameroon highlands as part of the emerging British 'protectorate' of the Oil Rivers. The Assistant Under-Secretary at the British Office, Villiers Lister, appreciated fully the advantages of

---

[1] F.O. 84/1739, Memorandum by Anderson on Pending Questions in Africa, 23 June 1885.

acquiring the Cameroons district, 'seeing that with a sanatorium upon it, many valuable lives might be spared and much
expense of home journeys saved'.[1] The British local agents did
everything possible to lay the foundations of a British colony
there. Hewett enjoined his assistant, in emphatic terms, to
secure a good site on the Cameroons Mountain and to obtain
the cession of the countries on the south and west through
which a road from Calabar and Victoria might have to pass.
The Vice-Consul, White, carried out his instructions. As stated
in chapter 2, he went to the extent of using two Poles to secure
for Britain all the treaties and 'cessions' that were thought
necessary for the British acquisition of the western and southern
slopes of the Cameroons Mountain.

The Anglo-German negotiations which culminated in the
agreement to accept Rio del Rey provisionally as the eastern
terminus of the British sphere of influence on the Atlantic
littoral were complicated at first by the fact that Lord Granville, the British Foreign Secretary, held on with unusual
tenacity to the plan which envisaged the Cameroons Mountain
as part of a British colony. Granville appeared to assume that
the Germans might not wish to extend their acquisition at
Duala inland towards the mountain, and that there might
therefore not be any question of inland demarcation. A formal
letter on this issue was addressed to the German Foreign Office.
The latter returned a very non-committal answer. It said that
the Germans had not yet defined the extent of the German
protectorate inland, but that they reserved the freedom of
decision, 'in the same way as the English do in the occupation
of portions of a coastline . . .'.[2] While the two governments
were indulging in exchanging notes, the German Governor in
Duala, Von Soden, decided to have German flags distributed
to the natives of the Cameroons Mountain slopes and thereby
counteract the work already done by British agents. Puttkamer, Krabbes, and two Swedes were the German answer to
Hewett, White and the two Poles.

---

[1] Basel Mission, op. cit., Collings to Derby, quoted pp. 24–5. Calprof
5/3, Memorandum of Instructions, 10 March 1885.

[2] S.P. vol. lxxvi, p. 758, Munster to Granville, 9 November 1884.

It may be recalled that in order to obviate an ugly diplomatic situation, Lord Granville formally repudiated the services of the Poles who were sustaining the British cause in the Cameroons. It became increasingly clear that the Cameroons Mountain was no longer an obstacle to an Anglo-German arrangement to demarcate the immediate hinterland. The potential boundary zone thus shifted to the region west of the mountain. This was the region dominated by the Cross River and its tributaries. The Cross River itself was certainly well known to Europeans. Beecroft had as early as 1842, and the Scottish missionaries regularly after 1870, sailed up the river as far as the 'rapids'. As for the territory between the Cross River and the Cameroons Mountain, it cannot be supposed that what the British and the German agents knew in 1885 was much in advance of Hutchinson's description:

> The Rio del Rey . . . flows through the Rumby country, and of which nothing is known. . . . The Kalabar native traders have some acquaintance with the natives . . . and they call them Arumbee [?][1]

On the whole there were two things which were clear to the British agents. The navigable portion of the Cross River must at all costs be on the British side of any hinterland boundary. The ramifications of Efik trading activities in the boundary zone could not be ignored, but then, from the German point of view, the trade which flowed towards Calabar could be diverted to Duala if Germany acquired a sizeable portion of this hinterland.

The preliminary manoeuvring by the two Powers before formal negotiations were resumed showed how boundary issues could never be completely insulated from the exigencies of European diplomacy. Just as Prince Bismarck used 'the colonial disputes as window-dressing to attract the French' in the period immediately antecedent to the Berlin West African Conference 1884–5, so now, after the conference, the failure of a rapprochement between France and Germany inevitably influenced Germany's attitude towards colonial boundary

---

[1] Hutchinson, *Impressions of West Africa*, 1858, pp. 166–7.

disputes with Britain. During this period, too, Britain relied heavily on German goodwill in her difficulties in Egypt, and the Germans were determined to exploit this dependence. But in this study of the boundary negotiations, no attempt is made to treat European diplomacy in all its bewildering ramifications.[1] Yet the diplomatic atmosphere of the negotiation of the Nigerian–Cameroons provisional boundary in 1885 was an auspicious one. As *The Times* explained, there was room enough in the world for the colonial enterprise of both Britain and Germany. The colonial aspirations of Germany could impair the friendly relations of the two Powers only if either of them failed to respect the 'just rights and legitimate interests' of the other. Lastly, neither Power should indulge in the 'perverse pursuit of a doctrinaire's will-o'-the-wisp'.[2]

Herbert Bismarck, the son of the 'Iron Chancellor', arrived in London on 4 March 1885 to negotiate a settlement of outstanding Anglo-German colonial differences. Thus began what he called rather cynically the Anglo-German 'colonial honeymoon'. Herbert was hospitably received by his friend Lord Rosebery and by the British Foreign Secretary, Lord Granville. The latter apparently thought it necessary to explain away his earlier letters on the Cameroons Mountain. They were supposedly 'not written in a very civil form'.[3] The mutual congratulations over, both sides got down to concrete work. The Germans based their arguments in respect of the Cameroons boundary on the 'hinterland' theory. Their acquisitions on the coast, and particularly Duala, ought to have an adequate region to exploit. Having abandoned the Cameroons Mountain project, the British negotiators were not disposed to dispute the German basis for a demarcation of spheres of influence. All the British wished to safeguard was what they assumed to be the Efik commercial empire.

---

[1] See Langer, *The Diplomacy of Imperialism, 1890–1902*, 1951. Taylor, *Germany's First Bid for Colonies*, 1938. Grey, *Twenty-Five Years, 1892–1916*, 1925. Rich and Fisher, eds., *The Holstein Papers*, 1957, vol. ii. Robinson and Gallagher, *Africa and the Victorians*, 1963.

[2] *The History of The Times*, vol. iii, 1947, quotes *The Times* of 12 January 1885, p. 17.

[3] *Die Grosse Politik*, vol. iii, pp. 449–50; vol. iv, p. 100.

Consequently, they suggested the Rio del Rey–Cross River provisional boundary and this line was readily accepted by the Germans.

The details of several agreements which included East Africa, the Cameroons, and the coast between Natal and Delagoa Bay were worked out by the German colonial 'expert', Dr Krauel, and the officials of the British Foreign Office. As far as the foreshadowing of the first section of the Nigerian eastern international boundary was concerned, in the 'Arrangement' arrived at between 29 April and 16 June 1885

> [Great Britain] engages not to make acquisitions of territory, accept Protectorates or interfere with the extension of German influence in that part of the coast of the Gulf of Guinea, or in the interior districts to the east of the following line: that is, on the coast, the right river bank of the Rio del Rey entering the sea between 8° 42′ and 8° 46′ longitude east of Greenwich; in the interior a line following the right bank of the Rio del Rey from the said mouth to its source, thence striking direct to the left river bank of the Old Calabar or Cross River, and terminating after crossing that river at the point about 9° 8′ longitude east of Greenwich, marked 'Rapids' on the English Admiralty Chart.[1]

Germany accepted similar conditions west of the line indicated above.

Within a year of the provisional boundary agreement designating the Rio del Rey–Cross River line, the Germans began to press for an extension of the line further into the hinterland. The German traveller Flegel had traversed extensively the neighbourhood of the Benue basin in 1879, 1882–3, and 1885. He was convinced that the region north of the Cross River 'rapids' was *res nullius* and was therefore open to German acquisition. The agents of the British Royal Niger Company were equally busy on the Benue and its main tributaries flowing from the south-east. These agents were particularly anxious to reach Yola and establish political relations with the ruler of a strategically-placed town. Besides, the company's interpreta-

---

[1] C.O. 806/242, Memorandum on Agreement, p. 110. Hertslet, *The Map of Africa by Treaty*, vol. iii, no. 260, p. 868.

tion of the principle of freedom of navigation of the Niger and the Benue stipulated by the Berlin West African Conference appeared to mean the company's exclusive control of the navigable portions of the two rivers. Thus, as soon as the company 'acquired' Yola, the British government was ready to accept the German suggestion for an extension of the Rio del Rey–Cross River boundary. Between 27 June and 2 August 1886 a Supplementary Arrangement was negotiated whereby Britain and Germany

> Agreed to an extended line of demarcation, which starting from the point on the left bank of the Old Calabar or Cross River, where the original line terminated, shall be continued diagonally to such a point on the right bank of the River Benue to the east of, and close to, Yola...[1]

This latter section of the boundary is however left for detailed analysis in the next chapter.

Undoubtedly the two provisional boundary arrangements contain ample reference to straight lines and longitudes. Here indeed would appear justification for Macdonald's 'blue pencil and rule' joke or for Oliver's claim that the imaginations of statesmen were preoccupied with concepts of coast and hinterland 'which tapered towards the centre into the vagueness of ignorance . . .'. These generalizations do not, however, tell the whole story. In respect of the provisional boundaries just outlined, it should be remembered that the British Prime Minister, Lord Salisbury, pointed out that 'when the geography of the country and the position of the various tribes are more accurately ascertained, it may be found practicable to settle a fresh line in accordance with their requirements'.[2] The following years were spent, on the British side, in 'ascertaining' the pattern of ethnic distribution and the geography of the boundary zone in the Cross River basin. The subsequent negotiations were technically based on the data which the British agents

---

[1] Ibid., no. 263, p. 880. Also see F.O. 64/1146, Despatches to Malet, July 1886.

[2] F.O.C.P. Confidential 5753, no. 13, Salisbury to Malet, 25 January 1888.

believed they could make available. It must, however, be confessed that there is no evidence to show that the British and the German governments deliberately enjoined their local agents to collect material on the indigenous ethnic and political landscape.

The extension of alien control to the hinterland was bound to result in considerable contact with the indigenous groups which occupied the boundary zone and close acquaintance with their geographical environment. The German administration in Duala achieved little success in hinterland penetration, although the governor, Von Soden, endorsed the policy of advancing from the coast through establishing friendly relations with the 'native kings' in the neighbourhood of Duala and the Cameroons Mountain. This was indeed the task originally undertaken by the Swedes as well as Puttkamer and Krabbes. Zintgraff also attempted, in 1886–7, the penetration of the hinterland from Rio del Rey. Success was negligible. Thus, poor resources on the part of the German local administration and hostility on the part of Duala trader 'kings' confined Germany to Duala.[1] It was not until 1889 that a German station was established at Bali on the Bamenda plateau. In the meantime the British Oil Rivers Protectorate had been promulgated. A lone British consul with his 'headquarters' at Calabar was too preoccupied with the affairs of the coast city-states west of Calabar to have the leisure or the compulsion to explore the Calabar hinterland. The coronation oath taken by King Duke of Duke Town, in the presence of the British consul Hewett, embodied the traditional Efik claim to political authority over the hinterland:

> I Orok Edem, Prince Duke . . . promise . . . that I will always govern and rule over Duke Town and its dependencies to the best of my ability.[2]

It is not clear how much territorial significance the British consul attached to the duke's declaration, but in the following year, he forwarded to the British government a memorandum

---

[1] Rudin, op. cit., pp. 54–6 and pp. 79–84.
[2] Calprof 5/7 (not dated).

in which the internal sovereignty of the ruler of Duke Town was challenged by the rulers of Henshaw Town. This was in connection with the receipt of 'duties'. The rulers of Henshaw Town, who also had extensive commercial dealings with the hinterland, demanded a share of the 'duties' for distribution to the 'adjacent tribes'. Without something from the 'duties' as presents, they feared that Efik traders would probably be expelled from the hinterland towns. The next British consul, Annesley, faced with a situation in which Efik traders were being molested in the upper Cross River described by the missionaries as the 'turbulence of the river', decided to invoke the authority claimed by the Efik rulers. The consul persuaded the latter to fit out a naval expedition against the people of Enyong. Their houses were duly burnt by the Efik, but a few days after the withdrawal of the Efik naval expedition the Enyong rebuilt their town and resumed their traditional policy of blockading the Cross River between Umon and Ikotana.[1]

The next British agent, Harry Johnston, was, as already mentioned, by far the most active of the early administrators in collecting data on indigenous ethnic and political organization. He was not merely an armchair ethnologist. He undertook an extensive exploration of the boundary zone to study the river systems and to ascertain the limits of Efik commercial activity. The proposed survey became for the British Foreign Office a matter of considerable importance, and a peremptory telegram from that office categorically stated that 'Delay Rio del Rey expedition most inconvenient'.[2] Johnston's exploration shortly revealed an important geographical fact which made nonsense of the provisional Rio del Rey–Cross River section of the Anglo-German agreement. Rio del Rey was not a river eighty miles long as had been assumed in the provisional boundary. It was indeed nothing more than the recipient estuary of a number of small streams connected with two larger streams, the Akpayafe and the Ndian. Which of the larger

---

[1] Ibid., 4/3, Memorial of Chief Henshaw to Granville, April 1885. Goldie, *Calabar and its Mission*, pp. 348–350.
[2] F.O. 84/1828, F.O. to Hewett, 14 February 1887.

streams represented the boundary?[1] A German official, Zintgraff, shortly afterwards confirmed Johnston's discovery. The German governor proceeded to observe in a letter to Hewett that

> You know as well as I that there is no Rio del Rey, at least no sources of such a river. . . . I do not know whether the rapids of the Cross River are to be found easier, or whether they have the same mythical existence.[2]

Time had apparently been wasted in London by British and German 'experts' in pretending to define a boundary.

For the benefit of the British Foreign Office, Johnston emphatically stated in his report that of the two coast rivers 'feeding' the Rio del Rey estuary, the Ndian and not the Akpayafe marked an ethnic boundary between Bantu-speaking Cameroons tribes, to the east, and the Efik people, to the west. There was a further consideration, argued Johnston: the Ndian also marked the eastern limit of the Efik commercial empire. The Efik man who had lent Johnston a well equipped boat for his expedition naturally provided a living proof of the achievements of the Efik traders.

> Yellow Duke, the house-slave of one of the 'Kings' of Old Calabar, had built up for his master a considerable trade. He sent his traders far away into regions between the basins of the Cross River and the Cameroons, trafficking with unknown natives for the two oils.[3]

The data thus provided formed the core of the British case during the negotiations for a more definitive boundary. It is hardly surprising that Johnston and his Foreign Office masters tried to insinuate political significance into what was no more than the role of Efik traders as middlemen. And according to Johnston, the trade and rule of the Old Calabar chiefs extended in 1887 considerably further than the Ndian River. The chiefs had reluctantly withdrawn their claims for damages against

---

[1] F.O. 84/1839, Johnston to Salisbury, 14 July 1887.
[2] F.O.C.P. Confidential 5753, Inclosure in no. 177, Salisbury to Malet, 28 July 1888.
[3] Johnston, *The Story of My Life*, 1923, p. 186.

the German government for 'really undeserved destruction of their settlements and the disposal of their followers'.[1]

Having completed his exploration of the river systems of the boundary zone, Johnston announced his intention of embarking on an expedition that might have embraced the region north of the Cross River bend and south of the basin of the Benue and its tributaries. Unfortunately this expedition never got under way, and this portion of the boundary zone remained a 'blank' during the renewed negotiations between Britain and Germany. What Johnston did achieve on the occasion was a trip up the Cross River. It was to confirm what the Calabar Scottish missionaries had always known. Apparently the original British treaty of protection with the Efik 'republics' was not enough to secure the compliance and cooperation of the many groups occupying the upper portions of the Cross River. Johnston attempted, therefore, to secure independent treaties of friendship and amity with Umon, Akunakuna and Iko-morut, 'besides making friends with and distributing English flags to the people right up to the borders of Atam'. He confirmed in his report that Calabar was at odds with Umon, Umon with Akunakuna, Akunakuna with Iko-morut. The 'wild state of freedom' which prevailed was demonstrated before Johnston, the presence of Efik war canoes notwithstanding, when

> In one instant, I was dragged out of the canoe by a score of cannibals, mounted on the shoulders of the biggest and carried off at a run to the town where I was put in a hut with the door open and had to submit to be stared at for an hour by hundreds of entranced savages.[2]

Johnston could not, in the face of this kind of experience, pretend that the Efik exercised any political authority over the peoples of the upper Cross River region. The reaction of the German administrators of the Cameroons to the exploring

---

[1] F.O.C.P. Confidential 6098, Johnston to F.O., no. 130, 23 October 1890. Also F.O. 84/1828, Johnston to F.O., no. 26, 3 December 1887.

[2] F.O. 84/1881, no. 6, Johnston to F.O., 9 February 1888. See also Minute by Anderson.

activities of Johnston revealed that they were very unlikely to attach any importance to the linguistic and other data which were being made available to the British government—except of course where they suited German imperialist designs.

The German acting governor rejected the claims made by the British that an Efik commercial empire existed in the region beyond the provisional boundary line. When a number of people, probably Bantu speaking, who were in debt to the Efik traders were enslaved as was customary, the German official went to Calabar and forcibly removed King Eyo Honesty VII of Creek Town. Here was an adequate answer to the pretensions of Efik rulers to regard German 'citizens' as Efik subjects. When Major Claude Macdonald arrived at Calabar in March 1889 as Lord Salisbury's Special Commissioner, he was faced with the local crisis created by this seizure and removal of a leading Efik king by the German acting governor of the Cameroons. His meeting with Krabbes at last secured the release of the Efik king, but their discussions revealed the Anglo-German divergence of views in regard to the interpretation of the extent of the Efik 'empire'. From this time onward, the German local officials pursued consistently and relentlessly the policy of confiscating Efik traders' goods in the region east and north-east of Rio del Rey.[1]

The Special Commissioner's proceedings in Calabar itself were not reassuring when it came to the claims of an empire put forward on behalf of the Efik. Macdonald discovered that in seeking to obtain local views about the form of British administration to be recommended to Lord Salisbury he had to deal, not with one king, but with different rulers who claimed to be equal in status: King Duke of Duke Town, King Eyo of Creek Town, Henshaw III of Henshaw Town and so forth. He conveyed his misgivings to the Scottish missionary Goldie, who informed him that the Efik kings had no political authority beyond the bounds of their small town-states.[2] In 1891 Macdonald was appointed commissioner and consul-general of the

---

[1] Calprof 6/1. Vice-Consul Wall to Macdonald, 9 November 1893; Casement to Macdonald, 18 July 1894.

[2] Confidential 5913, 1890. Report by Macdonald, 15 January 1890.

Oil Rivers Protectorate based on Calabar, and it was in this capacity that he took an active part in the renewed boundary negotiations of 1893.

Macdonald, as commissioner and consul-general of the Niger Coast Protectorate (the new name for the territory), had every opportunity to assess the ethnic and political realities of the Cross River region. A stern-wheeled steamer, the *Beecroft*, was now available for travel to the upper Cross River. The commissioner's subordinates undertook extensive overland journeys into Ekoi-land and beyond. The most remarkable of these overland excursions was that of Roger Casement through the Ekoi country from Okoyon to Okerike. Casement's report was hardly in the nature of an ethnographic survey. It was full of praise for the rich natural resources of the region, but had little to say about the existence or non-existence of Efik authority over what he called 'an utter wilderness of dense forest, uninhabited by man'.[1] Macdonald's successor in 1895 showed an active interest in the boundary question with regard to the Ekoi country. Sir Ralph Moor was aware that an Anglo-German survey was about to be undertaken in the region south of the Cross River bend. Moor's assessment of the indigenous political situation was simple and uncritical:

> many of these towns have, up to a late date, paid tribute to Efik kings as subjects.[2]

All that Moor had before him was the fact that there were many Efik traders to be found in the midst of the autonomous village communities in Ekoi-land. There was no evidence that the villages were disposed to accept Calabar political authority, let alone pay tribute to that authority.

From 1895, also, the reports of the British Consul-General began to include vague references to the ethnic groups which occupied the boundary zone to the north of the Cross River bend. The British administrators were quite right in observing

---

[1] Calprof 6/1. Casement to Macdonald, 18 July 1894. F.O. 2/63, Report on the Niger Coast Protectorate, 21 August 1894, pp. 33–43.

[2] F.O. 2/84, Report of an expedition up the Cross River, 11 September 1895.

that this region was dominated by the commercial activities of 'middlemen' Akunakuna traders. The latter attempted to tap the trade along the Aweyong tributary flowing into the Cross River from the north. The Akaju and the Atam peoples who lay astride this tributary were split into autonomous villages, and were so fiercely independent that the Akunakuna found it infinitely safer to conciliate than to cajole the riverain peoples, to enable them to carry on their enterprising trading transactions. The contact established by Moor and his subordinates with the peoples of this part of the boundary zone clearly revealed to the British agents the extreme ethnic and political fragmentation which characterized the region. The Ikwes regarded themselves as Ikwes and laughed at the question whether they were Ekoi or Boki. The British political officers noted that the ethnic pattern was so complex that they could not classify the multifarious groups they encountered or heard about. The reports named the Indem, the Atam, the Akaju, the Boki and the Yachi, but these were not indeed coherent ethnic groups. They were hopelessly intermingled.[1] The only reference, in the British reports, to the Bamenda plateau was that 'six days' journey north would bring the officers to the "Dama" country and the "Baminda" [Bamenda] peoples'.[2] The extent of the contact of British officials with the peoples of the boundary zone and the inadequacies of the material they assembled on the indigenous ethnic and political pattern help to explain the ease with which at the boundary conference table the Germans were able to dismiss British claims concerning an Efik 'empire' and Ekoi 'solidarity'.

The negotiations, conducted for the most part in Berlin, went on intermittently from 1888 to 1902. In the first place the illusion embodied in the 1885 provisional boundary line that the Rio del Rey was a river eighty miles long had to be replaced by something more real. Lord Salisbury, relying on the data assembled by Harry Johnston, made the preliminary suggestion to the German Ambassador in London, Count Leyden, that the River Ndian was 'a suitable boundary from an ethno-

---

[1] F.O.C.P. Confidential 6837, Moor to F.O., 21 December 1895.
[2] F.O. 2/85, Moor to Macdonald, 9 October 1895.

logical and commercial point of view'.[1] Salisbury went on to argue that on the other hand the territory through which the River Akpayafe flowed formed 'an integral part' of the Old Calabar country. The German Ambassador had apparently no facts at his disposal with which to agree or disagree with Lord Salisbury's exposition of the local situation in the Calabar–Cameroons boundary zone. He therefore merely forwarded to the German delegates to the boundary conference the suggestions made to him. The latter were apparently well briefed by the German Foreign Office to which the German governor of the Cameroons had forwarded his version of the local geographical and other conditions. The German delegates completely ignored Lord Salisbury's emphasis on the ethnological aspects of the question. As for commercial considerations, the advantages claimed by the British for the River Ndian equally applied to the River Akpayafe. The result was a deadlock in the 1888 negotiations, because the Germans refused to entertain the British claim that

> The land is ours by our Calabar treaties, because it all belongs . . .
> to Old Calabar Chiefs . . . it is important also that the trading
> frontiers of the Calabaree middlemen should as far as possible be
> repeated in the international settlement.

The Germans countered by insinuating that the provisional boundary of 1885 had been inspired by considerations of the river systems, not by the extent of the Efik empire nor by ethnology. They therefore concluded that since Britain had acquired the Cross River estuary, the logical and equitable thing was for the Germans to take control of the next river system beginning with the mouth of the Akpayafe.[2]

The negotiations in Berlin and events in the Calabar region interacted to a certain extent with one another. On the one hand, the local British officials urged the Efik traders to redouble their commercial activities, particularly in the region

---

[1] F.O.C.P. Confidential 5753, no. 226, Salisbury to Malet, 2 November 1888.
[2] Ibid., 6098, no. 325, Salisbury to Trench, 3 October 1890. Also 5945, Leyden to Salisbury, 1 January 1889.

between the Akpayafe and the Ndian rivers. This kind of energy on the part of the Efik might well convince the local Germans that there was indeed an Efik commercial empire which an international boundary should as much as possible respect. The new German governor of the Cameroons, Zimmerer, on the other hand decided to deal drastically with any Efik traders found on the German side of the provisional boundary. Efik traders were driven from the area north of the Rio del Rey estuary. In fact the Governor proceeded to grant concessions to the European firms of Messrs Knutson, Valdau and Heilbron, and the Ambas Bay Company in the very area from which Efik traders were being expelled. It was in vain that the British chief official lamented to the British Foreign Office with reference to the destruction of Efik posts that

> The ruins of these I have myself seen on the banks of the Ndian... the entire trade so far as Old Calabar is concerned has been destroyed.[1]

As was to be expected, the Anglo-German negotiations for a definitive boundary, when they were resumed in Berlin, became more involved. Every official who had been connected with the boundary zone, however vaguely, produced old and new arguments. It was at this point that the chief local administrators, Macdonald and Soden, were summoned to Berlin. Harry Johnston was available to refresh the minds of the British delegation on the racial and linguistic features characteristic of the area in dispute. Privately, though, Lord Salisbury urged the principal British representative, Trench, that all that Britain really wanted in the boundary zone was 'the retention of Mount Hewett [in the Ekoi country] as a favourable site for a sanatorium . . .'.[2] This was something apparently more important from the British standpoint than the Efik empire and the desirability of preserving Ekoi 'solidarity'. In the face of the impressive data on ethnography

---

[1] F.O.C.P. Confidential 6471, Macdonald to F.O., no. 8, 21 January 1893. Also Confidential 5945, Inclosure in no. 262, African Association to Salisbury, 13 August 1889.

[2] Ibid., 6098, no. 325, Salisbury to Trench, 3 October 1890.

and geography publicly marshalled by the British delegation, the Germans found it convenient to fall back on the provisional boundary agreement. Whether or not the Rio del Rey was a river, it was undoubtedly a body of water, and the head of the estuary was as good a boundary point as the source of the river that did not exist. The British delegates admitted privately among themselves that the Germans were on strong technical grounds. No agreement, however, was reached in 1890, but the Germans reminded the British boundary commission that

> The few square miles of bog, and one or two negro villages which would be added to German territory by giving up the present frontier, are quite secondary and subordinate . . . . 'These protected subjects' . . . easily rebuild their huts.[1]

The boundary negotiations were adjourned. In London, Anderson of the Foreign Office held private discussions with the German Ambassador, Metternich. These were inconclusive, and Anderson, reporting on the discussions, concluded with his misgivings that the territory in dispute 'might prove to be an Eldorado or a worthless swamp'. The doubts in Anderson's mind were soon dispelled when Macdonald assured him in a private letter that he himself had visited the place and found that 'the ground in dispute is a strip . . . of dismal swamp . . . peopled by a few miserable fisher folk . . .'.[2] Furthermore, Macdonald was not sure whether the inhabitants were Efik or 'Cameroons Bantu'. It is therefore hardly surprising that when the Anglo-German negotiations were resumed in Berlin, 1893, the British delegation gave in to the Germans. Macdonald was himself there to reiterate his conclusions about the worthlessness of the zone of contention. A point at the upper end of the Rio del Rey estuary was without much argument selected as the terminus. Thus for the time being the settlement of the Rio del Rey portion of the provisional boundary, in the

---

[1] Ibid., 6098, Trench to Salisbury, 23 October 1890.
[2] F.O.C.P. Confidential 6164, no. 3. Memorandum by Anderson on the Interview with Metternich (not dated). Also 6471, no. 32, Macdonald to Anderson, 26 March 1893.

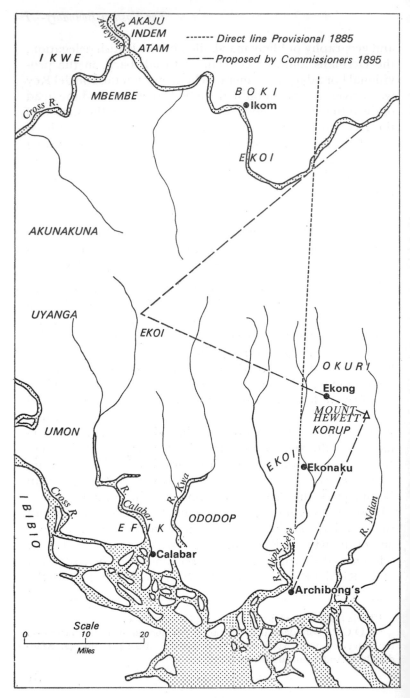

NIGERIA—SOUTHERN CAMEROONS BOUNDARY PROPOSALS
1885–1896

words of Trench's report, 'finally disposes of the Akpayafe controversy'.[1]

The second controversy about the definition of the boundary, to the north of the Rio del Rey estuary, centred on the question of whether or not the Ekoi groups should be split. The formal negotiations for this portion of the boundary zone did not begin until 1896. Meanwhile the British consul-general, Sir Ralph Moor, prepared the British case based on 'the interests of the people'. He concluded that

> I make the foregoing remarks purely in the interests of the natives who will be affected by the proposed boundary . . . and it will be a hardship to cut off the natives [of Calabar] from their markets.[2]

Moor's idea conveyed to the British Foreign Office was that the new boundary to be negotiated should skirt the Ekoi country—in favour of Britain—in order to preserve both Ekoi 'unity' and the markets of Efik traders. He did not say how he identified which towns were Ekoi in the boundary zone, and it seemed extremely unlikely that he would have favoured the wholesale transfer of 'Ekoi-land' to the Germans in order to safeguard Ekoi solidarity.

Two issues were constantly mixed up in the subsequent negotiations: Ekoi solidarity and Efik trade facilities. The Germans were not particularly concerned about what Ekoi groups they had, but were determined to put an end to the Efik trade caravans which diverted trade in the boundary zone towards Calabar. Their coast acquisition would be useless, economically, if Efik traders were allowed to continue their traditional practice of tapping the trade of Ekoi land. Lord Salisbury, who had always thought in terms of a survey on the spot, proposed a joint Anglo-German survey to determine the precise distribution of ethnic groups. As a result, Captain Close and Lieutenant Von Besser set out, towards the end of 1895, to make a survey of Ekoi-land between the Cross 'rapids' and the coast. The commissioners began their survey at Nsakpe in the

---

[1] Ibid., no. 38, Trench to Rosebery, 15 April 1893.
[2] Ibid., 6837, no. 50, Moor to F.O., 21 December 1895. Also *Cologne Gazette*, 22 July 1898 (for the German view).

neighbourhood of the 'rapids' and travelled southwards through Ekoi-land, visiting towns to the east and west of the provisional straight-line boundary. On the Cross River bend, the chiefs of Nsau and Nnasakang described themselves as Ekoi, and informed the commissioners that their trade was directed towards Calabar through the Cross River. At Otu, another Ekoi town, the commissioners encountered an Efik trader buying palm oil for King Duke of Duke Town. So far the commissioners' encounters appeared to have justified the two arguments of Ekoi solidarity and Efik commercial interests advanced by Britain.

The tidy human pattern came to a confused end. At Okuri, in the heart of Ekoi-land, the inhabitants described themselves to the commissioners as 'mixed Ekoi', and here was a type of ethnic categorization which conveyed little meaning to the European investigators. Thereafter, the commissioners increasingly spotted non-Ekoi villages located to the west and south of Mount Hewett. These villages belonged to Ododop (Bantu) groups and included Abong, Ekong and Ekonaku, the last village being exactly situated on the Akpayafe River. Towards the head of the Rio del Rey, the commissioners found Ifiang, an Efik colony of slave farmworkers belonging to King Archibong of Calabar.[1] The British local officials were apparently baffled by the outcome of the commissioners' survey. Apart from the one Efik town on the Rio del Rey, there was no evidence that Efik chiefs received tribute from the Ekoi and non-Ekoi villages in the boundary zone. Where too was the evidence of Ekoi solidarity which Moor appeared to have so much in mind? The commissioners on their own initiative proposed a boundary adjustment to reflect their findings. Instead of the straight Rio del Rey–Cross River 'rapids' line, the boundary should be deflected north-eastwards to Mount Hewett, then westwards to the Oban hills. From here the proposed boundary ran directly north-eastwards to the 'rapids'.

Sir Ralph Moor objected to the adjustment proposed by the

---

[1] F.O.C.P. Confidential 6837, Inclosure 5 in no. 50, Moor to F.O. 21 December 1895 (see the Commissioners' survey map attached).

survey team on two grounds. Firstly, Efik markets were still not accessible to Calabar traders. Secondly, Moor was not prepared to abandon his conviction that the boundary zone was Ekoi country and insisted that the westward deflection of the boundary from Mount Hewett amounted to splitting Ekoi groups. These arguments were advanced for the benefit of the German government. Sir Ralph had ended with another reason for opposing the boundary adjustment, but the British government kept this to itself: 'All the inhabitants in this country regard themselves as under British rule'.[1] There was no way of confirming Moor's claim, since no German official from the Cameroons had up to the time tried to establish German stations in Ekoi-land. The only post owned by Germany anywhere near the boundary zone was established in 1890 at Bali on the Bamenda plateau. In spite of German ineffectiveness in the area in dispute, it is significant that Moor's predecessor, an active member of the boundary commission in Berlin, Macdonald, wrote to the British Foreign Office and categorically stated that 'we shall do as well as can be expected if the Germans accepted the Close–Besser Line'.[2] On the other hand, the intelligence division of the British War Office upheld Moor's views as to the undesirability of splitting any ethnic groups, but feared that the Germans were unlikely to agree 'without material compensation'.

The Anglo-German negotiations on the Close–Besser joint report dragged on from 1896 to 1902. The old arguments were rehashed, and the joint report obviously invalidated many of the data on which the British based their case. As far as the Germans could see, the region was occupied by Ekoi and non-Ekoi groups not coherently distributed. If the Efik did extensive business in the area, traders in the German colony were entitled to the same facilities. In 1902 the German boundary commissioners proposed a new boundary line through the middle of the channel of the mouth of the Calabar River. The Ekoi groups would then not be split, as the British feared, but

---

[1] Ibid.

[2] Ibid., no. 36, Macdonald to F.O., 10 February 1896. (See Memorandum on the Boundary.)

they would become part of the German colony. If the British accepted, the Germans were prepared to offer territorial compensation in the unknown region north of the Cross River bend.[1] As was to be expected, the British turned down the German offer, and no agreement was concluded. It must also be borne in mind that there was at this time nothing resembling the 'honeymoon' of the earlier negotiations of 1885 and 1886. Chamberlain's efforts for an Anglo-German 'natural alliance' gave way to recriminations on both sides. The hostile diplomatic atmosphere as much as basic divergencies of interpretation of data on the local situation contributed to the breakdown of the negotiations for a definitive boundary.

The British local administrators became accustomed to speaking of British Ekoi and German Ekoi. They attempted to identify their subjects by distributing to them testimonials which read as follows:

> To whom it may concern—Notice is hereby given that in the village of . . . living within the limits of Her Britannic Majesty's Niger Coast Protectorate, the people are under the care and protection of that government.[2]

There is no way of knowing the manner in which the Ekoi towns reacted to this extraordinary document. At about the same time the Germans eased their way into the region. Keeping to their side of the original 'diagonal line', they moved into the Ekoi 'country' from Bali on the Bamenda plateau. Their first station was at Nsakpe established in 1899 on the River Awa. Shortly afterwards, a German officer, Captain Von Weiss, six of his soldiers and one hundred and twenty carriers were murdered at Otu. The murder provoked a punitive expedition which in turn precipitated what has been described, rather grandiloquently, as the 'Ekoi struggle for independence'.[3]

---

[1] Ibid., Confidential 7996, Inclosure in no. 102, Graham to Lansdowne, 19 November 1902. Also Newton, *Lord Lansdowne*, 1929, pp. 196–207.

[2] C.O. 444/1, Moor to C.O., no. 65, 13 April 1899. Also Talbot, *In the Shadow of the Bush*, pp. 151–2.

[3] Talbot, op. cit., p. 158. *Report on the Cameroons*, 1955, p. 9. Mansfeld, *Urwald Dokumente*, p. 21.

The rising revealed anything but Ekoi solidarity. It is true, however, that several Ekoi towns were involved in the fighting which went on till 1904. The British administrators were assured that none of the Ekoi towns on their side of the border had any hand in the fighting. No 'Ekoi' army took the field in reaction against the German invasion of their fatherland. In the same way, when the Boki villages on the German side of the provisional boundary decided to fight the Germans, there is evidence that they sought the assistance of the Boki on the British side, but that their solicitations produced no results.[1] These events are recounted to show the complete absence of comprehensive self-awareness among the Ekoi and the Boki, the major ethnic groups affected by the boundary which traversed this region. The groups were not only not homogeneous, but they were also not interdependent. It is reasonable to assume that if the local reaction to alien rule was based on tribal solidarity, the boundary negotiators might have had second thoughts in 1913 when a definitive boundary was agreed upon, to settle a vexing question 'once and for all'.

In the final settlement, the 'rapids' of the provisional boundary became the thalweg of the Cross River at the bend of the river about two and a half miles upstream from Obokun. The boundary southward followed the thalweg of the Cross River to its junction with the River Awa. The thalweg of the latter river continued the boundary, and thence to a number of hill-tops on the Oban Hills, demarcated with pillars. From these hill-tops, the boundary followed the thalweg of the Akpayafe River down to the coast. Here the boundary was coincident with the western bank of the Rio del Rey estuary, and it was agreed that the Bakassi peninsula, which bounds the Rio del Rey on the west should be treated as a commercial no-man's-land, although the fishing rights of the native population would remain as heretofore. All that was said in the agreement about the indigenous inhabitants, Ekoi or Bantu Ododop, was that they could, within six months, transfer with

---

[1] Calprof 6/1, no. 3, Roupell to Moor, 30 November 1899. C.S.O. 1/13, Rosebery to S. of S., 9 March 1904.

their property and harvested crops to whichever side of the boundary they wished, and that the representatives of the Powers 'may make deflections not to exceed one mile . . . in order that farms shall not be separated from villages to which they belong'.[1]

The boundary agreement concluded in 1913 was only briefly effective because in the following year British troops invaded and occupied the German Cameroons as soon as the First World War broke out. The end of the war saw the complete elimination of Germany as a colonial Power. The Cameroons was split between Britain and France in such a way that Britain acquired as a Mandatory Power the portion of the ex-German colony coterminous with Nigeria. The international boundary became virtually a regional boundary between Eastern Nigeria and Southern Cameroons. The new situation provided an excellent opportunity for the local British administrators to have a second look at the extent to which the Anglo-German boundary may have disrupted homogeneous ethnic groups in the boundary zone. For instance, in 1921 the first census ever conducted in Nigeria produced interesting statistics relative to the groups affected by the 1913 international boundary. The statistics for the relevant provinces are as follows:[2]

PROVINCE	TRIBES			
	Ibibio-Efik	Ekoi	Other Semi-Bantu	Bantu
Calabar ⎫ Ogoja ⎭ Nigeria	918,217 37	7,215 44,255	11,662 242,877	45 —
Southern Cameroons	2	38,279	1,613	83,132

The major group apparently split by the boundary, as the figures reveal, is the Ekoi tribe. The second table shows more precisely how Ekoi sub-tribes were affected:

---

[1] Hertslet, *Commercial Treaties*, vol. xxvii, pp. 220–5.

[2] Talbot, *The Peoples of Southern Nigeria*, vol. iv, Table no. 5, p. 26 and Table no. 25, pp. 60–1.

PROVINCE		THE EKOI BY SUB-TRIBE								
		Aka-ju	Nde	Nku-mm	Ekoi	Assu-mbo	Kea-ka	Man-ta	Ban-yang	Oba-ng
Calabar ⎱ Nigeria		—	—	—	7,046	—	—	—	—	—
Ogoja ⎰		7,575	9,212	13,894	10,957	—	—	—	—	—
Southern Cameroons		—	—	—	1,958	2,746	7,506	4,343	19,112	2,609

The figures set out above are not really helpful because Talbot worked at a time when it was fashionable to use undiscriminating collective terms such as 'tribes' and 'sub-tribes'. Unfortunately, later census reports did not provide a more precise picture of the ethnic complexity which characterized the human pattern. But another remarkable thing about the statistics is the smallness of the figures representing sub-tribes, and this helps to recall the fact that the boundary zone is one in which forests and elephants predominate and 'man seems to have no place in it'. It is therefore useless to imagine that the international boundary divided homogenous tribal communities and constituted 'a crime of the first magnitude'.[1] In any case, the British were shortly to embark on a major reorganization of local government on both sides of the international boundary. The whole exercise was one based on the assumption that 'a corporate tribal spirit under wise European guidance gives a most valuable impetus to the development of primitive communities'. The British political officers were therefore enjoined to discover not only village but also clan heads among the Boki, Ekoi, Bantu and other groups in the region. It was easy to find village chiefs or elders, but finding clan heads was another matter. The officers reported that they could not trace clan heads: this was so because obviously no clans existed.

The reports on the local government reorganizations spoke

---

[1] Confidential, no. 1049, no. 83, Governor of Nigeria to C.O., 11 February 1922.

of village councils working very satisfactorily. The artificially created district councils could not work because they lacked cohesion. The failure was rightly blamed on 'the antagonisms and petty jealousies between . . . village groups and in some cases between villages'.[1] The establishment of native authorities based on the amalgamation of clusters of towns and villages failed completely. A later inquiry conducted by a social anthropologist confirmed a situation already obvious. Each village recognized a chief who performed ritual rather than political functions. Political integration did not go beyond the limits of a village. A satisfactory demarcation of the intermingled ethnic groups was something impossible to describe.[2] In the circumstances, it would be far from objective to speak of 'tribal irredentism' in reaction against the international boundary. The last point is made with caution, because the boundary was not intended to function as an international barrier during the decades when the Southern Cameroons Trust territory was governed virtually as a portion of Eastern Nigeria. There was then the strong possibility that the adjoining administrative areas might amalgamate. Subsequent events decreed otherwise.

To begin with, the period of association with Eastern Nigeria witnessed quite early the influx of enterprising Ibo into the farms and plantations of the Southern Cameroons. The indigenous inhabitants found themselves in a position in which many of them had to buy articles of food cultivated by the Ibo. Those who abandoned farming had also to compete with the Ibo for jobs in the plantations. Nor was this all. The Ibo increasingly achieved ascendancy over retail trade in the major Cameroons towns. In view of these developments, the Cameroons people began to fear what they believed would end in Ibo domination. It was to allay this fear that the British administration in Nigeria decided, in the constitutional reorganization of 1954, to transfer the administrative 'capital' from Enugu to Lagos. It was also decided at a later consti-

---

[1] *Report on the Cameroons*, 1931, p. 6. See also Reports, 1926, pp. 18–20; 1929, pp. 15–17; 1955, pp. 33 f.

[2] Jones, *Report on the Position, Status, and Influence of Chiefs*, p. 49.

tutional conference that after Nigeria attained independence, the Southern Cameroons would become a separate Region of the Federation and enjoy a generous allocation of capital from the Federal Government. These inducements did not satisfy all the political parties in the Cameroons. They were beginning to be divided on the issues of union with or secession from Nigeria. The Kamerun National Democratic Party led by John Foncha preached secession, while the Kamerun National Congress and the Kamerun Peoples Party advocated a policy of continued but safeguarded association with Nigeria. The issue was therefore intimately bound up with whether the Anglo-German boundary would remain a regional boundary or become an international barrier separating Nigeria from the Cameroons. In the general election which took place in January 1959, Foncha's K.N.D.P. won with a small majority.[1]

During the election campaign much was made of slogans like 'all Cameroonians are brothers'. Some people indeed traced an entirely mythical history purporting to confirm the existence of an ancient empire and unity. The smallness of the K.N.D.P. majority was considered too inconclusive to decide the issue of secession. Foncha had won fourteen seats compared with the twelve of the opposing parties. The constituencies were unfortunately not arranged in a manner which might have enabled the pattern of voting to throw light on the sentiments of those ethnic groups, for instance the Banyangs and the Keakas, who are assumed to have close ethnic connections with the Nigerian groups, the Boki and the Ekoi. The Cameroons contains more than sixty ethnic groups, and large numbers in Wum and Bamenda Divisions as well as in the constituencies bordering what was then the French Cameroons voted for Foncha. These were enough to enthrone an 'anti-Nigerian' government. A broad analysis of the voting figures shows that the secession party won five seats out of six in Bamenda Division, three out of four in Mamfe Division, and one out of four in Kumba Division. Although these three Divisions border on Nigeria, no ethnic pattern could have been reflected in the above analysis. Another complicating factor arises from the

---

[1] *Daily Times* (Lagos), 2 February 1959.

fact that in an area of poor or non-existent communications between Nigeria and the Cameroons, the question of association with Nigeria meant little to the immediate neighbours of Nigeria. The significant thing, however, was that the new Southern Cameroons Premier issued a statement which, among other things, said that

> The assumption of power by the K.N.D.P. in the Southern Cameroons means the beginning of a new era of political and social changes long desired by Cameroonians . . . . The era of autocracy characterized by rebukes, intimidation and victimisation is being replaced by that of instruction, encouragement and demands for devoted service for the love of one's country. In short, there is the air of freedom in the Southern Cameroons now.[1]

The claim that a new era of political change had dawned was not quite true, because the territory had a second chance to decide its destiny.

The United Nations Mission which visited the Southern Cameroons after the 1959 election agreed that the election results could not be regarded as decisive. The administering Power, Britain, took the view that a plebiscite was necessary. The General Assembly of the United Nations proceeded to discuss the questions to be put before the Cameroons electors, and the two questions which emerged were whether the peoples wanted association with Nigeria or a continuance of the British Trusteeship to enable the government of the territory to 'explore [later] the possibility and suitable terms of reunification with an independent French Cameroons'. Foncha, the leader of the 'anti-Nigerian' party, again won. The plebiscite figures do not precisely reveal the choice of the Ejaghams and Overside people of Mamfe Division and the Balondos and Bakosis of Kumba Division bordering on Nigeria. In fact, one of the party leaders opposed to secession, Mr Mbile, spotted the problem, and argued that the votes should be counted 'according to tribal units. No one tribe, because of its numbers, should be allowed to force others into a

---

[1] Ibid., 6 February 1959.

system of government against their will and reason'. This was not done, and so the Anglo-German boundary became 'permanently' a section of the eastern international boundary of Nigeria.

4

The Eastern Boundary—II

The original international boundary drawn by Britain and Germany in the region south of Lake Chad has now been replaced by another one, following the decision of the peoples of the former British Trust territory of North Cameroons to amalgamate their country with Northern Nigeria. The old and the new international boundaries, however, traverse the same region—the region historically known as Adamawa. A fashionable interpretation of the nineteenth century history of this boundary zone is given in an administrative report on the former British Trust territory:

> The main event in the history of the Benue and Adamawa areas during the first half of the nineteenth century was the rise and consolidation of Fulani power under Modibo Adama. At the time of his death he had dominated an area of some 20,000 square miles from Madagali in the north to Banyo in the south, and from the river Ini in the west to the Lere in the east. He established his capital at Yola.[1]

The passage describes quite accurately the extensiveness of the boundary zone being discussed in this chapter. It also reveals, however, the complacency with which Europeans over-simplified the ethnic and political configuration of one of the most complex regions of the world. It is not difficult to explain why the German and then the British administrators found it very convenient to assume that Fulani rule was comprehensive.

---

[1] *Annual Report by H.B.M. Government on the British Cameroons*, 1955, p. 2.

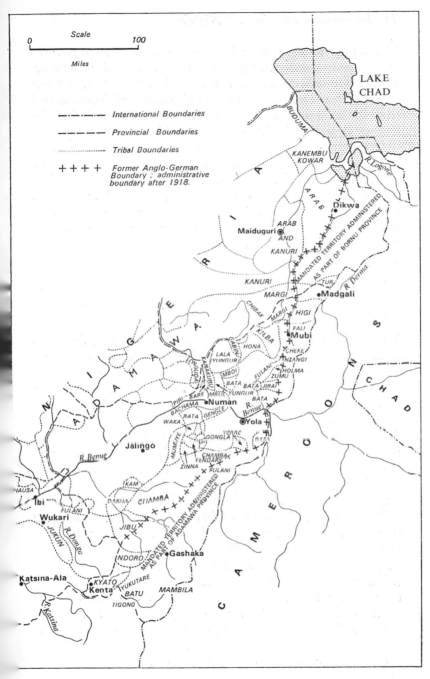

ADAMAWA ETHNIC CLUSTERS

In the task of establishing European organs of local government, contact was readily made with local Fulani leaders, many of whom were willing to become European tools. On the other hand, the innumerable 'pagan' groups which entrenched themselves in inaccessible mountain formations defied the Europeans as they had defied the Fulani before them.

One thing can be stated without equivocation. The European Powers who scrambled for the region and ultimately partitioned it could not pretend that an 'indigenous' political organization was not in existence. Whether they understood the precise character of this system is another matter. Dr Barth, the celebrated German traveller, who visited the Central Sudan and Adamawa between 1850 and 1855, left on record his view that

> [The Fulani] alone here succeed in giving to the distant regions a certain bond of unity, and in making the land more accessible to trade and intercourse.[1]

The agents of the European Powers who followed Barth understandably concentrated on establishing political and commercial relations with Yola and the Fulani 'provincial' rulers. In view of all this, an assessment of the international boundary should not concern itself simply with the manner in which the Fulani empire of Adamawa was broken up and partitioned. Such an assessment would have little historical value because it would ignore not only a critical inquiry into the true character of the Adamawa empire, but also the geographical and ethnic realities which a study of this section of boundary should take into account. Briefly, the region stretching from the Bamenda plateau to the Alantika mountain peak, south of Yola, is one of fantastic mountain formations, including plateaux, parallel ranges and innumerable hill-tops. These are broken into by deep ravines which provide the river systems through which tributaries flow north-westwards to the Benue and north-eastwards to the Faro. The Benue–Faro confluence is in the centre of a broad plain, some eighty miles by forty miles, dominated by Yola. Between the Benue and Lake Chad the

---

[1] Barth, *Travels and Discoveries*, vol. ii, pp. 510–14.

geographical configuration repeats the features of the region south of Yola. There are the same irregular masses and a broken sea of granite peaks. The Yedseram valley, however, provides uninterrupted access to the plains of Bornu. The irregular mountain formations, north and south of Yola, gradually disappear as one moves eastwards into the Cameroun Republic, to give way to a low plateau covered with grass in the north and thick tropical forest in the south. For the purposes of this study, the mountainous regions are more important because they were the ones in which innumerable, but often large, 'pagan' groups entrenched themselves after they were displaced in the plains by the Fulani.

During Dr Barth's journey from Bornu to Yola, he noted the following 'pagan' tribes: the Marghi, the Kilba, the Higi, the Fali, the Batta, the Chamba, the Jukun, the Tikar, the Daka, the Ding Ding and the Mbafu.[1] Recent ethnographic surveys have if anything increased the number of ethnic groups in the region, and there is abundant justification for speaking of tribes rolling upon tribes 'like the waves of the sea'. But no picture of Adamawa during the nineteenth century is accurate if it ignores the existence of important political systems which functioned outside of the Fulani empire.[2] 'Pagan' migrations and intermingling there certainly were, but 'pagan' empires had also risen and fallen, and had left results which the Fulani upheaval could not obliterate. Even Dr Barth was constrained to observe that, although the Fulani were taking steps to subjugate the region, they still had a great deal to do before they could regard themselves as the undisturbed possessors of the soil. This consummation completely eluded the Fulani in Adamawa. It is therefore necessary to locate the major ethnic groups and consider briefly the history of their past migrations and political activities. It is a history of successive waves of immigrants of whom the Fulani were the last. The interplay of historical and geographical forces produced the complicated ethnic and political picture which Adamawa presented during the nineteenth century.

[1] Barth, op. cit., vol. ii, pp. 510–14.
[2] Meek, *Tribal Studies in Northern Nigeria*, 1931, 2 vols.

It is largely a matter of conjecture who the aboriginal inhabitants of Adamawa were. Names quite out of the ordinary, like Ding Ding and Yem-yem, have been recorded, but these names have been shown to be nicknames for slaves and have not been identified with any ethnic groups that exist today. The most widely dispersed groups are the Mbum and the Baya (in the Cameroun Republic), the Fun, and lastly the groups collectively known as the Jirai, who are believed to be very early occupants of the region stretching from the Mandara highlands to the Southern Cameroons plateau and eastwards. The later major immigrants, in the order of their arrival, were the Jukun, the Chamba, the Batta, and lastly the Fulani. In the borderland south of Bornu, other major groups, destined to be affected by the political upheavals which accompanied the Fulani jihad, are the Marghi, the Kilba, the Fali and the Higi. It is to be noted that the Fun mentioned above were the ethnic group which supplied the name Fumbina to the area later named Adamawa, but as far as the history of the place is known, the first conquering and empire-building groups to appear were the Jukun.

The Jukun claim to have migrated from the 'north-east'—a claim which associates them with the much propagated Kisra legend.[1] There is also a tradition among these people which suggests kinship with the Bornu Berber ruling clan. This might perhaps explain why the Jukun were also called Bai-bai, as Dr Barth noted. Whatever the uncertainties regarding the origin of the Jukun, there is incontrovertible evidence that they were a remarkable people. They successfully established an extensive empire which in the days of its prosperity dominated a large portion of Hausaland and the Benue region of Adamawa. The present capital of the Jukun group in Nigeria is Wukari. The site of the traditional capital of the empire, Kororofa, has yet to be reliably identified. Nevertheless there is abundant evidence in Bornu chronicles to show that Kororofa had close political relations with Bornu which alternated in the characteristic phases of war and amity. The *Kano Chronicle* speaks of the extensive devastation wrought by Jukun armies in Hausa-

---

[1] Meek, *A Sudanese Kingdom*, 1931 ; see Introduction by Palmer, xvii.

land, including Kano itself.[1] It has been suggested that Jukun activities extended as far south as Calabar. In proof of this, reference is made to Sultan Bello's description of the Sudan which he gave to Clapperton in 1827. This description mentions an anchorage belonging to Atakpa, i.e. King of the Akpa. Ata is indeed a Jukun title, and not Efik.[2] It might well be that the extensive wars which the Jukun waged in Hausaland were intended to provide slaves which the Jukun exported through Calabar on the Atlantic. The term Ata is today also found among the Igara and other groups westwards to the Niger–Benue confluence and it would appear that Jukun political authority was also established over these groups.

The great days of wide-ranging Jukun conquests were soon over. The empire itself was exposed to attacks from outside, first by the Chamba and then by the Fulani. The decline of the slave trade across the Atlantic may also have contributed to the decline of Jukun prosperity during the nineteenth century. Another persistent element of weakness was the very structure of the empire. The empire was not centralized; it was a loosely-held confederacy of many groups which included the Igara in the west and the Mbums in the east, across the whole region of what is today southern Adamawa. In the absence of close ethnic and political cohesion in so extensive an area, disintegration soon followed the incursions of the Chamba. The final collapse of the empire was brought about by the devastations of the Fulani from three directions, north, north-east and east.[3] There are two conflicting traditions about the final collapse of Kororofa. A government anthropologist gathered these local versions and recorded them. The Fulani and Hausa informants maintained that the king of Kororofa had refused to acknowledge the suzerainty of Sokoto. The Shehu of the latter place, therefore, prayed to Allah for the destruction of the insubordinate Jukun ruler and his headquarters. The

---

[1] Palmer, *Sudanese Memoirs*, 1928, vol. iii, p. 116.

[2] The slim 'Atakpa' evidence must be seen against the background of the fact that the Efik imposed themselves on the aboriginal peoples known as the Qua and it would be easy to confuse the terms Qua and Akpa.

[3] *Gazetteer of Yola Province*, p. 15.

Jukun view was that the Shehu sent 'devils' who then proceeded to destroy Kororofa. These traditions have merely this value, that they show that for the larger part of the nineteenth century the Jukun rulers persisted in maintaining their independence where they could. This Jukun doggedness was specially strong in the triangle of the Central Cameroons–Nigerian border formed by Bakundi, Gashaka and Takum.

Apart from the area of Jukun political influence indicated above, the local traditions of widely dispersed ethnic groups point to close affinity with the major Jukun group. These groups have been identified at Pendiga, Gwana, Muri, Kona and in the region between Lau and Abinsi. It has in fact been argued that the Jukun language was at one time a kind of 'lingua franca' over an extensive area stretching to the Mbum of the Cameroun Republic. A few Jukun words have been selected in proof of this linguistic thesis. For instance, the word for salt in Bali is *ta Kona* (salt of the Kona), and Kona was a Jukun stronghold. The Mbum name for guinea corn is *nang Kona*. Meek did indeed give an impressive list,[1] but it is clear that a more detailed linguistic analysis involving many dispersed groups is necessary before firm historical conclusions can be made as regards the effectiveness of Jukun rule. In any case, the political effectiveness of the Jukun was seriously disrupted by the next conquering immigrants—the Chamba.

The Chamba who produced such a disrupting effect on the Jukun confederacy are themselves found today in scattered groups in Adamawa, Muri, and in the Cameroun Republic. As is to be expected, there is among them a tradition indicating a migration from the north-east. The first 'permanent' location of the major Chamba group appears to have been the central region of Adamawa, to the south of an area enclosed by the Benue and the Faro tributary.[2] The Chamba were sufficiently well organized to impose their rule on the former subjects of the Jukun empire. The later scattering of the Chamba from their

---

[1] Meek, *A Sudanese Kingdom*, pp. 18 f; also Migeod, *Through British Cameroons*, 1925, p. 217.

[2] *Report on the Cameroons*, 1955, p. 4. See also Passarge, *Adamawa*, 1895 (see ethnographic map enclosed).

centrally situated 'home' led to the migration of many Chamba groups to the Bamenda plateau, where they founded Bali. Others moved into the Donga basin, where they devastated the whole of the territory south of a line drawn between Yola and Katsina Ala. It was here that the Chamba subjected the Jukun centre of Wukari to deadly raids from new Chamba strongholds established at Takum, Suntai and Donga. By 1830 the Chamba had not only infiltrated the Jukun political area south of the Benue, but had successfully inaugurated their overlordship over the Zumperi 'pagans' of the hill-tops in the neighbourhood of the Cameroons source of the Donga River. It has also been discovered that the Chamba effectively imposed their suzerainty over odd tribal groups in the south-east of Gashaka and over the so-called 'Mbembe' in Bamenda Division. These conquering groups today occupy a distinct region known as Tigong, Ndoro and Kentu.[1]

The dislodging of the Chamba from central Adamawa was at first the result of the pressure due to the attacks of incoming Batta groups. The partial overthrow of their political ascendancy in widely scattered areas was the achievement of the Fulani. The Batta claim to have begun their journey from Mandara. Their ruling classes swept southwards along the valley of the Yedseram and into the plains of the Benue–Faro confluence and basin. These remarkable empire builders conquered all before them, leaving Batta clans in places as far apart as the Bornu border and the Alantika hills in Central Cameroons. Today Batta offshoots occupy both banks of the Benue from Garua to Muri, and also Holma, Gudu and other points along the Yedseram, although many of these have become islamized and resent being called Batta.[2] The most celebrated of the achievements of the Batta was the foundation of the powerful state of Fumbina. The fame of the powerful Batta prince, Kokomi, was still remembered when Dr Barth visited Adamawa in 1851.[3] It was this state of Fumbina situated on the Benue–Faro plain that the Fulani leader

---

[1] *Gazetteer of Muri Province*, pp. 39–41.

[2] Meek, *Tribal Studies*, vol. i, pp. 69 f.

[3] Barth, *Travels and Discoveries*, vol. ii, pp. 510–13. Kirk-Greene, *Adamawa*, 1958, pp. 16–20.

Adama decisively conquered after the jihad. Many Batta groups submitted, but others fled to continue resistance from the surrounding mountains.

Apart from the Batta 'strongholds' north of the Benue, the boundary zone between the Benue and the southern Bornu highlands were, and still are, occupied by four large tribal groups—the Marghi, the Kilba, the Higi and the Fali. The first two are separated from the last two by the Yedseram River valley. These groups therefore lie conveniently on either side of the first international boundary between Yola and Lake Chad. The only problem this boundary might seem to create was in connection with Fulani conquests, which were confined to the narrow plains. The new international boundary runs across the territory of the Higi and the Fali and so involves ethnological problems.[1] It is however necessary to discuss briefly the antecedents of the groups mentioned in this paragraph, partly to show that the peoples often dismissed as 'pagans' were not incapable of effective political organization and resistance, and partly in order to complete the picture of the indigenous background against which the precise character of the Fulani conquest can be understood.

The Kilba occupy the hill country to the west of Nubi. Their neighbours to the north and north-east are the Marghi. Both groups speak related languages and may indeed include many clans which had close affinities in the remote past. The Kilba were in the past uncommonly well organized and recognized a central authority in the person of the chief of Hong. The choice of the supreme Kilba chief was made by the members of a particular kindred at Hong, headed by the Hedima (Prime Minister), who was also responsible for the maintenance of the national cult. The other senior officials were also drawn from the royal Hong kindred. The Kilba lived in clearly demarcated villages, each of which was under the control of a 'shel' or headman who was himself also a member of the royal house of Hong. The political organization of the Kilba and the aura of divinity surrounding their chief resembled those of the pre-Muslim Sudanic kingdoms. The Kilba were on the whole too

---

[1] Kirk Greene, op. cit., pp. 67–8.

warlike and independent to submit to the Fulani. These were the people to whom the British administrators in Nigeria would apply 'a reputation for lawlessness . . . robbery, murder and inter-village battles'.[1] The Kilba neighbours, the Marghi, were less well organized. For this reason, the Fulani were able to consolidate their strongholds at Madagali, Michika, and Uba, which were formerly Marghi towns on the 'plains' of the Yedseram.

The Higi belong to a large group of peoples inhabiting the southern slopes of the Mandara hills between Uba and Madagali. They describe themselves as 'the people of the mountains'. The Higi claim close ties with two other groups, the Sukur and the Gudur of the Cameroun Republic. They used to send regular gifts to the priest-chief of Gudur. One problem about the Higi and related groups is that they did not form a single homogeneous whole. They fell into a number of groups with considerable differences both in dialect and in custom. Apart from this element of weakness, the Higi had never evolved a system of secular chieftainship. Each community—usually a collection of kindreds—was under the spiritual authority of a chief-priest who owned the cult by which successful harvests were safeguarded and epidemics were averted. But the most remarkable feature of Higi villages was the defensive stone walls behind which the Higi warriors could use their bows and arrows and spears with deadly effect. Like Higi, the term Fali is applied to many groups which have very little connection with one another. They differ in language and custom. The heterogeneity of these groups should be borne in mind in assessing the effects of the second boundary which runs through the territory of the Higi and the Fali.

The Fulani, whose jihad transformed the ethnic and political landscape of the boundary zone, were not new to the territory. From a period that cannot be determined with exactitude, various Fulani clans with their cattle had unobtrusively moved into widely scattered parts of the Central Sudan. From the Mandara highlands to the Central Cameroons pockets of Fulani settlements came into existence. At that time

---

[1] Meek, *Tribal Studies*, vol. i, pp. 181–2.

the Fulani were preoccupied with their cattle and seem to have shown no disposition to organize themselves politically or to question the authority of the 'pagan' princes in whose territory they lived. In some of the well organized 'pagan' states the Fulani were employed by the native chiefs as herdsmen.[1] For instance, the Kilba ruling princes at Hong and other Kilba centres had for many centuries enjoyed the services of the Bororo Fulani. In the Batta state in central Adamawa, Kokomi had exercised undoubted sovereignty over the Fulani, including the vexatious privilege of *jus primae noctis*. It is very likely that among the Higi and the Fali where the unit of effective government was the kindred, the Fulani enjoyed greater freedom from native interference. Whatever the degree of subordination to local princes, the Fulani clans which settled among the Kilba, the Marghi, the Higi, the Fali, the Batta, the Chamba, the Dama and the Mbum have been identified as the Garr'en, the Bewe-en, the Ylaga-en and the Walarbe'en.[2] At the beginning of the Sokoto jihad, many more Fulani clans were ejected from Bornu and they moved into the regions north of the Benue to reinforce the Fulani already settled there. The Adamawa Fulani groups had kept very much to themselves. There was apparently no intermarriage between them and the ethnic groups among which they lived. There was therefore lacking that remarkable product of intermarriage and intermingling known as the Town Fulani in Hausaland.

As already mentioned, many Fulani clans were expelled from Bornu four years after the beginning of the Sokoto jihad. These Fulani were already animated with the new conquering zeal, and it was this new ambition which was destined to transform the local political scene on a gigantic scale. The jihad in the boundary zone is associated with the Fulani Mallam, Modibo Adama, from whose name Adamawa is derived. Adama's Fulani group had originally settled in the Batta country contiguous with the Verre Hills. There were excellent

---

[1] *Gazetteer of Yola Province*, p. 10.

[2] Boyle, 'Historical Notes on the Yola Fulani', pp. 73–4 in *The Journal of the African Society*, vol. x, 1910–11.

pastures there, and so the Fulani were reasonably prosperous. Adama's family could therefore afford to send him to Bornu to study under the celebrated scholar, Mallam Kiari. It was while studying in Bornu that Adama first heard rumours that a purified and true religion had been launched in Hausaland by Usuman dan Fodio. He left Bornu determined to follow the good example of dan Fodio. Whether or not Adama first proceeded to Sokoto and personally received a 'flag' from dan Fodia is a subject very much wrapped up in controversy. Yola Fulani naturally insist that the founder of the empire which they still claim received a 'flag', because this obviously conferred prestige and sanctified the otherwise material considerations which motivated Fulani action in Adamawa.[1]

With or without a 'flag', Adama proclaimed himself, in 1806 at a place called Gurin, the leader of the local Fulani. He was apparently accepted as such, for other Fulani leaders flocked to him from all directions to receive his blessing for the prospective task of conquering the 'pagans' in whose territories they had hitherto lived peacefully. It should be pointed out, though, that significantly there were other Fulani leaders who began their own conquest of the surrounding 'pagan' country independently. The distinction is an important one for a proper understanding of the true structure of the Adamawa 'empire', because, for one thing, it helps to explain the relationship which persisted between the rulers of Yola and other powerful Fulani rulers who controlled vast areas to the east and south of Adamawa. According to available records, only twelve Fulani leaders, including Mallam Shabana of Zumu, Dembo of Holma, Haman Danraka of Marua, Mallam Haman of Mubi, Dembo of Mallabu and Yaiya of Uba personally received Adama's blessing for the work of spreading the new Islam which they undertook. For this reason, it is reasonable to assume that the Fulani conquests north of the Benue, whatever their size, were accomplished under the direct leadership of Adama, whose personal campaigns were invariably in the regions to the north-east and north of Yola. Modibo Adama's

---

[1] Meek, *A Sudanese Kingdom*, p. 23.

jihad opened in 1809 in the Batta state of Demsa. The native capital was soon overwhelmed. Some of the Batta submitted, but their ruling kindred and many followers took refuge in the neighbouring hills. North of Yola, Malabu and Song fell to the Fulani, and over these Adama appointed his personal representatives.[1] The next expedition directed from Yola was the celebrated Mandara campaign of 1820–23, in the course of which the Fulani captured many strongholds along the Yedseram plains. These included Zummu, Holma, Mubi, Uba, Michika and Billa Kilba. How much territory these conquests represented cannot be determined with exactitude, but, at the time of Dr Barth's visit in 1851, they consisted mostly of the plain surrounding the Fulani strongholds. The German traveller indeed left in his accounts a very clear picture of the state of affairs in this region north of the Benue. He came to the conclusion that the Fulani had still a great deal to do before they could consider themselves the undisputed possessors of the soil. For instance, at Uba, Barth noted 'cultivated fields, where as the slaves of Mohammedans, they [the "pagans"] . . . all neatly dressed in long aprons of white clean gābagā . . . (were) marched out to their daily labour in the field'.[2] But even here, at no great distance from the plains of Uba, there were 'pagan' villages which defied the Fulani and intermittently raided them for cattle. Barth's journey to Yola took him through the other Fulani strongholds at Mubi, Mbutadi, Segero, Badanijo, Sarawa, Holma and Belem. The situation as regards the 'pagans' and the Fulani was substantially the same as the one described above. As to the precise control Yola had over these northern strongholds, it can be shown that on the two occasions when Ardo Haman of Garua and Lamedo Abba in the Marghi country tried to defy Adama's authority, the local rebellions were crushed and Adama appointed new representatives.[3]

As Barth approached Yola he noted that 'the country now became quite open to the east and south, and everything

---

[1] Boyle, op. cit., pp. 81–4. Kirk-Greene, op. cit., pp. 131–2.

[2] Barth, op. cit., vol. ii, pp. 414–17.

[3] Boyle, op. cit., pp. 76–8.

indicated that we were approaching the great artery of the country which I was so anxious to behold'. It was on this plain, the region of the Giri district, that Modibo Adama's son concentrated his colonizing activities. New Fulani towns were founded, at each of which fighting men were left to hold back the Batta 'pagans' and prevent them from raiding into the fertile fields and pastures used by Yola slaves and Fulani herdsmen. Something of an armed, but beleaguered, state centrally controlled from Yola emerged here. But while Yola consolidated its authority immediately to the east and to the north, other Fulani leaders were independently carving out their own domains to the south of the Benue–Faro confluence. Ardo Jobdi, whose clan had settled in the Batta state of Bundang, overran that state. He then pushed his conquests southwards into the territory of the Mbum and founded Ngaundere on the ashes of the native capital, Delbe. Another Fulani leader, Ardo Jedda, conquered the Dama and Laka 'pagans' on the upper reaches of the Benue, and made Rei-Buba his capital. Other fighting Fulani leaders unassisted by Yola included Haman Sambo, who conquered the Chamba of the Faro basin and established Tibati, and Haman Gabdo Dandi, who drove his horde down the Deo River and seized Koncha from the Kotopo 'pagans', then extended his conquests to Banyo, and finally turned his attention to the Mambila plateau, where he founded Gashaka as his capital. These conquests in the south of Adamawa raise two basic questions. First, to what extent did these independent Fulani leaders regard themselves as the lieutenants of Modibo Adama and their acquisitions as mere fiefs of Yola? Second, which areas here became Fulani and which remained under independent 'pagan' control? The course of the Fulani conquests here, as in the region east and north of the Benue, reveals one uniform pattern. The plains and the river basins afforded the Fulani horsemen ideal fighting ground against the 'pagans', whose main weapons of war consisted of spears, bows and arrows. These weapons were miserably inadequate against Fulani horsemen. The low-lying plains and plateaux were therefore the 'pagan' areas conquered and politically dominated by the Fulani. The intermediate country and the vast mountainous tracts remained in 'pagan' hands. No accurate description of the general political situation can make a coherent picture.[1]

It must be conceded that Modibo Adama, who founded Yola, undoubtedly enjoyed tremendous spiritual prestige even among his turbulent Fulani compatriots who independently consolidated their own capitals at Ngaundere, Tibati, Rei-Buba and Gashaka. It is nonetheless extremely questionable whether it can realistically be claimed that Modibo Adama, at his death in 1848, handed over to his son, Mohammad Lawal, a 'well consolidated kingdom'.[2] What probably survived Adama's death was the spiritual leadership of Yola. It was during Lawal's reign that Dr Barth made his celebrated journey to Yola. As has been mentioned, Lawal concentrated his attention on the 'armed' state immediately to the east of Yola, and there was ample evidence in Barth's accounts that the ruler of Yola had effective authority over the Fulani in the strongholds north of the Benue River. Dr Barth was however not allowed by Lawal to travel to south Adamawa because the Yola ruler feared that Barth's presence there might intensify the spirit of independence already crystallizing in the powerful southern Fulani 'provinces'. But Barth collected considerable information about the state of affairs and came to the conclusion that the ruler in Yola was not the most powerful man in Adamawa. His explanation is very interesting.

> [Lawal] has all his slaves settled in slave villages, where they cultivate grain for his use and profit, while [the other Fulani rulers], who obtain all their provision in corn from subjugated pagan tribes, have their host of slaves constantly at their disposal for expeditions [and for sale].[3]

Barth also attempted to divide the southern provinces into those which acknowledged some sort of allegiance to Yola and those which enjoyed quasi-independence. Chamba under Sambo and Koncha under Jobdi sent regular presents of slaves

---

[1] *Report on the Cameroons*, 1926, p. 10. Frobenius, *The Voice of Africa*, vol. ii, p. 669.

[2] *Gazetteer of Yola Province*, p. 18.

[3] Barth, op. cit., p. 408, pp. 507–10.

and ivory to Yola, but even these presents were no more than gestures of friendship. On the other hand, Buba of Rei-Buba, situated on the upper course of the Benue River, not only exhibited open hostility to Yola but also sought to confirm his independence by obtaining direct Sokoto recognition. The attitude of the governors of Bubanjidda remained intransigent, and in 1872 the governor Jedda refused to take the oath of allegiance to the Modibo of Yola. The powerful governor of Ngaundere made no pretence of being a lieutenant of the incumbent of the Yola throne. He dealt with foreigners without any reference to Yola. Neither at the time of Dr Barth's visit nor subsequently did there emerge a representative council in Yola which might be expected to attempt to co-ordinate affairs, military or political, throughout Fulani-dominated Adamawa. The Modibo of Yola himself had no officials charged with the task of supervising what there were of provincial organs of government.

As the religious zeal which certainly animated the original founders of the empire faded, and weak rulers came to occupy the throne in the Adamawa 'capital', Fulani rule degenerated still further into raiding for slaves. Further expansion of the area of political control ceased, because the Fulani rulers were apparently content with the luxury of the life in the towns into which slaves and ivory flowed from the surrounding regions. Lamido Sanda, who succeeded Lawal in 1872, conducted raids against the Lala 'pagans' in the north, but these adventures ended in disaster and in the complete discomfiture of the Fulani raiders. There is ample justification for the view that Sanda's reign from 1872 to 1890 was 'unfortunate for Adamawa'.[1] Yola and the Fulani districts to the north of the Benue became increasingly isolated from the southern provinces, whose governors could now export their slaves and ivory to North Africa through the southern tributaries of the Benue, and thus bypass Yola. Under Zubeiru, the last independent Lamido of Yola, there was a belated period of activity to reduce Adamawa to a coherent feudal state. But then Europeans were already at the gates. Thus Zubeiru succeeded in achieving no

---

[1] Kirk-Greene, op. cit., pp. 140–1.

more than a nominal and short-lived submission of his powerful colleagues.[1]

There was one other factor which contributed to the
complicated political picture which Adamawa presented.
Fulani thrusts into Fumbina were also directed from Sokoto
and its fief, Bauchi. Muri on the middle Benue became the
headquarters of independent Fulani military and political
activities south-eastwards along the Benue tributaries, the
Teraba and the Donga. It was during the reign of Hamman at
Muri, oriented towards Sokoto rather than towards Yola, that
the Chamba and the Jukun began to pay tribute to Muri. The
political influence of the latter was projected increasingly
towards the hillsides and ravines of the Central Cameroons
mountains. The result was naturally a further disorganization
of tribal life in the Adamawa and Benue regions, as ethnic
groups were scattered over large areas.[2]

Dr Barth's last thoughts on Adamawa were a remarkable
exercise in prognostication. In full view of the Benue River, he
had written as follows:

> Hence I cherish the well founded conviction that along this
> natural highway European influence and commerce will pene-
> trate into the very heart of the continent, and abolish slavery, or
> rather those infamous slave-hunts and religious wars, destroying
> the natural gems of human happiness, which are spontaneously
> developed in the simple life of the pagans, and spreading devasta-
> tion and desolation all around.[3]

Barth saw enough evidence of devastation in the activities of
the Adamawa Fulani. These were individual Fulani who
owned as many as a thousand pagan slaves, noted Barth. He
therefore asked himself the second question 'whether it be their
[Fulani] destiny to colonize this fine country for themselves, or
in the course of time to be disturbed by the intrusion of Europeans'. The forebodings of Dr Barth materialized, and it was
the intrusion of Europeans, either as missionaries or as agents

---

[1] *Report on the Cameroons*, 1929, pp. 13 f.
[2] *Gazetteer of Muri Province*, pp. 18–34.
[3] Barth, op. cit., pp. 507–10.

of European imperialism, which provided the occasion for the boundary arrangements. The genesis of European interest is therefore briefly discussed next, in order to see to what extent the ups and downs of the relations established between the European Powers and the Adamawa rulers influenced the boundary decisions which ultimately emerged.

For two main reasons Yola was bound to become the focus of European activities in the Adamawa region. All the evidence available to the European agents, including that of Barth, conveyed the impression that Yola was the capital of a potentially rich and extensive Fulani kingdom. Commercially, Yola was strategically situated for tapping the trade of the region through the excellent trade arteries, the Benue and its tributaries. After Barth, the British explorer Beecroft attempted, but without success, to reach Yola from the lower Benue. In 1879 an expedition organized by the Church Missionary Society under the command of Ashcroft in the ship *Henry Venn* reached Yola and made its way to Garua, also on the Benue. Significantly enough, a German, Flegel, who was later to become a very active German agent, accompanied the missionary enterprise on the Benue.[1] Subsequently, in 1882–3, Flegel visited the Lamido of Adamawa and had two audiences with him. According to his own account, he spent some six months in Yola before being ordered to leave. As Germany had not officially decided on colonial ventures, it would appear that Flegel did not attempt to enter into political relations with Yola on behalf of Germany. In the next few years, when European Powers began to assume that the greatest power in the Central Sudan was controlled from Sokoto, Flegel was forestalled in an important 'diplomatic' mission to the Shehu of Sokoto by an agent of the British Niger Company, Joseph Thomson. The latter's success formed the basis of the initial British claim to the political control of Yola, which was itself assumed to be a dependency of Sokoto.[2]

The relations between the Niger Company and the Lamidos of Adamawa were from the very start rather puzzling and

---

[1] C.M.S. *Intelligencer*, 1880, pp. 475–88.
[2] F.O.C.P., no. 76, Royal Niger Company to Rosebery, 15 June 1893.

contradictory. For instance, if the company believed, as it claimed then and afterwards, that the Thomson treaty with Sokoto secured Yola and with it Adamawa for Britain, it is then difficult to explain why another agent of the same company thought it necessary in the same year to obtain independent treaties with Muri and Yola. This agent, William Wallace, made his first appearance in Yola in 1883 and reported that he was favourably received by the Lamido, Sanda. He exchanged presents with the Lamido, and believed that he also received permission to lease a portion of land in Yola for a factory (i.e. trading post). In the following year, this permission was repudiated by the Lamido who, on this occasion, received Wallace with extreme coldness.[1] Then in 1885 the company's hulk *Emily Waters* was taken up to Yola, but was ordered away. Later again in the same year permission was given for trade from the hulk. No records are available to explain the vagaries of Yola politics, but it should be observed here that these irregularities in the relations between Yola and the British company persisted until 1893, and make intelligible the ease with which both French and German agents attempted to establish a foothold in the region of Adamawa.

Meanwhile the agents of the Niger Company pursued their basic trade interest in the region immediately west of Yola, on the Benue and its tributaries. It was essential to control the navigable portions of the rivers. Within a short time important and effectively held trading centres were established at strategic points, Ibi, Bakundi, and Kunini, for trade in ivory, beniseed, gum-arabic and tin. These achievements helped the company in the long run to tighten its hold on the Benue and to defy attempts, particularly by France, to carve off a block of territory west of Yola. It was however the Germans who presented the first challenge to the Niger Company's claim to ascendancy over the region. The German administrators in the Cameroons attached great importance to the Benue and its tributaries as the best, quickest and most profitable way of

---

[1] R.G.S., vol. xiv, 1899; see Moseley, 'The Regions of the Benue', pp. 630–6.

gaining access to the hinterland of their colony. The attempts at penetrating this hinterland from the Cameroons coast failed disastrously. The officials could not help recalling that the extensive travels of the Germans, Nachtigal, in 1869–74, and Flegel, in 1879–83, all pointed to the fact that the German colony could have little value without Adamawa and the rivers which afforded easy access to it.[1] Thanks too to the activities of Hausa traders, the Germans came to know that there were vast ivory markets at Banyo and Ngaundere. The trade caravans went north-westwards and westwards to Yola and to other centres on the tributaries of the Benue.

Flegel indeed did more than just explore the Benue basin. In Bakundi he had sought land for a German factory. The emir of the town, having been fed with glittering presents, gave Flegel the permission he solicited. The German began to build a factory, but shortly afterwards the emir changed his mind and ordered that the uncompleted factory should be pulled down. A British commissioner reported later, rather gleefully that 'this was done'.[2] In view of the disheartening difficulties the Germans encountered in trying to gain the hinterland of their coast colony, it was only natural that they should be the first to ask for the extension of the 'coast' boundary to the hinterland, such extension to be based primarily on the 'hinterland theory'. Thus, shortly after the Rio del Rey–Cross River line was agreed upon, Bismarck began to press for a line up to the Benue. German pressure arose directly out of the fact that their agent Flegel was proposing to make another journey inland, and his supporters pretended to regard all the region north of the latitude of the Cross River 'rapids' as no-man's-land.[3] The views of the Royal Niger Company were naturally dominated by considerations of trade. The navigable Benue and its tributaries which flowed north-westwards mattered most. In spite of the fact that the British and the Germans were aware of the existence of the Sokoto and Adamawa empires, they made no reference to their political frontiers in the

---

[1] Rudin, *Germans in the Cameroons (1884–1914)*, pp. 76–8.
[2] Confidential 5913, Macdonald to Salisbury, 13 January 1890, p. 13.
[3] Rudin, op. cit., pp. 65–6.

negotiations which produced the Cross River–Yola line in 1886.

The preliminary agreement covering the southern Adamawa region was conveyed in a letter to the German Ambassador in London. Rosebery agreed to

> an extended line of demarcation, which starting from the point on the left bank of the Old Calabar or Cross River, where the original line terminated, shall be continued diagonally to such a point on the right bank of the river Benue to the east of, and close to, Yola, as may be found on examination to be practically suited for the demarcation of a boundary.[1]

The agreement clearly revealed no concern for the possible reactions of the Lamido of Yola. The arguments about Yola came later, but in 1886 all concerned appeared satisfied with this preliminary boundary. At the time, the efforts of the Royal Niger Company to exert pressure on Sokoto in the interest of the company's ambitions with regard to Yola and, to the eastward of Yola, Garua, had produced no results. In any case, the British believed that the boundary line separated 'mountains, torrential streams and sparsely inhabited areas from wide fertile plains, great navigable waterways, and densely populated districts'.[2] Britain had the better of the bargain in 1886, and that was apparently all that mattered. All the evidence shows that the British thought that the Cross River 'rapids'–Yola line was up to a point a very satisfactory one, geographically speaking. The three great tributaries of the Benue, the Teraba, Donga and Katsena rivers, which rise on the plateau of the Central Cameroons, only become navigable at the boundary line, and here canoes entered Nigerian territory without interruption. The line also, the British believed, coincided with the pattern of human distribution, for, while the groups designated 'pagan' tribes had withdrawn to the almost inaccessible hill-tops, the more 'civilized' agricultural and trading peoples kept to the well-watered plains on the

---

[1] Hertslet, *Map of Africa by Treaty*, vol. i, p. 85, vol. iii, no. 263 Supplementary Agreement, 27 July–2 August 1886.

[2] R.G.S., vol. xliii, 9 March 1914, Nugent, 'The Geographical Results'.

British side.[1] Whether or not the 'pagans' had close affinities with the plain peoples was an issue to which nobody paid any attention until 1919, when the British assumed responsibility for the administration of the ex-German region. In 1886, however, the British had reasons to be happy with the boundary arrangement, but the Germans were shortly to have second thoughts.

After 1886 Yola and the Benue were destined to become increasingly important in the schemes of the European agents interested in establishing spheres of influence in that region. As far as British interests were concerned, it should be noted that the relations between the Royal Niger Company and the Lamido of Adamawa had continued to deteriorate. No agent of the company was allowed to show his face in Yola, and this was not owing to any awareness on the part of the Lamido that the British and the Germans had been engaged in partitioning his 'empire'. The first crisis which developed was not directly bound up with the question of the Cross River 'rapids'–Yola provisional boundary line, but, potentially, the underlying situation was the political one of a possible linking up of German Adamawa with Nupe through the Benue. This contingency would have affected fundamentally the disposition of the boundary between Yola and Lake Chad. A German trader, Hoenigsberg, after overcoming petty obstacles placed in his way by the officials of the Royal Niger Company, had made his way to the Fulani province of Nupe which lay astride the confluence of the Niger and the Benue. There he successfully persuaded the emir, Maliki, to challenge the notion that the Royal Niger Company claimed the Nupe country as its own. The Nupe ruler forthwith summoned the company's senior agent and asked for a clarification of the company's political status in that region. William Wallace's evasive strategy of offering to increase the subsidy to Nupe proved abortive. In the presence of all, including the German trader, the emir reaffirmed that he was an 'independent' ruler and was entitled to enter into political relations with anyone he

---

[1] F.O.C.P. Confidential, 5753, Salisbury to Malet, 25 January 1888; also Calvert, *The Cameroons*, 1917, pp. 62–3.

liked. A German enclave in Nupe was therefore not in-conceivable.

The Germans were foiled in this by the officials of the Royal Niger Company, who proceeded to deal drastically with Hoenigsberg.[1] A charge was trumped up that he had been trading with Nupe without paying duties to the company which was the custodian of the Lower Niger. For this offence the goods carried by Hoenigsberg were confiscated, and he himself was taken to the company's headquarters at Asaba to be tried by the company's Chief Justice. He was found guilty of attempting to provoke disorder in British territory and was sentenced to deportation. If he returned to the 'Niger Terri-tories' he would face imprisonment.[2] The Germans naturally felt very annoyed at the manner in which the Royal Niger Company had treated a German national, and particularly in a region which was presumably 'open to all'. The British government however decided to stand firm by the Royal Niger Company and thereby won an important principle when it came to an agreement with the German government to the effect that Hoenigsberg could return to Nupe to trade, pro-vided that he did not engage in political intrigues against the Royal Niger Company.[3]

This agreement was not the end of German complaints in regard to the Niger and the Benue. The Royal Niger Company claimed to control, to its own interest, all the navigable rivers in the region, and such a claim was inconsistent with the 'free navigation' stipulated by the Berlin West African Conference. Germany attacked many aspects of the Royal Niger Company's administration, and came to the conclusion that it was time to appoint her own consul on the rivers. Alternatively, Britain should send an independent commission to investigate the state of affairs in the region. Britain naturally accepted the latter proposition.[4]

In the meantime the German government of the Cameroons

---

[1] See Flint, *Sir George Goldie*, pp. 114–16.

[2] F.O. 84/1894 Memorandum by Hatzfeldt, 5 March 1888, and enclosures.

[3] F.O. 84/1935, F.O. to R.N.C., 20 December 1888.

[4] F.O. 84/1987, F.O. to R.N.C., 31 January 1889.

colony persisted in its attempts to penetrate the hinterland of the colony into Adamawa. The indomitable Zintgraff proposed that a line of stations running into the hinterland by way of the high plateau should be established to provide a route for trade caravans to operate southwards to the German coast. In 1888 he undertook a hazardous journey in an effort to enter Adamawa, keeping to the German side of the provisional boundary line of the 1886 Anglo-German agreement. Apart from founding a German station at Bali on the Bamenda plateau, Zintgraff could achieve nothing else. He subsequently appeared, after passing through Bakundi, at Ibi. From here he made his way to Yola, where he reported later that he was hospitably entertained by the Lamido. However, the German traveller was not given permission to travel directly from Yola to Banyo. The Lamido of Yola might have had his own reasons for refusing to allow Zintgraff to visit southern Adamawa, but the German's reaction to the Lamido's unrelenting attitude is interesting. He lamented that 'two days were enough in the English capital of German Adamawa to convince me that under no circumstances would permission be granted to me to travel to Banyo'.[1] It seemed reasonable to the Germans to argue now that the power which had Adamawa should also have Yola, the capital. It would be misleading, however, to draw the conclusion that the Germans were sincerely regretting that what they believed to be the territorial framework of an indigenous empire was being disrupted by the Anglo-German boundary. German concern over Yola, and indeed over the Benue, was basically commercial. It was also political to the extent that the Germans were convinced that a letter of introduction from the Lamido of Yola would facilitate their prospective 'transactions' with the Fulani provincial governors of central and southern Adamawa. For the reasons indicated here, the German government awaited with impatience the report of the special commissioner appointed by Lord Salisbury to investigate 'questions affecting imperial interests' on the Niger and the Benue.

The report by Macdonald throws considerable light on the

---

[1] Kirk-Greene, op. cit., quoted p. 32.

activities of the Royal Niger Company on the Benue and on the confused interpretation of the political status of Yola. The Moslem emirates on the Benue, particularly Muri, did not countenance the political pretensions of the Royal Niger Company. The company's relations with the Lamido of Yola were very strained, and the Yola ruler would not allow the company to 'build or trade in any part of his country'. In spite of this, the company had gone past Yola and established a hulk at Garua, in the province of the Emir of Ribago.[1] With reference to the Anglo-German boundary agreement, which was described as ending a 'little to the east of, and near, Yola', the special commissioner indicated that

> [The Royal Niger Company] evidently read this as in no way affecting the north bank, for, as I have said, they have a station or trading hulk at Garua, in the Ribago Province, on the north bank, 80 miles to the east of Yola.[2]

If the Lamido of Yola effectively controlled Adamawa, his refusal to allow the Royal Niger Company to operate in Yola should automatically have excluded the company from the provinces of Adamawa. The commissioner's report made it clear that technically the Germans could strive to add the northern bank of the Benue River to their Adamawa acquisition. If they had had any serious intention of implementing this, they would have encountered the bitter opposition of the British government, determined as it was to support the position of unchallenged ascendancy which the Royal Niger Company claimed on the Benue. In 1890 a suitable diplomatic climate existed for the settlement of outstanding Anglo-German boundary questions. It all began with Salisbury's offer in 1889 to cede Heligoland, an island dangerously close to an important German naval base, to Germany in exchange for German South-West Africa. Bismarck turned down the offer, but his successor was prepared to enter into general negotiations with Britain.

---

[1] Confidential 5913. Report of the Special Commissioner, p. 14.
[2] Ibid. See also Rudin, op. cit., pp. 110–11.

It is clear from available evidence that the British and the German negotiators of the 1890 Agreement at no time considered the question of the precise political structure of Adamawa or the status of Yola vis-à-vis the region south of Lake Chad. Lord Salisbury was for his part primarily anxious to safeguard the British position in Uganda. The navy-minded German emperor was successfully tempted with another offer of Heligoland. As to the region south of Lake Chad, the Germans were satisfied with a vague recognition of their rights to a territory in which no German had set foot. The Anglo-German Agreement usually known as the Heligoland Agreement dealt also with East Africa, South-West Africa and Rio del Rey. Clause V referred specifically to the region north of the Benue.

> No Treaty or Agreement, made by or on behalf of either Power to the north of the River Benue, shall interfere with the free passage of goods of the other Power, without payment of transit dues, to and from the shores of Lake Chad . . . . All Treaties made in territories intervening between the Benue and Lake Chad shall be notified by one Power to the other.[1]

The agreement undoubtedly foreshadowed an Anglo-German intention to draw a boundary through the region stretching from Yola to Lake Chad, but before its precise location could be decided, another international crisis developed on the Benue.

The Anglo-German 1890 Agreement aroused French fears primarily because it made a vague reference to the region south of Lake Chad. The French press insinuated that the British aimed at extending British territories in the region to the Nile. The thing to do was therefore to frustrate the 'evil' designs of Britain by intensifying the Saharan ambitions of France, including wedging a French enclave in the region between the Benue and Lake Chad. In any case the Anglo-French Agreement of 1890, known usually as the Say–Barrua line, lent itself to irreconcilable interpretations as regards

---

[1] Hertslet, op. cit. vol. i, p. 85; vol. iii, no. 270, pp. 899–906.

Adamawa and Yola. The French Prime Minister, Casimir-Perier, indeed emphatically stated that the Say–Barrua Agreement 'could not be interpreted as governing the question of Adamawa . . . and the Benue'.[1] In addition to this consideration, both the Germans and the French were agreed that the free navigation of the Lower Niger and the Benue guaranteed by the Berlin West African Conference left it open for them to enter into political relations with independent native potentates whose territories bordered on the rivers. There was nothing therefore to stop the French from establishing a French protectorate in the regions of the Benue and Adamawa. The resources and the will were there. Lieutenant Mizon was there, too, to champion the French cause. The only obstacle the British could interpose was the unsubstantiated assertion that 'the Benue, up to a point above Yola, is a British Protectorate'.[2] The activities of Mizon provide therefore an essential background for the precipitate location of the Anglo-German boundary which emerged in 1893.

The first Mizon mission to the Benue region was not sponsored officially by the French government. A 'colonial group', which included journalists and other French expansionists, was prepared to finance the first expedition. The objectives of the group and those of the French government were, as far as the region south of Lake Chad was concerned, in close accord. Mizon with twenty-five armed men sailed up the Niger delta. After a hazardous encounter with the people of Patani, Mizon allowed himself to be taken to the Royal Niger Company's station at Akassa, partly to be treated for wounds and partly to afford the agent-general of the company an opportunity to warn the Frenchman against landing anywhere until he had passed Yola. In due course Mizon made his way to Yola, where he was favourably received by the Lamido. He received presents and permission to trade, which was more than any agent of the Royal Niger Company had so far achieved in Yola. In December, Mizon left Yola for southern Adamawa, to the

---

[1] F.O.C.P. Confidential 6572. Inclosure in no. 11, Dufferin to Rosebery, 10 February 1894.

[2] Ibid., Rosebery to Dufferin, January 1894.

120

temporary relief of the local British agents. The Frenchman traversed southern Adamawa, calling at Ngaundere, the powerful provincial capital of that part of Adamawa. There was much for him to publicize when he arrived back in his own country. The economic potentialities of Adamawa were vast. The independent potentates of Yola and southern Adamawa had received the French mission very hospitably. All that was left was to consolidate the gains of France through the formal establishment of a French protectorate of Adamawa.[1] Mizon became a national hero, and banquets were held in his honour in various French cities. These banquets were attended invariably by representatives of the French government.

The second Mizon mission to the Benue received the support of substantial money contributions from French patriots and colonial societies. There was also to accompany the lieutenant an accumulation of French goods for trade in Adamawa. Thus, with a strongly equipped expedition, Mizon set out once again for the Benue in August 1892. There was now real alarm in London. The head of the Royal Niger Company, Sir George Goldie, tried in vain to persuade the British government that the Mizon mission was a political one and threatened the British position on the Benue. The Salisbury Government, which was shortly to resign, refused to be drawn into precipitating a major diplomatic crisis, and in any case the French government had already given an 'assurance' that the French mission to the Benue was 'essentially commercial and scientific'.[2] Away from all the fuss his expedition had provoked, Mizon quietly made his way up the Niger and the Benue. Goldie left nothing to chance, for he instructed the local agents of his company to be prepared to use force against the Frenchman if the latter provided the slightest conceivable excuse. Thus it was that Mizon was followed up the Benue by an armed contingent of the Royal Niger Company's forces.

Mizon stopped at Muri, an emirate on the middle Benue,

---

[1] *Le Temps*, 23 June 1892; *République Française*, 6 July 1892. Also Hanotaux and Martineau, *Histoire Des Colonies Françaises*, 1939, vol. iv, pp. 486 f.

[2] F.O. 84/2209, Phipps to Anderson, 29 July 1892. F.O. 84/2257, F.O. to R.N.C., 24 August 1892.

and signed a treaty of friendship with the emir, who was very hostile to the Royal Niger Company. The French armed party was placed at the disposal of the Fulani ruler, who was at the time engaged in attacking the 'pagan' village of Kwana for slaves. The village was burnt to the ground, and all its surviving inhabitants were enslaved. Although Mizon now significantly headed his correspondence 'The French Protectorate of Muri', his actions in Muri proved the undoing of the French cause. The agents of the Royal Niger Company were not slow in pointing out to the Lamido of Yola the danger inherent in Mizon's policy of military alliance with a none too friendly neighbour. The Lamido, in the circumstances, undertook to inform the company that he no longer wished to have any dealings with the French. He was now willing to deliver to the Queen of England the protection of 'all that portion of land belonging to Adamawa, upper and lower, on the River Benue, of my boundary'.[1] Despite this concession to the Royal Niger Company, a comical struggle for the Lamido's favour developed between the agents of the company and Mizon when the latter showed up at Yola. Mizon apparently proved the better negotiator, because the Lamido signed another treaty placing himself under French protection also.

The agent-general of the Royal Niger Company came to the conclusion that diplomacy would no longer serve, and that more drastic methods were called for. The French stations at Muri were forcibly closed down and all the goods there were confiscated. Mizon's ship moored at the French 'base' of Yola was also confiscated, although Mizon was allowed to leave Yola without molestation. The British government endorsed the actions taken by the Royal Niger Company. If Mizon thought that his government would take appropriate action to safeguard 'French Adamawa', he was mistaken. The news of his connivance at a Fulani attack on a pagan village had reached France. The French press took the lead in denouncing Mizon:

Mizon went to Africa to make French influence penetrate there.

---

[1] F.O. 27/3160, R.N.C. to F.O., 15 June 1893; see enclosed Zubeiru to Wallace.

He has compromised it. He has allied himself with the Moslems against the pagans, whom the more practical English have always taken care to protect. Let us hope that the Ministry will take measures to withdraw from Mizon's authority his unfortunate subordinates and to recompense as it merits his extraordinary conduct.[1]

The British government for its part complained that the Frenchman had 'engaged in treaty-making within the British sphere of influence and . . . committed acts of war in British territory'. The French government willingly gave an assurance that a successor to Mizon would lead the French expedition out of Muri and Yola 'with the least possible delay'. The British government even insisted on the unequivocal clarification of the expression in the French note, '*Continuer, si possible, sa marche sur Yola.*'[2]

French activities in the Muri and Yola regions caused the Germans as much alarm as it caused the British. It will be recalled that Mizon traversed southern Adamawa and was received at Ngaundere, which no German had succeeded in visiting. Another Frenchman had also in 1893 travelled without mishap through the Adamawa provinces of Chamba and Koncha. Since 1886 when the Anglo-German provisional boundary was committed to a terminal position east of Yola, all German attempts to penetrate Adamawa from the coast had yielded few results. In spite of substantial financial grants from the Reichstag, Morgen, Gravenreuth and Ramsay failed to obtain a political footing for Germany in southern and central Adamawa. The partly successful expedition led by Von Stettin only served to prove to the Germans that the occupation of Adamawa was bound to be an extremely hazardous undertaking.[3] French ambitions in the area threatened what hold the Germans had. The vital thing was therefore to define more precisely the Anglo-German provisional agreement

---

[1] Mockler-Ferryman, *British West Africa*, 1898, quoted on p. 423.

[2] F.O. 27/3131, F.O. to Dufferin, Africa, no. 115; F.O. to Phipps, 4 July and 26 July 1893; see minutes by Rosebery and Anderson.

[3] Townsend, *The Rise and Fall of Germany's Colonial Empire 1884–1918*, 1930, pp. 164–5.

around Yola, and if possible, extend it to Lake Chad. Britain was equally interested in securing Yola and in interposing German territory between herself and French ambitions in the region south of Lake Chad. The general situation was a propitious one for an Anglo-German boundary agreement.

Before the formal boundary discussions began, the Royal Niger Company's chief in London was approached by a private German 'Committee for the protection of German interests in the Hinterland of the Cameroons against French encroachments' for assistance on behalf of an expedition into Adamawa by way of the Benue. Goldie promised to help, subject to an undertaking that

> The expedition will not make Treaties or take any political action in the region which lies to the west of longitude 15° east and to the north of the latitude of Yola.[1]

The immediate result of this exchange of private letters was that Goldie and Vohsen, the president of the German committee, initiated private negotiations for the boundary around Yola and to the north of Yola. Both sides, nevertheless, kept their governments informed. It is to be noted that it was the Anglo-German negotiations for the definition of the boundary of the Yola district which at last seriously brought up the question of the pre-existing political frontier of the 'Yola Kingdom'. When the negotiations came into the open, the Germans expressed regret that the previous provisional boundary had ignored historical antecedents. They alleged that Goldie had agreed that Yola, as the capital of Adamawa and the residence of its sultan, should be ceded to Germany. They indicated a boundary line to run from the Cross River rapids to a point twenty kilometres downstream from Yola. Its northward continuation would go to Mubi and thence to a point on the Shari River. Such a line, the Germans argued, would preserve the territorial integrity of the Adamawa and Bornu empires. Goldie, whatever the local political merits of his alleged proposals, stoutly denied that he had ever agreed to the

---

[1] Confidential 6471, R.N.C. to F.O., 6 May 1893; see Inclosure 1, Vohsen to R.N.C., and Inclosure 3, R.N.C. to Vohsen. See also Flint, op. cit., pp. 180–2.

cession of British Yola. The British government agreed with Goldie on the ground that 'we do not admit that the whole of Adamawa, with the exception of the capital, is in the German sphere'.[1] It is easy to understand that when in 1893 the Royal Niger Company at last succeeded in obtaining a treaty placing Zubeiru, the Lamido of Yola, under its protection, it would argue that

> No more fruitful source of trouble in these regions can be imagined than that the powerful Emir of Yola, who has now thrown in his lot altogether with England, should be informed that this country has drawn a frontier-line with Germany almost within sight of his walls.[2]

The company did not say what it considered to be a boundary which might satisfactorily respect the empire of Yola. The reports forwarded by the company's agents styled the Lamido 'Sultan de l'Adamawa'. A German memorandum on the political status of Yola reveals why the German government in the end gave up its struggle to secure Yola as part of German Adamawa. Dr Kayser, the Director of the Africa Department of the German Foreign Office, put the position as follows:

> In order to facilitate a speedy settlement of the matter . . . Germany is prepared to desist from the claim to include Yola, which, owing to an erroneous appreciation of local conditions . . . was reserved for the English . . . . However desirable it might accordingly be to correct that mistake and to avoid separating districts which are naturally and historically connected with one another . . . I will refrain from pursuing the matter further.[3]

In the circumstances, the important criterion in circumscribing Yola was what 'would be a reasonable line, fair to both sides', Britain and Germany—not to the Lamido of Adamawa and his provincial lieutenants.

The boundary arrangement agreed upon between Britain and Germany in November 1893 in regard to the frontier around Yola was indeed as Dr Flint claimed 'an intricate piece

---

[1] Ibid., no. 53, Trench to F.O., 13 May 1893.
[2] Ibid., no. 205, R.N.C. to F.O., 10 August 1893.
[3] Ibid., Inclosure in no. 174, Malet to Rosebery, 21 July 1893.

of armchair geography'. The phrase in the 1886 provisional boundary 'a point to the east of, and close to Yola' had to be more precisely described. The British government first suggested that the point should not be nearer Yola than the junction of the Faro and the Benue, because, otherwise, the boundary 'would be a serious interference with the freedom of circulation of the people of Yola'. What was meant by 'the circulation of the people of Yola' was not explained. The Germans, on the other hand, wished to know whether a point twenty miles south of Yola would satisfy the requirements of the Royal Niger Company. The outcome of these farcical discussions was 'a line running straight towards the centre of Yola, on condition that it ends at a point equally distant from Yola as the Confluence of the Faro is, and thence follows to the confluence the arc of a circle', with Yola for its centre and having a radius of five kilometres.[1] The last German request regarding Yola was quite extraordinary. Having successfully and completely dismembered Adamawa, Dr Kayser requested that the Royal Niger Company should give an undertaking to use its influence with the Emir of Yola, as paramount chief of Adamawa, to induce the Fulani provincial chieftains within the German sphere to acknowledge the German protectorate. The British Foreign Office, however, thought the German request reasonable, but objected to its formal inclusion as Article IV of the Anglo-German Convention.

The negotiations for a provisional boundary between Yola and Lake Chad produced little controversy. Neither Germany nor Britain had established a firm hold on that region. As long as Germany obtained direct access from Adamawa to a portion of Lake Chad she was content. She was also willing to give Britain an assurance that a boundary would not bar Britain from Darfur, Kordofan and Bahr-el-Ghazal, so all was well. Without much haggling, then, Article II of the Anglo-German Agreement of November 1893 carried the Yola boundary northwards

> to a point where the 13th degree of longitude east of Greenwich is intercepted by the 10th degree of north latitude. From that point

---

[1] Ibid., no. 14, Telegraphic, Rosebery to Gosselin, 14 August 1893.

it shall go direct to a point on the southern shore of Lake Chad, situated 35 minutes east of the meridian of the centre of the town of Kuka.[1]

The German reaction later to the Anglo-German agreement which defined this section of the eastern international boundary of Nigeria is interesting because it shows that the two Powers were fully aware that they had dismembered an indigenous empire which was described as Adamawa. In a debate in the Reichstag, the government spokesman confessed that they regretted that Germany had not acquired Yola, the capital of Adamawa. He conceded, however, that 'England has spent far more than we have in capital, men and expeditions, and yet . . . we have obtained lands in which no German has as yet set foot'.[2]

The following years did not throw much light on the precise nature of Yola reaction against the partitioning of Adamawa. The Lamido however began to complain that the British flag had been flying in his capital for six years and yet no taxes had been paid to him. This point is mentioned because it is easily mistaken to identify the revival of Zubeiru's hostility to the British with a growing awareness that Britain had co-operated in dismembering his empire. It is therefore useful to examine briefly how Germany set out to consolidate German Adamawa and to show that Zubeiru gave no help to his supposed provincial lieutenants. The German request that the Royal Niger Company should persuade Zubeiru to exhort the provincial governors to accept Germany achieved nothing because the company had no influence over Zubeiru and the latter very little over the powerful Adamawa provincial rulers. German occupation was bound to be military, and a man appeared in the Cameroons colony determined to carry through this policy with characteristic German ruthlessness.[3] Chancellor Hohenlohe and Governor Puttkamer were, unlike their predecessors, believers in a 'forward policy' in the Cameroons. Such a policy

---

[1] Hertslet, *Map of Africa by Treaty*, vol. i, p. 86; vol. iii, no. 275, pp. 913–15.

[2] F.O.C.P. Confidential 6572, no. 21, Malet to Rosebery, 1894.

[3] Rudin, op. cit., p. 91.

was to be both commercial and political. Thus in 1895, for the first time, a caravan of Hausa traders was enabled to take trade goods to the coast, instead of to Yola, from Yaunde. In 1899 Kamptz captured Tibati, capital of the Chamba province, to the south of Yola. Two years later, Dominic established military stations at Garua and Marua. Throughout all these operations in which the Germans were overrunning Adamawa, no leadership for concerted Fulani resistance came from the Lamido of Adamawa.

In 1900 Zubeiru refused to accept the authority of the British government, which superseded that of the Royal Niger Company. In September 1901, the British High Commissioner, Lugard, decided that the time had come to end what he described as 'the semi-fanatical obduracy of the Emir of Yola'. A British expedition, comprising fifteen officers, seven N.C.O's, 365 rank and file plus heavy guns, was organized against Yola. The direction of the flight of Zubeiru is significant. He fled northwards, and the governors who rallied to his support were the 'fief' holders in the Fulani strongholds of the region north of the Benue. The governors included the Ardo of Moda, the Ardo of Holma, and Ardo Bakari of Madagali, the last being later shot by the Germans for giving assistance to Zubeiru.[1] It is clear therefore that it would be unhistorical to base an assessment of the effects of this section of the international boundary on the indigenous political systems on the assumption that there was indeed a coherent political entity known as Adamawa. It will also be unrealistic to consider the partition from the standpoint which regards Adamawa as a province of the Sokoto empire. It is of course true that the Royal Niger Company had originally sought to stake its claim to the area on the 1885 treaty with Sokoto. It is also true that from time to time the Lamido of Yola sent slaves to Sokoto probably as a gesture of friendship and mutual admiration. In terms of practical politics, only two letters have been recovered which throw any light on the relationship which existed between Sokoto and Yola during the critical periods in the relations between the Fulani potentates and the Europeans. The first

---

[1] See *Annual Reports* (Northern Nigeria), 1902 and 1904.

letter was written by the Sultan of Sokoto, prompted, no doubt, by the Royal Niger Company, to persuade the Lamido of Yola to permit the company to establish trading stations. The letter produced no results, as Macdonald's report shows.[1] The second letter was written in 1897 after the Royal Niger Company had invaded Ilorin. The sultan warned Yola 'not to allow the company to remain in any part of the country over which you have jurisdiction'.[2] This letter cannot be taken very seriously, because when Britain overwhelmed Yola, Sokoto forces were not rallied against the intruders. Zubeiru went down fighting, without assistance either from Sokoto or from his provincial potentates. The events associated with the effective European occupation of Adamawa have been briefly summarized in order to show that the traditional basis for criticizing the boundary is untenable. The analysis of the objective political situation which prevailed during the closing years of the nineteenth century leads to two conclusions. Yola was not the centre of a co-ordinated Adamawa empire. The second conclusion was accurately stated by Lugard when, on the occasion of the enthronement of a British puppet emir of Yola in 1902, he observed that

> The Fulani . . . succeeded only in gaining the submission of the [pagan] towns in the plains where their horsemen were effective. The pagan tribes in the hills and broken country and even in large areas of the plains maintained their independence . . . and frequently carried the war up to the gates of the Fulani walled towns.[3]

The reports of the Survey and Demarcation Commissions to some extent provide material for a realistic assessment of the effects of the international boundary on the local political and ethnic groups. The picture that emerges is inevitably a complicated one. The region of Yola and to the north of it was surveyed by an Anglo-German Demarcation Commission in

---

[1] Confidential 5913, op. cit., p. 14. Kirk-Greene, op. cit., pp. 43–44.

[2] Ibid., quoted p. 49.

[3] Ibid., quoted p. 24.

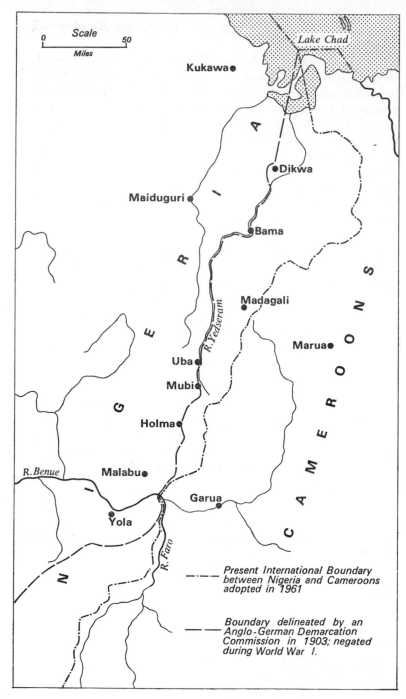

THE BOUNDARIES NORTH OF THE BENUE

1903.[1] It is expedient to avoid becoming involved in the technicalities of the work undertaken by the commissioners and to concentrate on the historical aspects. These technicalities are no doubt only of peripheral interest to a historian. And the discussions here are confined to the regions of Adamawa, although the commissioners dealt also with the question of Southern Bornu. The commissioners began by attempting to determine the location of the Yola arc described in the provisional boundary. They decided to abandon the arc geometrically described and to substitute a line through the confluence of the Benue and Faro rivers. North of the Benue, the commissioners opted for the River Tiel, a tributary of the Benue, and the Yedseram, which runs to Lake Chad. The final Anglo-German agreement for a definitive boundary, based on the report of the Demarcation Commission, authorized the local European administrators to make an allowance of up to one kilometre on either side of the boundary in order not to split farm land belonging to towns and villages. Lastly, the inhabitants of opposite sides of the rivers were to enjoy equal rights on the rivers concerned.

It is clear that as far as the demarcation of Yola was concerned, the broad plain of the Benue-Faro confluence, some eighty miles by forty miles, which Dr Barth described as the 'armed state' of Yola, was shrunk to a tiny area in which, according to the British, the former Lamido of Adamawa was allowed enough space for his people to gather firewood and to pasture Yola cattle.[2] Thenceforth the Germans in charge of German Adamawa did everything to undermine Yola as the political and commercial capital of Adamawa. The British co-operated by pointing out to their puppet ruler in Yola that the old days were over. As for the region north of the Benue, the boundary which ran through the river plains separated almost neatly the major Higi and Fali 'pagan' groups from those of the Kilba and the Marghi. But it cut through Fulani strongholds, often separating the towns from the surrounding plain districts

---

[1] R.G.S., vol. xxvi, 1905; see Jackson, 'The Anglo-German Boundary Expedition in Nigeria', pp. 28–42.

[2] C.S.O. 1/192, Lugard to C.O., 30 March 1902.

which the towns dominated in every sense of the word. In other words, the boundary here was 'a geographical one, and had no regard for political positions'. Thus, until the disappearance of German rule, there was considerable friction in the boundary zone, and this arose from the fact that Fulani rulers whose fiefs had been sundered by the Anglo-German boundary continued to exact tribute from the plain 'pagans' who were on the wrong side of the boundary. Another source of friction was the un-inhibited manner in which plain-dwelling 'pagans' decided to rejoin their kith and kin on the plateaux and mountains. In so doing they crossed the boundary which meant nothing to them. They would thus be British subjects in one year and German subjects in another.

The Adamawa boundary zone south of the Benue was not traversed until 1907, when an Anglo-German Survey Com-mission arrived. Then in 1912–13 a Demarcation Commission covered the same zone. The two reports prepared by the com-missions provide material for a realistic assessment of the effects of the Anglo-German boundary on the local ethnic and political groups involved in the 1893 arrangement. The picture that emerges is inevitably a complex one. Immediately south of the Yola plain, the boundary traversed the Fulani Chamba province. The inhabitants of this province comprised the Fulani conquerors and the 'pagan' Chamba and Dakka who had submitted to the Fulani. The boundary cut the M'bulo plain and followed that river to its source in the Shebshi mountains. The splitting of effective areas of Fulani political power ended here. At the Shebshi hill-tops, the 1912–13 com-missioners found independent 'pagans' 'entirely ignorant of the world beyond the next village to their own . . . the "kings" of all the towns on the English side and a good many from the German side came to salute us, generally bringing a present'.[1] All of them were blissfully unaware that a boundary had separated them. From the Shebshi mountains, across the Dakka, to the valley of the Teraba tributary of the Benue, the region through which the boundary ran was indeed a wild one.

---

[1] R.G.S., vol. xliii, 9 March 1914; see Nugent, 'The Geographical Results'.

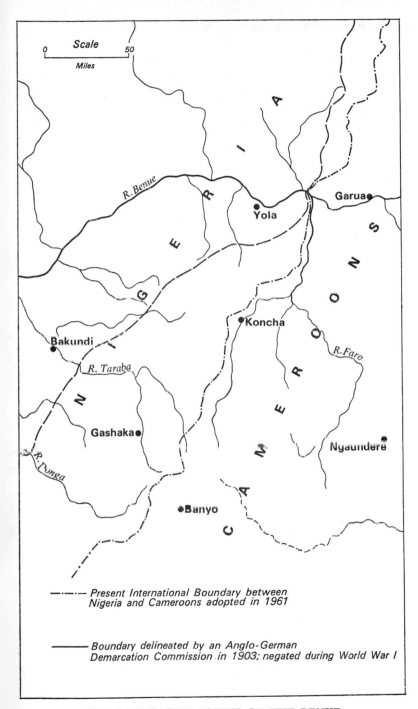

Scale
0   50
Miles

R. Benue

Yola

Garua●

Koncha●

R. Faro

Bakundi●

R. Taraba

Gashaka●

Ngaunderé●

R. Donga

●Banyo

N I G E R I A

C A M E R O O N S

—··—··— Present International Boundary between
Nigeria and Cameroons adopted in 1961

———— Boundary delineated by an Anglo-German
Demarcation Commission in 1903; negated during World War I

THE BOUNDARIES SOUTH OF THE BENUE

There were a few villages on the hill-tops and the inhabitants were, in the words of the 1912–13 commissioners, 'wilder and the houses smaller and more squalid than those previously described'. In one or two ravines which marked the course of the rivers, for instance at Gankita in the valley of the Kam River, there were Hausa settlements for collecting rubber. If there was any sovereignty here, it was the one exercised by the Hausa (not the Fulani) who controlled the trade routes through the river valleys in an area of wild mountain formations, 'alive with everything except humanity'.

The boundary then dropped into the plains of the Donga valley, an area of considerable 'pagan' political activity and definable ethnic grouping. The aboriginal inhabitants gave their name to the region known as Tigong, Ndoro and Kentu. During the nineteenth century, the Jukun and the Chamba who dominated the Benue region came under pressure from the Muri Fulani. The result was that many Chamba and Jukun ruling clans followed the Dongo River into the Ndoro plain, but without severing their close connections with the Jukun–Chamba of Wukari and Donga. The boundary which sundered the Ndoro plain from the Wukari district had the result of disrupting a reasonably homogeneous 'pagan' community. This evil was recognized in time, for in 1933 the Ndoro plain ceased to be administered from Gashaka and was transferred to Wukari, with which Tigong, Ndoro and Kentu traditionally had close cultural and ethnological association.[1] South of the Ndoro plain, the boundary crossed the plains and highlands of the Katsina Ala river system, and then followed the tops of successive parallel ridges until it reached the edge of the Bamenda plateau. The only 'pagans' encountered here were the Zunperi who lived on the hill-tops and were described by the commissioners as 'cannibals'.[2] The last stretch of the boundary being discussed here was a 'happy' one because it generally separated Tiv elements from the plateau dominated by Tikar, Bali and Widekum groups.[3] The British

---

[1] *Report on the Cameroons*, 1933, p. 11. Also *Gazetteer of Muri Province*, p. 41.

[2] Nugent, op. cit., pp. 630–51.

[3] *Report on the Cameroons*, 1936, pp. 19–20.

member of the commission came to the conclusion that the boundary between Yola and the Cross River, running south-west, followed the western limits of the highlands and, in doing so, successfully divided mountains, torrential streams and sparsely inhabited regions from fertile plains, great navigable waterways and densely populated Nigerian districts. He apparently forgot that the Yola and M'bulo plains contained two important Fulani provinces which the boundary disrupted. There was also the Ndoro plain which sundered the Jukun and the Chamba of the Donga River.

The Anglo-German boundary through Adamawa ceased to function at the outbreak of the First World War. The German colony was invaded by the British and the French, the latter from French Equatorial Africa. Having successfully elimi-nated German local opposition, the two allies agreed at a meeting in London in February 1916 to draw a 'temporary' line to demarcate their respective administrative areas. This 'temporary' line came to be known as the 'Picot line', named after the French chief delegate to the London meeting.[1] The negotiations between Britain and France for a definitive boundary went on from 1919 to 1920. Available material on the negotiations suggests that the British government, relying on data supplied by the British officials in the British Came-roons, was anxious to reunite political groups as it understood them. It had in mind primarily Bornu and the Fulani strong-holds split by the Anglo-German boundary. The French, on the other hand, seemed to hold the view stated in 1906 by Major Hill that a frontier defined as following the limits of occupation of a tribe or the boundary of an indigenous state would be arbitrary because it would depend upon 'such a shadowy thing as the rule of an African potentate'.[2] French objectives were both territorial and commercial. They wished to obtain as much of Adamawa as possible. They were also determined to secure a navigable portion of the Benue by obtaining Garua. The latter acquisition would enable them,

---

[1] See *West Africa* 1049, no. 410, 25 June 1918; and no. 46, 6 December 1918.

[2] R.G.S., vol. xxviii, 1906, pp. 145–54.

under the provisions of the Berlin West African Conference, to import goods duty free into French Adamawa by way of the Niger and Benue rivers. The negotiations for the new partition of Adamawa were carried on side by side with the negotiations for the division of other German colonies which the allied Powers had confiscated. In the circumstances, British gains in other parts of the world had to be counterbalanced by concessions to France in Adamawa.

The Milner–Simon Agreement which emerged gave Britain the western ranges of the Mandara highlands, and the 'lands' of Uba, Billa Kilba, Holma, Zummu, Malabu and Gurin. The British believed they had thus restored the territorial integrity of Fulani districts. South of the Benue, the Anglo-French boundary did nothing to restore the state of Yola and the Fulani provinces. It left the provinces of Gashaka to the British and gave the French Banyo and Ngaundere. In all this the British local administrators were still preoccupied with the concept of an Adamawa empire tidily divided into Fulani provinces, and so their criticisms of the boundary dwelt largely on the assumption that the Fulani provinces of Chamba, Koncha and Banyo were split by the boundary. These arguments had no effect on the French. According to the chief British delegate to the Anglo-French negotiations,

> The French laid great stress on the need for the [trade] road from Bare via Chang and Bagam to Fumbun, thence via Banyo . . . Koncha, Laro and Chamba to Garua, thence via Murua to Mora. . . . Having regard to considerations connected with other parts of the Peace Arrangements, the French view was not opposed.[1]

The new boundary certainly restored the districts which the Fulani strongholds along the Yedseram plain allegedly controlled. In doing this, it split the Mandara 'pagans', the Higi and the Fali. It is however true that the 'pagan' groups were diverse and that there was little justification for the Nigerian governor's claim that the northern territories in question were 'inhabited by homogeneous tribal communities . . . [who] are

---

[1] *West Africa*, 1049, 50641, C.O. to Gov. of Nigeria, 19 September 1919.

animated by strong sentiments of homogeneity and a love of tribal unity under a hereditary chief'.[1] In the central regions of Adamawa, the British, although still preoccupied with thinking in terms of Fulani provinces, began in due course to realize that the boundary also split 'pagan' groups. For instance, the Bamum lived on either side of the Anglo-French boundary, and villagers from the British side visited Bamum markets on the days when special markets were held on the French side. There was a corresponding movement of Bamum people in the opposite direction. The Bamum chief who was on the French side appealed to the British section of the tribe to join him, but the British decided not to allow this wholesale migration to take place.

Little material is available on the manner in which the French organized local government in their part of Adamawa. The British proceeded, however, in pursuance of the policy of indirect rule, to divide British Adamawa into Fulani emirates and districts. Little contact was at first made with the 'pagans' entrenched in the mountainous regions. The situation was graphically summarized by Dame Margery Perham as follows:

> My approach even to the lowest villages had the effect of a tornado sweeping out nearly the whole population, so that little could be seen of them but black heads peering round the rocks . . . while on the further boulders naked figures were poised, scissors-like, on tiptoe for flight.[2]

The view prevailed that these 'pagans' should come under Fulani districts because the Fulani district heads had 'a certain amount of authority derived from a previous conquest of the "pagans" '. Some administrative reports, however, conceded that in other 'pagan' areas Fulani authority was non-existent.[3] The Emir of Yola, for his part, held on to the belief that the Anglo-French boundary was 'politically mortal', He complained to the British resident that 'they have left us the head, but they have cut off the body'. On another occasion he

---

[1] Ibid., 17278, Gov. of Nigeria to C.O., 11 February 1922.
[2] Perham, *Native Administration in Nigeria*, 1937, pp. 136–8.
[3] *Report on the Cameroons*, 1926, p. 10.

lamented that 'they have left me merely the latrines of my kingdom'.[1] There was no way of knowing at first the precise basis of the Emir's complaints. He might be referring to the Yola plain, most of which lay in French Adamawa. He might also have had in mind the fact that the Fulani districts of the Yedseram valley restored by the Anglo-French boundary and traditionally the fiefs of Yola were being administered by the British, but not as part of the truncated Emirate of Yola. The point of view of the Emir was clarified during the presence in Yola of the visiting missions of the Trusteeship Council in 1949 and 1955. On both occasions the then Lamido of Adamawa made the following ominous pronouncement:

> It is still a mystery to the inhabitants of Adamawa that their country is composed of two Territories, viz., a portion being British and another held in trust. . . . A change of policy is requested, i.e. the total dissolution of Trusteeship, and annexation to Adamawa Emirate of all the portion now British and French Territory formerly belonging to Adamawa.[2]

No evidence is available to indicate the reaction of the visiting missions to the request, but the British Secretary of State for the Colonies was willing that the wishes of the inhabitants of the British Trust Territory as to the question of organic union with Northern Nigeria should ultimately prevail. The British, however, could not speak for the French government.

Up to 1955 it was not certain whether the Anglo-German boundary or the Anglo-French line would become the second section of the eastern international boundary of Nigeria. Many of the British administrative officers complacently forecast that the separation of the British Trust Territory from Nigeria would be a shock to many communities. The communities they talked about were the Fulani and not the many 'pagan' groups split by the Anglo-French boundary. The latter, like similar groups in the Southern Cameroons, might prefer union with their kith and kin in the French Cameroons. The British failed to advert to the possibility that the 'pagans' might not be

---

[1] Kirk-Greene, op. cit., pp. 67–8.
[2] Ibid., quoted p. 86. See also *Report on the Cameroons*, 1955; Attachment B.

willing to be finally delivered into the hands of Fulani rulers whom the 'pagans' had always hated. Many of the 'pagan' hill countries were still declared 'unsettled' by the British because of the hostility of the 'pagans' to strangers, among whom the Fulani were included. In the Mambila plateau, some 5,000 ft. high, the British administration was not exactly dealing with the 'pagans' as independent groups whom the Fulani never conquered. The main problem here was the difficulty of wiping out the lions that had invaded the plateau. Nobody therefore anticipated the results which emerged from the 1959 plebiscite.

The United Nations Trusteeship Council decided that in the case of the Northern Cameroons, two questions should be put in the plebiscite for November 1959: 'Do you wish the Northern Cameroons to be part of the Northern Region of Nigeria when the Federation of Nigeria becomes independent?' or 'Are you in favour of deciding the future of the Northern Cameroons at a later date?' No reference was made to the issue of probable union with the French Cameroons. The plebiscite was therefore not exactly testing the fundamental questions of Fulani provinces separated from Yola and of the 'pagan' groups cut in two by the Anglo-French boundary. In realistic terms, what was being tested was merely whether the Anglo-German frontier should become an internal administrative boundary or an international boundary. The pattern of voting which emerged is interesting but not conclusive. The constituencies into which the territory was divided revealed the extreme ethnic complexity of the region. For obvious reasons the districts dominated by the Fulani voted in favour of union with Nigeria. On the other hand the 'pagan' districts in Gwoza, Adamawa north-east, Chamba and Mambilla voted overwhelmingly in favour of the second alternative. Thus the 'pagan' majority in Adamawa registered their opposition to integration with Nigeria primarily because they feared subordination to a Fulani bureaucracy backed by the British administration in Northern Nigeria.[1] The outcome was not

---

[1] See *West Africa*, 7 November 1959 and *The Daily Times* (Lagos) 10 November 1959, for voting figures.

necessarily a vote against the Anglo-French boundary. The results in two areas are worth noting because they showed that the 'pagans' were fully aware of the implications of the way they voted. In the Donga valley, all the stations in the Ndoro plain voted in favour of union with Nigeria. It will be recalled that here the Jukun–Chamba groups were sundered by the Anglo-German boundary. South of Yola, in the broken country of the Shebshi mountains and the Vere hills—a region in which the Batta 'pagans' had been split into mountain Batta and plain Batta by the Fulani conquest of the plain—twelve of the fifteen stations voted against union with Nigeria. The voting patterns in these two areas certainly had considerable correlation with ethnic distribution.

The peoples of the Northern Cameroons had a second chance in 1961. This time the choice was between union with Nigeria or secession. The complacency which marked the attitude of the leaders of Northern Nigeria in 1959 gave way in 1961 to intensive propaganda among the 'pagans'. The latter were promised social and political amenities if they joined Nigeria. They were asked 'to forget their personal animosities for their betterment'. The issue was not long in doubt. The results showed a substantial majority in favour of union with Nigeria. The Premier of Northern Nigeria greeted the results in these words:

> I most sincerely welcome you to Nigeria and assure you at all times of the friendship of my Government. The journey was long but thank God we have reached the end. Our brothers and sisters of the Trust Territory will now rejoin us in peace and amity.[1]

The Premier did not explain what he meant by 'brothers and sisters', but it is reasonable to assume that the resultant elimination of the Anglo-German boundary was welcome. The Milner–Simon line thus became Nigeria's international boundary in the Adamawa region.

---

[1] *Sunday Times* (Lagos), 23 April 1961.

5

The Western Boundary—I

The zone traversed by the first section of the western international boundary affords two significant contrasts with the region of the eastern boundary in comparable latitudes. One is ethnological and the other political. In the west, no one can speak without manifest absurdity of unclassifiable ethnic or linguistic groups, nor can one write in terms of a political vacuum. There was indeed excessive political activity which was the direct result of well developed state systems. These systems had functioned effectively for many centuries, but when disintegration set in, especially during the nineteenth century, warfare became the predominant feature of political relations. The zone discussed in this chapter was described in simple terms in 1890 by Governor Moloney of Lagos as follows:

> Geographers have continued the name Slave Coast, originally given by the Portuguese, to that portion of West Africa situated between the Volta and the Oil Rivers. This territorial wedge is linguistically divided between the Ewe and Yoruba or Yoruba-speaking peoples.[1]

We know today that the groups found east of the Volta include the Fon, the Egun, the Popo and the Adja, as sub-divisions of the Ewe linguistic cluster,[2] but for the purposes of studying indigenous frontiers and state systems the two-fold classification into Ewe and Yoruba groups is adequate. Whether or not

---

[1] R.G.S., vol. xii, 1890; see Moloney, 'Notes on the Yoruba'.

[2] Murdock, *Africa, its Peoples and their Culture History*, 1959, pp. 252–4. See also Newbury, *The Western Slave Coast and its Rulers*, 1961, pp. 3–5.

a common language also implied a common origin as well as a common culture is another matter.

The neat and simple classification into two groups comprising the Yoruba and the Ewe may indeed suggest a relatively easy background for an assessment of the discordance between the 1889 colonial boundary and the indigenous frontiers. There were however four complicating factors which individually and collectively upset what might otherwise have been a coherent ethnic landscape. The first was the wide dispersion of Yoruba groups of which the earlier writers were understandably unaware. The formation of linguistic enclaves in widely separated regions created a situation in which 'kinship of language [existed] over a wide area without bringing about a political unity of commensurate extent'.[1] The Ewe speaking peoples were not content to remain in their own territory either. Many Ewe groups thrust their way eastwards to create areas of mixed linguistic communities. The linguistic duality already noted with regard to Badagri and Porto Novo on the coast extended to the hinterland and over districts of considerable area. The political situation which developed during the nineteenth century produced the two remaining factors which intensified the complication of the ethnic configuration of the boundary zone. Oyo was traditionally the dominant political power centre of the Yoruba and had controlled an empire which gave a large part of Yorubaland both cultural coherence and political unity. When Oyo authority was undermined, the empire entered upon a phase of progressive disintegration, with the result that there emerged a congeries of states of varying size and degree of independence. Lastly, the decay of Oyo hegemony was accompanied by the rise of a dominant 'Ewe' state, Dahomey; and Dahomey was to become a military kingdom which devastated but did not assimilate conquered territories. Thus, quite apart from the linguistic overlapping, Yoruba groups fought one another, and Dahomey ravaged and dominated both Yoruba and Ewe groups without discrimination. A detailed analysis of the confused situation

---

[1] Dowd, *The Negro Races*, 1907, p. 195, pp. 202–3. See also Fortes and Evans-Pritchard, eds., *African Political Systems*, p. 23.

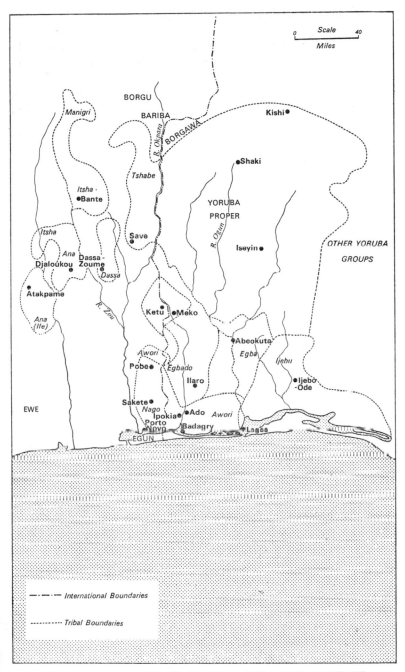

THE DISTRIBUTION OF YORUBA-SPEAKING PEOPLES

created by the factors enumerated above will provide the background against which the international boundary can realistically be criticized.

The name Yoruba is a corruption of the word Yarriba, given to the people by the Hausa. The name is now of course applied to a large group which inhabits Western Nigeria. The language has many dialects which are mutually intelligible. In spite of this close dialectical affinity, the Yoruba speak of themselves as Oyo, Egba, Ijebu, Ijesha, Ekiti and so forth. Fadipe divides the Yoruba groups into those who descended from the aboriginal inhabitants of Ife, and the Oyo groups held to be the descendants of later immigrants from the east.[1] Ife remains the spiritual headquarters of the Yoruba, and according to tradition it was from Ife that the seven grandsons of Oduduwa spread to the 'four corners' of Yorubaland. To determine whether among the Yoruba speaking peoples there were aboriginal groups on whom later immigrants imposed a language or from whom the immigrants borrowed a language is a task awaiting linguistic and historical research. Thus the question of origin is still a matter wrapped up in myth and speculation. Like many other groups in Nigeria—for instance, the Jukuns and the Borgawa—the Yoruba are associated with the much propagated Kisra migration.[2] It has been mentioned already that the earlier writers and European administrators did not realize that groups speaking Yoruba dialects were dispersed over wide areas. Thus for instance, Governor Moloney of Lagos, in an address to the Royal Geographical Society in 1890, asserted that the Weme River might be viewed as 'the old geographical boundary between Yoruba and Ewe speaking peoples'. Two years earlier, the same governor, in emphasizing his solicitude for Yoruba solidarity, described Yorubaland as 'comprised traditionally as regards its corners... of Yoruba proper, Egba, Ketu, and Ijebu. . . . People to the west and to the north are not Yoruba'.[3] The remarkable thing

---

[1] See Fadipe, *Sociology of the Yoruba*.

[2] The Western Regional Government provided funds for research into Yoruba origin or origins. The project was directed by Dr S. O. Biobaku, but the results have not been published at the time of writing.

[3] Johnson, *History of the Yorubas*, reprint 1957, quoted pp. 571–6.

was that the Alafin of Oyo, 'Head of all Yorubaland', agreed with the governor's demarcation of Yoruba speaking groups. Ellis, writing on the Ewe speaking peoples in 1890, attempted a rather undiscriminating generalization. He claimed that

> The Ewe language prevails from that river [the Volta] for a distance of 155 miles eastward along the coast, and inland to an unknown distance, probably about 200 miles.[1]

The above assessments ignored the overlapping of Yoruba and Ewe speaking peoples referred to already. They overlooked too the Yoruba enclaves in countries today known as Togoland and Dahomey.

Recent ethnographic studies show that there are considerable areas of Yoruba speaking peoples right across central Dahomey to as far west as Togoland. Daryll Forde describes the groups identified in Dahomey and Togoland as the Tsha, Ife and related groups. Rough estimates of their numbers are as follows: Savalou, 55,566; Togoland, 13,000.[2] These numbers are impressive, considering that the districts are poorly populated. The important thing to note, therefore, is that the territorial distribution of Yoruba speaking peoples, west of the Okpara River, embraces the districts of Save, Dassa, Bantc, Djaloukou and Atakpame. There are various traditions in explanation of this dispersion. In Dassa the present dynasty claims an Egba origin. French ethnological maps describe Yoruba groups as Nago, i.e. 'the lousy', a derogatory term applied by the Ewe of Dahomey. Johnson suggested rather vaguely that the far-flung groups speaking dialects of the Yoruba language were not Yoruba, but aborigines over whom the ruling clans of the Yoruba imposed their rule and culture. He went on to point out that Yorubaland itself was not empty of peoples when Oduduwa and his party entered 'from the east' to conquer and to absorb.[3] His

---

[1] Ellis, *The Ewe-speaking Peoples of the Slave Coast of Africa*, 1890, p. 8.

[2] Forde, *Ethnographic Survey*, Western Africa, part iv, pp. 1–4 and 43–4. *Africa*, xvii, 1947, see Parrinder, 'Yoruba Speaking Peoples in Dahomey', pp. 122–8. Murdock, op. cit., pp. 244 f.

[3] Johnson, op. cit., pp. 15–16. For a realistic assessment of the extent of a Yoruba empire which flourished during the 17th and 18th centuries, see Ajayi and Smith, *Yoruba Warfare in the Nineteenth Century*, 1964, pp. 3–4.

further observation that the knowledge of the Yoruba language existed only among the ruling houses in areas now known as Popo, Ga and Dahomey country is not true, as demonstrated by the results of ethnographic studies to which reference has already been made.

For the present study, it is reasonable to suggest that the Yoruba groups now being identified far to the west of the boundary zone should be ignored. They had ceased for at least two centuries to have any political connection with the main Yoruba groups. Of more consequence for the study are the Yoruba groups located immediately east and west of the Okpara River. Two other rivers, the Yewa (Ado) and the Ogun, may be noted on the map. The region of crucial importance may therefore be described as a rectangle bounded by the sea-coast on the south, the Okpara River on the west, the Ogun River in the east, and a line somewhere between the eighth and ninth degrees of north latitude. The Yewa runs through the middle of this rectangle. The northern portion is occupied by Yoruba speaking Ketu. South of Ketu are mixed populations of Ewe and Yoruba refugees. These mixed communities occupying territories to the west and the east of the Yewa River are described usually as Egun (Ewe) and Anago (Yoruba). The problem created by the overlapping of Ewe and Yoruba speaking peoples in the boundary region described above was further aggravated by the political situation created by the disintegration of the Oyo empire and the rise of vigorous states, particularly the state of the Egba and the military empire of Dahomey. The result is the extreme difficulty of defining indigenous political frontiers during the nineteenth century. To understand this problem, attention must be turned to the fortunes of Oyo, Dahomey and Egbaland.

It has been claimed that at the time of its greatest prosperity the Oyo empire extended from the Niger, in the east, to the Volta in the west. At one time the number of vassal princes exceeded 1,000. As to how this extensive empire was controlled, Johnson observed that

> The entire Yoruba country has never been thoroughly organized into one complete government in a modern sense. The system

that prevails is that known as the Feudal, the remoter portions have always lived more or less in a state of semi-independence, whilst loosely acknowledging an overlord.[1]

There is however evidence to show that some Yoruba groups—the Ijesha, Ekiti, Ondo and Akoko—never became part of the Oyo empire.[2] As to the administrative system, Johnson's observation means that for practical purposes the old Oyo empire was highly decentralized. In the provinces the local rulers were allowed freedom of action to manage their own affairs as long as they recognized the suzerainty of the Alafin and paid the annual tribute. Conquered towns were usually supervised by political 'residents', who collected for the Alafin the annual tribute. Apart from the annual tribute, the provincial rulers were expected to participate in the Bere festival which took place every January. On this rare occasion the provincial rulers turned up or were required to turn up at the capital to pay homage to, and 'cut grass' for, the Alafin.

The chiefdom of Oyo was theoretically very well organized. This central region administered directly by the Alafin and the Central Council, the *Oyo misi*, included the Oke-ogun districts (the area north-west of present day Oyo) and most of the Osun division. There is evidence also that the Egbado were closely linked, administratively, with Oyo. The two main Egbado chiefdoms, Ilaro and Ijanna, were uncommonly dependent on the Alafin. The senior Egbado chiefdom was Ilaro, which at one time had no fewer than four hundred ruling chiefs under it. The chief or Olu of Ilaro was unequivocally a crowned vassal of Oyo, to which he retired after ruling for three years. On the other hand, the ruler of Ijanna was not a crowned head, but he came second in importance to the Olu of Ilaro. It is worth noting that when the days of Oyo hegemony were already numbered, Clapperton and his companions were told in 1825 by the chief of Ijanna that the Alafin of Oyo was the supreme head.[3] West of the Egbado country, the authority of Oyo was accepted as far as Porto Novo and Whydah. Oyo, which

---

[1] Johnson, op. cit., pp. 40–1. Forde, op. cit., pp. 19–21.
[2] Ajayi and Smith, op. cit., p. 4.
[3] Clapperton, *Journal of a Second Expedition*, London, 1829, pp. 10–11.

possessed in the eighteenth century the most feared military machine, periodically harassed the Aja states of central Dahomey to exact tribute.[1] In the absence of a centralized council embracing the whole empire, the outlying parts of the empire were held by Oyo as long as the provincial rulers or the political 'residents' were willing to remain loyal to the Alafin. As the history of Europe during the Middle Ages amply demonstrated, feudalism as a basis of political relationship was always susceptible of instability.

Apart from the weaknesses inherent in a feudal administrative structure, the Oyo empire was saddled with other peculiarities which were destined to accelerate the process of disintegration during the early years of the nineteenth century. Three examples will suffice to indicate these additional weaknesses. First, the succession to the chiefdom of Oyo was not strictly by primogeniture. The councillors, headed by the *Basorun*, could elect a successor from the members of the royal family belonging to the male line. It is therefore hardly surprising that succession often became an occasion for intrigues and internal strife. Second, the chief councillor could at any time get rid of an Alafin by requiring him to take the customary 'parrots' eggs'. This meant that the Alafin had to kill himself because he was no longer pleasing to the gods.[2] Third, the Alafin was held in great awe and respect. For this reason, he was confined to the palace except on special occasions. He was seen in public only during the annual festivals in January (the Bere) and in July (the Egungun), and possibly also in September (the Awrun). This dangerous confinement of the head of the Oyo empire was slightly offset by the appointment of a commander-in-chief, the *Are-Ona-Kakanfo*. This leader was expected to deal with disaffected areas or with regions exposed to external danger. He was also expected to go to war once in three years and to return successful or commit suicide. As the career of Afonja was to show, the Alafin used the appointment of a commander-in-chief as a means of getting rid of a dangerous

---

[1] Akinjogbin, 'Agaja and the Conquest of the Coastal Aja States' (*J.H.S.N.*, vol. ii, no. 4, 1963, pp. 555–7).

[2] Talbot, *The Peoples of Southern Nigeria*, vol. iii, pp. 566–70.

rival. In any case, there was nothing to prevent the *Are-Ona-Kakanfo* from refusing to commit suicide and consolidating his position in some outlying province. The Oyo army was not one controlled centrally from Oyo. The military force consisted of the 'caboceers' and their immediate retainers.[1] In the circumstances, it is difficult to discern a machinery for maintaining in the Oyo empire anything but fluctuating political frontiers.

On the eve of the political decline of Oyo hegemony, marked by internal strife and disruption, the elements of weakness indicated above were manifest. Johnson's explanation of the threshold of the unhappy new era, during the nineteenth century, is interesting:

> The cup of iniquity of the nation was full; cruelty, usurpation, and treachery were rife, especially in the capital. . . . The nation was ripe for judgement, and the impending wrath of God was about to fall upon it; hence trouble from every quarter, one after another.[2]

It is clearly unwise to enter into a discussion of divine wishes in human affairs, but Johnson was quite right in saying that trouble developed in many directions. There is indeed evidence that the Alafin's agents perpetrated acts of increasing oppression in the districts originally occupied by the Egbas. The Aja states to the west of the Oyo imperial frontier were finding Oyo demands increasingly vexatious and were determined to shake off Oyo hegemony.

The first decade of the nineteenth century is generally regarded as the turning point in the fortunes of the Oyo empire. The last powerful Alafin of Oyo, Abiodun, died in the closing years of the eighteenth century. His successor committed suicide. Two other ineffective rulers reigned for short periods, to be followed by an interregnum. Those on whom authority should have developed were themselves either weak or selfish. The actual break-up of the empire began under Alafin Arogangan. His personal weakness as much as what

---

[1] Clapperton, op. cit., p. 57; Talbot, op. cit., p. 829.

[2] Johnson, op. cit., p. 188. See also Hambly, *Culture Areas of Nigeria*, Chicago, 1935, p. 391.

Johnson called 'the . . . iniquity of the nation' contributed to the new state of affairs. The first sign of serious trouble arose out of the treasonable behaviour of the commander-in-chief, Afonja, who was in charge of Ilorin, a potentially dangerous northern frontier zone. If we accept the story that has been handed down by tradition, the successor of Arogangan reigned for four months only. The next successor, Maku, received no traditional congratulations from Afonja in Ilorin. A deputation was therefore sent to inform Afonja formally that a new Alafin had been enthroned. 'The New Moon has appeared,' Afonja was told. 'Let that New Moon speedily set,' was Afonja's ominous reply.[1] At about the same time, the independence movement among the Egba had already begun under the leadership of Lishabi. The reaction of the Aja states in Dahomey will be discussed later, but because it was impossible to organize any forces effective enough to suppress the rebellion of Afonja in Ilorin, the virus of discontent spread to all the provinces of the Oyo empire. In the Oshun part of the central chiefdom, the Owu war broke out. Then followed the destruction of the former Egba towns. In the general confusion consequent on the breakdown of the old constitution, powerful Yoruba leaders attempted to establish new centres of political power.

The years up to the Fulani sacking of Katunga, the old Oyo capital, were taken up with one inconclusive campaign after another. Clapperton and Lander left a fairly clear picture of the air of despondency which seems to have engulfed the capital during those years of trouble in every part of the empire. During the interview Clapperton had with the Alafin during the former's sojourn in Katunga the ruler reportedly said that he was glad 'that white men had come at this time; and now he trusted his country would be put right, his enemies brought to submission, and he would be enabled to build up his father's house, which war had destroyed'.[2] With touching

---

[1] Johnson, op. cit., p. 196; Ellis, *The Yoruba-speaking Peoples of the Slave Coast*, 1894, pp. 9–19. For a recent study of the nineteenth century warfare in Yorubaland, see Ajayi and Smith, op. cit., pp. 11–12.

[2] Clapperton, op. cit., pp. 39–41.

poignancy the Alafin recalled that Badagri, Allada (the former chief Aja state) and Dahomey, 'all belonged to him', and, rather more arrogantly, declared that if he ordered the king of Dahomey to desist from the notorious annual custom of human sacrifices, 'he must obey him'. Clapperton had however seen the depressing realities of the true political situation clearly enough not to be deceived by the Alafin's truculent declaration. Four years later the Lander brothers passed through Katunga on their way to Bussa. The political situation was, if anything, worse. Town after town was found by the Landers to be in complete decay. Of the capital itself, the Landers noted that

> The walls of the town have been suffered to fall into decay. . . . The people cannot, surely, be fully aware of their own danger, or they never could be unconcerned spectators of events which are rapidly tending to . . . totally annihilate them as a nation.[1]

The Landers came to the conclusion that the Yoruba people were a simple, honest, inoffensive but weak, timid, and cowardly race—a notoriously unfair assessment of a people who for many centuries controlled an extensive empire. The judgement is, however, useful in showing how the situation in the first three decades of the nineteenth century must have impressed itself on external observers.

The most serious threat to the capital was indeed the one bound up with Afonja's activities in Ilorin. Afonja declared himself independent in or about 1824. By promising slaves their freedom he attracted to Ilorin many slaves who deserted their masters in the Oyo districts. The Fulani and Hausa elements who had hitherto tended their cattle or traded peacefully now rallied to Afonja. An event which probably permanently changed the course of Yoruba history occurred when Afonja invited a Fulani leader called Abdul Alimi to assist him in his fight against his own kith and kin. Alimi was shortly afterwards to overthrow Afonja, make Ilorin a Fulani province, and carry the jihad into Yorubaland. One by one the northern

---

[1] Lander, *Narrative of an Expedition*, New York, 1843, vol. i, pp. 178–188.

Yoruba towns fell to the Fulani. These included Offa, the Igbomina towns, Ikoyi and Gbogun. Katunga was to follow. But before calamity materialized, a belated effort was made by the Yoruba to crush the Fulani threat. The Alafin entered into a military alliance with the king of the Bariba,[1] who were also exposed to Fulani expansionism. The upshot was a decisive war against the Fulani. The war, named the Eleduwe war after the Bariba king, ended catastrophically for the allies.[2] The final political humiliation of the Oyo empire came when the Fulani ruler of Ilorin ordered that the Alafin should come in person as a vassal of Ilorin to pay homage. According to Johnson, this was done.

A second summons from Ilorin met with a firm refusal, and it was this refusal on the part of the Alafin, Amodo, which provoked a Fulani expedition which culminated in the sacking of Katunga or old Oyo, probably in the year 1835. The leading Oyo families moved south with what was left of their followers to rebuild Oyo at Ago. The ruins of the impressive walls of the once great metropolis of Katunga tell a sad story and are still there for the inquisitive and historically-minded tourist. With the flight of the Oyo ruling families, other Yoruba war leaders who had participated in the disastrous war against Ilorin made their way to new rallying points in Yorubaland. It was thus that Ibadan and Ijaye came into existence as new power centres. Whatever solidarity had existed among the major Yoruba groups came to an end.

The disruption of Oyo hegemony produced far-reaching consequences for the western frontiers of the empire. The Egba led by Lishabi consolidated themselves in the vicinity of the *Olumo* rock and declared their independence of Oyo. The Egbado, traditionally very loyal to Oyo, were shortly to be exposed to the territorial ambitions of Abeokuta and to the devastations of Dahomian armies.[3] To understand the fluctuations and uncertainties of the western frontiers of Yorubaland in the nineteenth century, it is vital to discuss the

---

[1] Bariba is another name for the Borgawa mentioned on pp. 11–12.
[2] *Gazetteer of Ilorin Province*, pp. 122–5. Johnson, op. cit., pp. 260–8.
[3] Forde, op. cit., pp. 32–44.

fortunes of the most vigorous Yoruba state in the colonial boundary zone. The new Egba state (i.e. Abeokuta) and its expansion were of much greater consequence than the mocking shadow of the former Oyo empire. The intermittent strife involving Ibadan, Ijebu, the Ekiti and the Egba undoubtedly contributed to the difficulty of new Oyo becoming a political rallying centre for the Egbado and the Yoruba towns situated west of old Oyo—groups most exposed to Dahomian military domination. But to go back to the Egba. The Egba, who were expelled from their former towns and who rallied around the *Olumo* rock, comprised originally four sections, each under its own chief. As the government became more centralized, the Alake was recognized as the senior chief.[1] Abeokuta, the nucleus of the new Egba state, was described as follows:

> That town, then much talked of in English missionary circles, is situated on the Ogun River, and is about eighty miles due east from Kana [an Oyo tribute-collecting centre in Dahomey]. It is sixteen miles in circumference, surrounded by a mud wall six feet high, and defended by a ditch five feet wide.[2]

The region that attracted Egba expansionist leaders was the Egbado country lying south and south-west. The new state needed direct and uninterrupted connection with the sea, and to achieve this it was vital to dominate the Egbado towns that stood along the route. The Egba began by soliciting the friend-ship of the strategically placed Egbado town of Otta. But the chief of Otta apparently thought more highly of himself than the true facts of his military power warranted. He demanded tribute from the Egba. The consequence of the chief's arro-gance was the reduction of Otta to vassalage by the Egba. Ado, another Egbado town, soon shared the fate of Otta. The greatest Egba successes in the Egbado country were achieved against the leading Egbado towns of Ilaro and Ijanna. It will be recalled that these towns had represented Oyo supremacy over the Egbado. Now the Egba found an excuse for imposing their authority on the Egbado towns on the allegation that the

[1] Biobaku, *The Egba and their Neighbours*, 1957, p. 26.
[2] Ellis, *The Ewe-speaking Peoples*, p. 314.

towns had co-operated with the Ibadans and the Ijebu in anti-Egba activities. In any case, the people of Ilaro were further alleged to have solicited Egba aid in order to get rid of a tyrannical Olu. The inhabitants of Ilaro and Ijanna fled at the approach of Egba forces, and their towns were sacked. Ilaro in due course came under Egba suzerainty when the inhabitants agreed to install a pro-Egba Olu in 1857, and to receive an ajele or consul from Abeokuta.[1] The Egba did not, however, dominate all the Egbado towns. Those they sacked added to the refugee communities fleeing into the 'borderland' of the Ewe and Yoruba speaking peoples. It was indeed difficult to determine the precise political frontier of the Egba state in this direction. The fluid situation was to lead to difficulties with the British in Lagos when Oke–Odan and Ilaro appealed for British protection against the Egba and Dahomey.

There is abundant evidence to show that the effective western frontier of the Egba state was the Ogun River. The situation created by Dahomian military activities west of the river was admirably summarized by Johnson:

> Almost every year their [Dahomian] expedition would come as far as Ibara, ten miles from the town [Abeokuta, capital of the Egba], the inhabitants deserting that place for Abeokuta, and sometimes they [Dahomians] would camp on the Atta hills, five or six miles distant, remaining for a couple of months, and devastating the country all around. The Egbas would remain day and night keeping watch on the walls till the beginning of May, when the rains had set in, and the rivers began to rise. The Ogun river at this time became a wall of protection for them as the Dahomians could not ford it, nor bridge it and they had no canoes. . . . The Dahomians therefore invariably raised their siege and returned home before the rains had fairly set in.[2]

The Egba Yoruba neighbours to the west of the Ogun River included many towns traditionally subject to Oyo. These were Ilesan, Ibise, Oke Amu, Ago, Iluku, Gbagba, Ago Sabe and so forth. The Alafin of Oyo could now not afford them any pro-

---

[1] Biobaku, op. cit., p. 20; Johnson, op. cit., p. 255.
[2] Ibid., p. 362.

tection. It was with reference to them that the Alafin of Oyo lamented in a letter to the governor of Lagos that

> All my frontier towns are in great panic now, and if I make no stir to protect them they will all scatter.[1]

The Alafin indeed made no stir, and it was left to the Dahomian armies to carry away into slavery those of the Alafin's subjects they could capture. There was also west of the Ogun River the Yoruba state of Ketu. This Yoruba state, the chief of which was (and is) called the Alaketu, was, according to the tradition of the place, formed by one of the ancient offshoots from Ife. Little or no material is available on the part played by Ketu in the turbulent decades that witnessed the collapse of Oyo hegemony.[2] Relations between Ketu and the Egba state were hostile. For instance, in 1868 the Egbas besieged Meko, an important Ketu town, because the Egbas believed it engaged in spying for Dahomey and also for Ibadan against the interests of Abeokuta. Apart from the siege of Meko there is hardly any justification for speaking seriously of Egba frontier policy in this region. Thus neither Ketu nor any of the Yoruba towns west of the Ogun were effectively protected from Dahomey. One isolated example of Egba concern rather proves conclusively the contention that the effective western frontier of the Egba state was the Ogun River. A town called Ishagga, situated ten miles west of the River Ogun, sympathized with the Egba cause. It became, however, the first halt of the Dahomian forces in the periodic assaults on Abeokuta. The town was not defended by the Egba.

The consequences of the break-up of the Oyo empire, particularly in the regions of the western frontiers of the empire, have been discussed in detail in order to show that in the nineteenth century, when the Alafin of Oyo described himself as 'Head of Yorubaland, the four corners of which are and have been from time immemorial known as Egba, Ketu,

---

[1] Ibid., p. 463.
[2] See Parrinder, *The Story of Ketu*, 1956; and Akinjogbin in *Africa in the Nineteenth and Twentieth Centuries*, 1966, edited by Anene and Brown, pp. 267–8.

Jebu, and Oyo . . . embracing all Yoruba speaking peoples',[1] he was merely indulging in memories of a glorious period which had become a thing of the past. At the time the Alafin was making the claim quoted above, Oyo was relying on militant Ibadan to keep back the Fulani from further southward advance and to regain paramountcy over the Ijeshas and Ekitis. It was the Egba state, the most vigorous Yoruba political unit in the region of the western boundary, which bore the brunt of Dahomian attacks on Yorubaland.

The nature of the military ascendancy of Dahomey is a factor of indisputable importance for understanding the political landscape of the western boundary zone. This is so for three reasons. First, the Dahomian kingdom was too impressive a political reality to be ignored by the European Powers which negotiated the partition of this portion of the slave coast. Second, the military aggressiveness of Dahomey intensified the flight eastwards of splinter Ewe groups to add to the Yoruba–Ewe intermingling in mushroom states which claimed to be independent of any suzerain. Third, Dahomey conquered, sacked and ravaged, but she did not assimilate the conquered territories. In the circumstances, the eastern frontier of Dahomey was fluid, and any precise assessment of such a frontier would appear extremely conjectural.[2] The origins of this remarkable kingdom deserve a brief discussion.

Dahomey was originally an insignificant member of the Aja family of states dominated by Allada (Ardra). Throughout the second half of the seventeenth century the entire region was harassed by Oyo troops, and in the end Allada accepted the paramountcy of Oyo and paid regular tribute on behalf of the Aja states. Because of the servility of Allada to Oyo, its preeminence in the Aja country progressively declined. The sister states attempted to rebel against the hitherto dominant state. The consequent state of internal chaos in the Aja family of states provided Dahomey with an excellent opportunity to assert her separate political identity and later to attempt to fill

---

[1] C.O. 806/299, Moloney to Knutsford, 31 July 1888.

[2] R.G.S., vol. xii, 1890, Moloney. Ellis, *The Ewe-speaking Peoples*, p. 6. Skertchley. *Dahomey as it is*, 1874, p. 36.

the political vacuum created by the eclipse of Allada. The precise course of events is shrouded in obscurity. There are, however, two prevailing traditions, which, whatever their historical authenticity, certainly foreshadowed in their bloody details the character of the kingdom which emerged. One version is briefly this. The sons of the king of Allada or Ardra were engaged in a struggle for succession to the throne. One ultimately proved supreme. The second fled to Da, the king of the Aja state called Abomey. The third fled to Porto Novo (for a long time after known as Little Ardra). The fugitive to Abomey in due course superseded, through treachery, the king of Abomey. He cut open the stomach of Da and built his palace over the spot where Da was buried. Hence the name Dahomey which means 'the belly of Da'.[1] The second version of the tradition is that one of the contestants for the Allada throne invited Agaja, the king of Dahomey, to intervene. The king obliged and destroyed Allada. From then on the usurper began the process of reorganizing the Aja states under his own authority. This version of the origin of Dahomey obviously lacks the etymological significance of the first.

During the early years of the eighteenth century, Dahomey achieved very little success because of the military pre-ponderance of the Oyo empire. The Dahomian attacks on the Aja states, including Whydah, were frustrated by the inter-vention of Oyo armies. As a matter of fact Dahomey bought peace in 1730 by agreeing to pay tribute to Oyo. Kana, south of Abomey, became the historic collecting centre of the tribute sent annually to Oyo.[2] This setback did not long deter the Dahomian kings from their destined career of conquest. During the first half of the eighteenth century, Whydah, an important outlet to the Atlantic, had been absorbed into the Dahomian kingdom. The manner in which Whydah was con-quered was characteristic of Dahomey. Whydah, like many of the petty states on the coast, had grown very prosperous as a

---

[1] Norris, *Memoirs of the Reign of Bossa Ahadee, King of Dahomey*, 1787, pp. xiii–xiv. Also Dalzel, *The History of Dahomey*, 1793, p. 2.

[2] Burton, *A Mission to Gelele, King of Dohamey*, 1864, vol. i, pp. 196–8. Dalzel, op. cit., p. 14, pp. 44–5 and pp. 52–3.

result of the transatlantic slave trade. Dahomey needed free access to the coast for the sale of slaves in exchange for European guns and powder. If war was needed to achieve this objective, Dahomey would not shrink from it. What transpired between Dahomey and Whydah was graphically described by Ellis as follows:

> The Whydahs had, after consulting their priests, confided the defence of the ford to their chief god, the python; and the Dahomians, discovering this, crossed over, killed the serpent, and . . . fell suddenly upon the town. . . . The Whydahs excused their cowardice by charging the Dahomis with cannibalism, saying that they did not fear death in battle, but could not support the idea of being eaten.[1]

As already indicated, it was the growing Dahomian menace which accelerated the movement eastwards of Ewe speaking groups. Appa, Badagri, Katanu or Fra, originally inhabited by aboriginal Yoruba speaking peoples, became mixed communities with the arrival of Ewe refugees. To the north of the towns mentioned here, other Ewe groups took refuge in the swamps in and around the sheet of water known as the Denham waters. The situation here was noted by the agents of the European Powers interested in the region:

> These tribes are the Katenus, Esos, and Whemians (all speaking the Ewe or Dahomey language), who live in large native villages and towns built entirely out and over the water . . . where safety was sought from their more powerful fellow-countrymen.[2]

Porto Novo, founded according to tradition by the 'brother' of the king of Dahomey and known as Little Ardra, was originally inhabited by the Yoruba under the name of Ajase-Ipo. The ruling Yoruba chief had welcomed the immigrant Ewe but was in due course treacherously murdered by the Ewe chief, who then made himself the king of Porto Novo. Dahomey

---

[1] Ellis, *The Ewe-speaking Peoples*, pp. 286–7. See also Herskovits, *Dahomey, an Ancient West African Kingdom*, New York, 1938, vol. i, pp. 5–7, and Burdo, *A Voyage up the Niger and Benue*, 1880, p. 273.

[2] Moloney, op. cit., pp. 596–614.

refrained from attacking a 'sister' state and indeed relied on a close alliance with Porto Novo for the subjugation of the petty states of Badagri, Appa and Frah. The nineteenth century, which witnessed the crumbling of the Oyo empire, left Dahomey the undisputed master of the region. Even before Katunga or old Oyo was sacked by the Fulani, the Dahomian nation under Gezo, who became king in 1818, had repudiated the obligation to pay tribute to Oyo. Gezo sacked Kana, the tribute-collecting centre, and instituted the ceremony which 'opens as it were the customs of Abomey. The victims are made to personate in dress and avocation Oyos'.[1] The centralization of Dahomey state and its army provided not only stability but also the instrument for extensive continental conquests.

In contrast with the traditional Oyo political organization, the king of Dahomey was absolute, and the person of the king was sacred. No councillor or priest had the right to suggest that the gods demanded the death of the Dahomian king. He was not confined to the palace, as the Alafin of Oyo traditionally was. If the Dahomian king lost a battle or a war, he was not required to commit suicide. The Dahomian state was, even by modern criteria, very well organized.[2] The principal officers of state were the servants of the king. They included the *Megan*, principal adviser and head of village chiefs; the *Mehu* or *Meu*, a sort of treasurer and foreign minister; the *Gau* and the *Kposu*, the ministers of war; the *Jahu*, the supply minister; and a host of palace officials headed by a eunuch. The provincial governors, for instance, the *Yevo-gan* of Whydah (Captain of the White-men), ranked below the royal ministers and were never powerful enough to lead successful rebellions against the centralized authority of the king. Another significant feature of Dahomey governmental hierarchy was that none of the offices was hereditary, and although the Megan and Meu could appoint a royal successor from among the late king's sons, they remained the creatures of the reigning monarch, whose wishes in the matter of succession were scrupulously observed. The

---

[1] Burton, op. cit., vol. i, pp. 196–8; Ellis, *The Yoruba-speaking Peoples*, p. 169.

[2] Murdock, op. cit., p. 257.

most powerful instrument of policy at the command of the
Dahomian monarch was undoubtedly a standing army. In
thus possessing a permanently equipped army, the kingdom
was very different from her eastern neighbours, who relied on
irregular 'feudal' levies. The standing army of Dahomey comprised two corps, the male and the female, the latter being the
redoubtable Amazons. Forbes, in 1850, and Borghero, in 1861,
were eye-witnesses of the prowess of these Amazons at mock
battles and military reviews in Abomey.[1] Various estimates
were made of the size of the Dahomian army. Beecroft probably exaggerated in his view that Dahomey could muster
between 20,000 and 25,000 troops. A possible justification for
Beecroft's guess was that the standing army was usually aug-
mented by provincial levies under their own chiefs when a
major expedition was contemplated.

There was another important difference between Dahomey
and her eastern neighbour, the Oyo empire. Rightly or
wrongly, Burton, in deploring the civil war that sapped the
very fabric of the Oyo empire, charged the Yoruba with an
absence of patriotism because, as he put it, 'greed of gain—not
the pious and patriotic aspiration to recover the lands of their
forefathers—has sustained [them] . . .'.[2] No one, however
prejudiced, could on the other hand refuse to recognize and
admire the fanatical love of king and country which animated
the Dahomian army. Dalzel noted that the Dahomians
reverenced their king with a mixture of love and fear, little
short of adoration, and recorded a remarkable interview:

> When I asked a Dahomian, just before his going to battle, if he
> was not apprehensive of finding the enemy too strong: 'I think of
> my king . . . and then I dare to engage five of the enemy myself . . .
> my head belongs to the king; not to myself; if he pleases to send
> for it, I am ready to resign it; or if it be shot through in battle, I am
> satisfied—it is in his service.' Even at this day, after a tyranny of
> forty years, every Dahomian possesses the same sentiments.[3]

---

[1] See Ellis, *The Ewe-speaking Peoples*, chapter xii, pp. 182 f. and Forbes,
Dahomey and the Dahomians, 1851, preface x.
[2] Burton, *Abeokuta and the Cameroons Mountains*, 1863, vol. i, p. 266.
[3] Dalzel, op. cit., p. 69.

Burton, who undertook an unsuccessful mission to Abomey, referred to Dahomey as 'this small black Sparta'.[1]

Dahomey's career of conquest during the nineteenth century was under the leadership of two remarkable kings, Gezo, 1818–58, and Glegle or Gelele, 1858–89. It is to be noted that the Anglo-French colonial boundary through the zone under consideration was made in 1889, after the death of Gelele. The precise extent of Dahomey as a well organized political unit will probably remain no more than a matter of conjecture. Abomey and Kana, more directly under the king, were the centres of Dahomian political power and religious life. Herskovits enumerated the following as the provinces: I Whydah, II Allada, III Zagnanado, IV Save, V Atakpame, VI Adja, and observed that no details could be recovered concerning the administration of the provinces, the very area of which varied with the fluctuations of the fortunes of war.[2] To the west of Dahomey lay the powerful Ashanti confederation. Between Dahomey and Ashanti, expediency and wisdom dictated relations of caution and amity. To the north and north-west of Dahomey, the Mahi invariably retired into the neighbouring highlands and wilderness at the approach of Dahomian troops. They were never conquered, and they denied Dahomey the slaves she primarily sought. In the circumstances, the region east and south-east of Dahomey offered her great attractions. A routine which became an annual affair for Gezo and Gelele reveals the extent to which the eastern frontier was exposed to Dahomian ravages and domination:

> In January or February, he [the king] marches with the army on the annual marauding expedition, to return in March or April to the capital. About May he moves to Kana and there performs the customs in memory of the defeat of the Yorubas and the cessation of tribute. In October or November he summons his officers and chiefs, leaves Kana . . . [for] entry into the capital. He then holds the Annual Custom, and remains in Agbomi [Abomey] till the time for the annual expedition has once more arrived.[3]

---

[1] Burton, *A Mission to Gelele, King of Dahomey*, 1864, vol. ii, pp. 231–2.
[2] Herskovits, op. cit., vol. i, pp. 23–6. Also Forbes, op. cit., pp. 12–20.
[3] Ellis, *The Ewe-speaking Peoples*, p. 169.

Dahomey was primarily interested in capturing slaves for export and for the 'annual custom' of butchering human beings in keeping with her religious rites. She overran territories and then abandoned them, and made no attempt to organize them politically. This practice persisted throughout the nineteenth century. It is indeed extremely doubtful whether Dahomey was seriously concerned with territorial acquisitions at the expense of Oyo or Abeokuta; hence the difficulty of indicating the eastern frontier of Dahomey with preciseness. Between Dahomey and her eastern neighbours there were at times frontiers of separation and at other times frontiers of contact. For this reason no study of the indigenous political frontiers in the zone should ignore a brief reference to the grim strife between Dahomey and the Egba state. It is to be noted that in this encounter, particularly in regard to military activities, linguistic affinity progressively ceased to be a factor in differentiating political allegiance. The Egba attacked Yoruba speaking communities that barred them free access to the sea. Dahomey ravaged Ewe speaking and Yoruba speaking states indifferently. As was to be expected the clash between Abeokuta and Dahomey first occurred in their attempt to dominate the mushroom states that lay between them and the Atlantic. The mushroom states included Egbado towns and others of combined Yoruba and Ewe elements. The internal confusions which prevailed in many of these petty states arose partly from the decay of the Oyo empire and partly from the usual squabbles associated with succession disputes. Many of them clung to their ephemeral independence, whilst in others ambitious contenders to the throne played into the hands of Abeokuta and Dahomey, or perhaps played Abeokuta against Dahomey. Their behaviour added to the political fluidity which baffled European observers.[1]

There were indications that up to 1850 the slave trade was still a very profitable activity along the slave coast. Abeokuta therefore sought to control Ilaro, Ijanna, Otta, Ado and even Ikorodu. Dahomey, already in control of Whydah, attempted to extend the sea-board she could dominate to Badagry, and

---

[1] C.O. 806/281, W.O. to C.O., 1 July 1887.

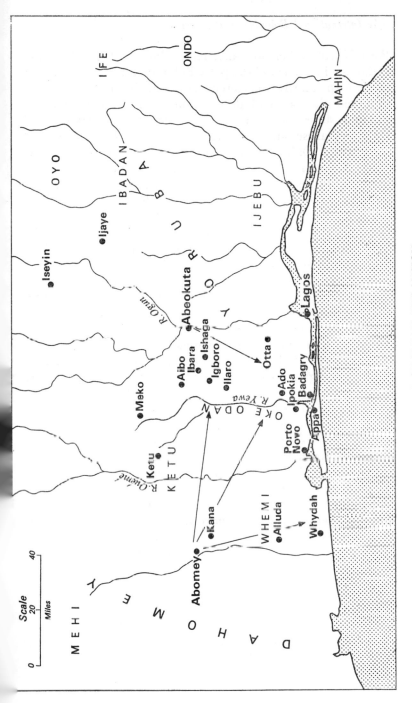

EGBA AND DAHOMIAN EXPANSION

Porto Novo was her close ally. The ambitions of Abeokuta and Dahomey in respect of the petty Egbado and Ewe states were therefore primarily commercial, although they necessarily presupposed the political domination of the 'inconveniently' situated states. The actual clash between Abeokuta and Dahomey arose out of the Egba siege of the Egbado state of Ado, which Dahomey believed to be tributary to her ally, Porto Novo. It was Dahomey's failure to save Ado that was presumably responsible for the implacable hostility which marked Dahomey–Egba relations for the remainder of the century.[1] On the occasion of the Ado siege, Gezo, the Dahomian king, not only suffered military defeat but lost to the Egba warriors important royal symbols in his precipitate flight from imminent capture. The umbrella, the stool, and war charms seized by his enemies could not be redeemed for the simple reason that the Egba burnt them. From this time, circ. 1846, it became the consuming ambition of Dahomey to destroy the capital of Egbaland. It was the defence of the capital as well as continued aggressive policy in the Egbado towns directly to the south that absorbed Egba political and military energies during the second half of the century—so far, that is, as the boundary zone was concerned. The Egba more or less abandoned to Dahomey the Egbado states immediately east and west of the Yewa River. At Ijanna, one of the candidates for succession, a man called Dekun, invited Dahomey, not Abeokuta, to intervene. Dekun found asylum in Dahomey and the forces of Gezo proceeded to reduce Ijanna to ashes.[2] In the same manner, Olikiti, a chief in Oke–Odan, invited in the Dahomians. The result was precisely the same. Dahomey, however, destroyed and withdrew, thus confirming the view that she did not seek the political consolidation of her conquests. The peoples of Ijanna and Oke–Odan who fled at the approach of the Dahomian forces invariably returned to rebuild their houses and await the next annual Dahomian expedition.

---

[1] Biobaku, op. cit., p. 31 and pp. 33–4; Johnson, op. cit., pp. 296–7. Newbury, op. cit., pp. 36 and 48.

[2] Johnson, op. cit., p. 228.

The lower region of the Yewa River was therefore a frontier of separation between Dahomey and Yorubaland. In this region lay the Egbado states of Ipokia, Ado, Oke-Odan, Ilaro and Ijanna. The political reality in this frontier was the complete domination of Dahomey, which took no account of similarities or divergencies of language and culture—a point which should be kept in mind in assessing the colonial boundary which later emerged. In the upper reaches of the Yewa River, the contest between Dahomey and Abeokuta was a more direct confrontation. But between them lay the Yoruba state of Ketu. The view that Ketu was originally an Ewe state is clearly untenable in the face of available evidence.[1] The place seems, however, to have been badly organized politically. The Alaketu (king) exercised an authority which did not seem to extend beyond the town of Ketu. The surrounding villages, theoretically subject to the Alaketu, enjoyed virtual independence. For instance, Meko (or Mekaw) on several occasions defied the claim of pre-eminence on the part of the Alaketu, and its local Bale styled himself 'king'.[2] In the political confusion which engulfed Yorubaland, Ketu and Meko took opposite sides. Meko became the ally of Ibadan forces usually ranged against Abeokuta. The extraordinary situation which emerged was that while Abeokuta was attempting to ravage Meko, Ibadan forces were organizing raids against Ketu, the capital of the state. The fate of Ketu, viewed politically and culturally, is an important question in the study of the colonial boundary.

In her expeditions against Abeokuta, Dahomey did not encounter any organized opposition in the Yoruba state of Ketu. It was indeed likely that one Ketu town after another sought to buy peace by spying for Dahomey and by promising supplies for the troops that traversed their country. Johnson asserts that in 1880 one chief in Ketu called Afin acted as Dahomey's guide in an enterprise in which Dahomey ravaged the western districts of Yoruba proper. The Dahomian achievement (if the word is appropriate) which was long

---

[1] Parrinder, *The Story of Ketu: an Ancient Yoruba Kingdom*, 1956, p. 16.
[2] Ibid., p. 33; Ajisafe, *History of Abeokuta*, 1924, p. 130.

remembered was the destruction of Ketu itself in 1886. Johnson ascribed the fate of Ketu to what he described as 'retributive justice', probably on the ground that a chief of Ketu had on a previous occasion acted as a Dahomian spy during the Dahomian devastations of the western regions of the Oyo chiefdom.[1] The treachery of a Ketu chief did not however prevent Ketu, in her extremity, from dispatching messengers to Abeokuta and Oyo to solicit help. None came, and Ketu was razed to the ground by Dahomian forces. The macabre sequel to the sacking of Ketu has been described as follows:

> The prisoners of Ketu were taken off to Abomey on long files, tied to one another. The heads of those who had been killed were piled in heaps and left to putrefy for some weeks, after which they were strung on bamboos and taken away for the admiration of the public at Abomey.[2]

According to the evidence collected by Dunglas, the final destruction of Ketu has been preserved in mocking songs still heard in the old capital of Dahomey. One such song is worded as follows:

> War has broken Ketu
> Agidbigo Hungbo is taken
> . . . .
> War has broken Ketu for ever.[3]

The story of the heroism of the Egba in the defence of Abeokuta and the equally heroic fanaticism of the Dahomians in assault is too well known to need repetition in detail. Between 1851 and 1886 the threat of capture and annihilation hung over Abeokuta. The most celebrated assaults on the Egba capital occurred in 1851 and 1864. On the latter occasion the triumphant Egba defenders pursued the routed Dahomian forces as far as the Yewa River. This Egba victory had, however, no long-lived effect on the dominating position of

---

[1] C.S.O. 1/1, 10, no. 6. Barrow to Young, 11 January 1885.

[2] Parrinder, op. cit., p. 57. See also *Church Missionary Intelligencer*, 1885, Appendix.

[3] Parrinder, op. cit., quoting from Dunglas, p. 60. See also Waterlot, *Les Bas-Reliefs des Bâtiments Royaux d'Abomey*, 1926.

Dahomey in the frontier region west of the Ogun River. Gelele of Dahomey, who succeeded Gezo in 1858, also inherited his father's inflexible determination to crush Abeokuta. In this ambition he was to be no more successful than his predecessor. Nevertheless Gelele successfully pursued his father's policy of making an annual expedition in order to ravage all the Yoruba and Ewe villages situated between the upper Yewa and the Ogun rivers. The villages thus pillaged included Ibiyan, Aworo, Tobolo, Ezio, Alazi, Iwere and so forth.[1] Neither Oyo nor Abeokuta reacted actively against the outrageous Dahomian despoliation of the villages enumerated above. The nearest Abeokuta came to the solace of the Dahomian victims was in offering temporary asylum to the refugees from the villages nearest the Ogun River. These, as often as they had adequate warning, invariably harvested the produce of their farms and fled across the Ogun into Egbaland. The precipitate flights were one way in which the Egba themselves knew that the Dahomians were again on the march.

In view of the military preponderance of the Dahomian forces which went unchallenged in the region west of the Ogun River, it would be reasonable to suggest that the Ogun River was the eastern frontier of Dahomey. There are, however, many snags in thus ascribing to the Dahomian empire a definable framework. Ketu and many other towns west of the Ogun were destroyed, but it is doubtful whether, politically, they submitted to Dahomey. Many of the inhabitants, when they could, withdrew into Abeokuta. As soon as the Dahomian forces left, the villages were reoccupied by their fugitive owners. The most objective way to interpret the resulting situation is indeed to consider the region between the upper Yewa and the Ogun rivers as an elastic frontier, with Ketu and the neighbouring towns serving as a buffer between the powerful neighbours to the west and to the east, that is, between Dahomey and what was left of the old Oyo empire.[2] Nearer the Atlantic

---

[1] Ajisafe, op. cit., pp. 125–30. Johnson, op. cit., pp. 454–6 (for full list).
[2] *American Geographical Society of New York, Bulletin*, vol. xxxix, 1907; see Semple, 'Geographical Boundaries', pp. 385–97. (The points made by Semple are applicable to indigenous political frontiers.)

coast and east of Dahomian Whydah, Porto Novo had a special relationship with Dahomey and was therefore regarded as an ally of Dahomey. North-west of Porto Novo there were petty states peopled by Popo, Aja and Egbado refugees which enjoyed considerable independence and security from Dahomian forces because of their swampy and creek-encumbered environment. It is against the background of the foregoing facts that the evolution of the colonial boundary must be described.

The political fluidity produced by excessive and, in a sense, negative political activity on the part of the indigenous states was paralleled at first by the uncertainties which characterized the genesis of European involvement in the region. The relevant indigenous states, it may be recalled, were Dahomey, Porto Novo, Whemi, Katenu or Frah, Ipokia, Appa, Ado, Oke-Odan, Badagry, Lagos, Ketu, Egbaland, Oyo, and a host of Egbado 'states', claiming dubious independence.[1] The European Powers which became involved in the politics of the region were Britain and France. It can be claimed that in no other boundary zone of Nigeria did the realities of the local political posture of affairs play as decisive a role in determining, generally, the location of the colonial boundary. The ups and downs of the relations between the European Powers and the indigenous states are therefore important for an understanding of the evolution of the boundary. Apart from the temporary French hold of Porto Novo as a protectorate in 1863, the British dominated the whole coastal region up to 1883, and at a time when there were for many years no European rivals to exploit the fluctuating political conditions prevailing on the coast and in the hinterland, the British showed an incredible lack of foresight. Generally speaking, the British attitude towards Dahomey and Abeokuta and solicitude for the trade of Lagos set the pattern which foreshadowed the colonial boundary that ultimately emerged.

Two things, above all others, dominated British policy after 1851. Dahomey was 'an odious stronghold of slavery and human sacrifice'. Abeokuta, on the other hand, was looked

---

[1] See C.O. 806/281, Memorandum by W.O., already cited.

upon as the 'Sunrise within the Tropics'. The great hope pinned upon Abeokuta by the humanitarians was reflected in Miss Tucker's assertion that 'The rapid progress of the Gospel among the benighted Egbas has been like the dayspring in their own sunny land.'[1] The Church Missionary Society, the Wesleyans and the Baptists arrived one after another from 1846 onwards to begin missionary work in Abeokuta. In 1848 Townsend, the C.M.S. pioneer, took back to England a letter and a present of native cloth from the ruler of Egbaland to Queen Victoria. The latter naturally expressed great pleasure and authorized the President of the C.M.S., the Earl of Chichester, to write an acknowledgement and to exhort the Alake of Egbaland to 'wean his people from illicit to lawful commerce'.[2] While these proceedings reflected the underlying attitude of Britain to the most active political unit in Yoruba-land, it would be misleading to suggest that the British local agents invariably behaved in conformity with the sentiments of the missionaries. As will be shown later, at least one of the British rulers of Lagos became quite disenchanted with Abeo-kuta and was not loath to describe Abeokuta's people as 'impudent freebooters'. Thus British interests in the work of the missions were often at cross-purposes with the requirements of Lagos trade.

During the whole period, Dahomey was sacking and plundering and enslaving her neighbours. The events of 1850–1 serve, in spite of temporary set-backs, to illustrate the pattern of relationships which continued to exist between Britain, Dahomey and Abeokuta. It should also be borne in mind that at a period described in British colonial history as one of 'colonial apathy' to territorial expansionism, Britain might blockade and bombard Lagos, Whydah and Porto Novo, yet she was unwilling to embark on what Lord Salisbury described at a later date as 'these expensive Western African expeditions'. Peaceful and inexpensive protectorates involving the occasional presence of naval squadrons were considered

---

[1] Tucker, *Sunrise Within the Tropics*, 1853, p. 268. Burton, *Abeokuta and the Cameroons Mountains*, 1863, vol. i, see Preface.

[2] Ibid., pp. 241–2.

adequate to support the beneficent effects of legitimate trade in undermining the slave trade. Subsidies might also have to be held out to the local potentates. Dahomey remained insensitive to such overtures. In May 1850 Beecroft, the British consul for the Bights of Benin and Biafra, accompanied by Commander Forbes (who had visited Abomey the previous year), went on an official visit to Gezo of Dahomey. Instructions from the British government authorized Beecroft to promise Gezo a subsidy of £3,000 for three years, and at the same time to warn him against further raids on the Ewe and Yoruba neighbours. The mission failed.[1] As a matter of fact, Gezo demanded that the British should remove all the European factories from Lagos, Badagry and Porto Novo to his own port at Whydah. The request was naturally unacceptable to the British mission. Before Beecroft left Abomey, Gezo gave him to understand that Dahomey planned a colossal attack on Abeokuta in the following year. The British answer was to maintain the blockade of the coastal towns except Badagry.[2]

In addition to the blockade of 'Dahomian' ports, the British government instructed Beecroft to give the Egba an early warning of the projected Dahomian attack, and for this purpose Commander Forbes was despatched to Abeokuta. The attack, when it materialized, completely failed. Whether or not Gezo suspected that Britain had a hand in the defeat of his forces is not known. But the greater the friendship Britain showed Abeokuta, the more was Dahomey antagonized. Then the expulsion of Kosoko, Gezo's friend, from Lagos and the reinstatement of an Egba ally, Akitoye, reinforced the antagonism. Gezo indeed was for a time shaken by the drastic British action in Lagos. Thus in 1852, he agreed to an anti-slave-trade engagement between himself and Commander Forbes.[3] The blockade of Whydah was raised, and prospects of good relations between Britain and Dahomey appeared very good. Lagos was apparently destined to be the great

---

[1] Newbury, *The Western Slave Coast*, pp. 50–3.

[2] F.O. 84/816, Palmerston to Beecroft, 12 February; Beecroft to Palmerston, 4 May and 22 July 1850.

[3] Hertslet, *Map of Africa by Treaty*, vol. ii, pp. 647 f; see also no. 65, Notes on Dahomey, etc., 1847–93.

base of operations to extend British influence over Dahomey and Yorubaland.[1] However, Gezo died in 1858.

It was Gelele, Gezo's son, to whom another British mission was sent in December 1862. The British visitor, Wilmot, was favourably impressed by Gelele. In his report to Rear-Admiral Walker, Wilmot asserted that

> If we can only prove that we are really sincere in our wishes to be friendly with him, I am quite certain that he will think very seriously of our proposals to him for giving up the Slave Trade, as well as the 'human sacrifices'.[2]

The British government and the House of Commons were sufficiently impressed to be prepared to propose another mission under Consul Burton at the end of 1863. Presents asked for in advance by Gelele were procured, except for a carriage and horses, and Burton was asked to explain to him that horses could not survive in Africa. On the whole, the Burton mission afforded Britain another opportunity for entering into peaceful relations with the king of Dahomey. Lord Russell indicated to Burton that

> [If the Dahomian king wished] to enter into an engagement with Her Majesty's Government to encourage lawful trade, and to promote, as far as lies in his power, the development of the resources of his country, Her Majesty's Government would be willing to appoint an agent at Whydah to be an organ of communication with the king.[3]

The circumstances were auspicious, especially since relations between Abeokuta and the Lagos administration under Glover had worsened to breaking point. Gelele's logic, however, led to a different conclusion. If Britain no longer supported the Egba, then the occasion was one for a final reckoning with the defiant capital of Egbaland.

In Abomey, Burton was hospitably received, but it was not easy for him to get down to the main business of his mission.

---

[1] F.O. 2/31, Baikie to Malmesbury, 2 March 1859.
[2] Burton, *A Mission to Gelele, King of Dahomey*, vol. ii, quoted in appendix iii.
[3] Ibid., F.O. letter quoted in preface x–xiii.

When he finally obtained a formal interview with the king, it became clear that Dahomey nursed a deep-rooted grievance against Britain. It was briefly this. Some British people had maliciously represented the Dahomians in books as a bad people. It hurt because books never died. If Britain did not want any more slaves, as she certainly had done before, she should tell the truth frankly and say that the slaves Britain already possessed were enough for the country for which they bought them.

> But for a parcel of men with long heads to sit down in England, and frame laws for us, and pretend to dictate how we are to live, of whom they know nothing . . . is to me somewhat extraordinary.[1]

Burton's mission was a failure, and the last chance for a British *rapprochement* with Dahomey was gone. Burton's anger knew no bounds, and he did exactly what the Dahomian king had complained about. He wrote that the Dahomians were a 'flatulent, self-conceited herd of barbarians . . . in fact, a slave race— vermin with a soul apiece'.[2] Gelele refused to accept a British agent at Whydah, and in fact did not disguise to Burton his resolve to attack Abeokuta in 1864. If Burton's mission to Dahomey had succeeded, the history of Nigeria's western boundary might conceivably have been a different story.

The missionaries, who had indeed never been happy about the worsening relations between the British administration in Lagos and the Egba, took alarm at the news of the new Dahomian threat to Abeokuta. Prayers were offered in places as far apart as Switzerland and Syria 'for the deliverance of the Egba'.[3] In London the C.M.S. Committee and 'other friends of Africa', including the Earl of Harrowby, went on a deputation to the Colonial Secretary, the Duke of Newcastle, to urge a reversal of the anti-Egba policy of the Lagos administration. The reasons were clear to the C.M.S. Committee. Abeokuta was 'one of the dearest spots on earth'. A special circular there-

---

[1] Ibid., see 'Note', pp. 211–15; also pp. 274–9.
[2] Ibid., p. 250.
[3] Biobaku, op. cit., pp. 74–5.

fore invited prayer 'that Dahomey might be restrained and compelled to return to her own land, if it might be without blood-shedding'.[1] The Egba successfully defeated the Dahomian attack and guaranteed their own independence. It would however be misleading to suggest that missionary sentiments exactly reflected the policy pursued by the British agents on the spot. The exigencies of Lagos trade were an important consideration. The Yoruba civil war adversely affected Lagos trade, and the British administrators believed that the thing to do was to stop the civil war. If, as Glover believed, the Egba were the main obstacle to the free flow of trade to Lagos, then the Egba should be dealt with. Another factor in British policy in the region was concerned with eliminating the French at Porto Novo. Admiral Didelot had declared the state to be under French protection in February 1863, but the French withdrew in 1864. Glover suggested at once that Britain should move into Porto Novo. He proceeded to sign treaties with Ipokia, Ado and Oke-Odan with a view to defending them from Dahomian attacks. Such expansion was however unauthorized and was described as 'utterly extravagant'.[2]

In the end, Glover was dismissed by the Governor-in-Chief, John Pope Hennessy, in 1872. Another aspect of Glover's policy should be noted. The energetic administrator believed that Lagos was destined to be the main African port of the trade of the hinterland of West Africa stretching beyond the Niger to the Nile basin. He therefore attempted to bypass the Egbas in order to open alternative trade routes through Ilaro and Ketu. His ambitious plans came to nothing, because the Colonial Secretary was not prepared 'for a crusade in West Africa on behalf of trade, civilization and Christianity'.[3] Although British policy towards the Yoruba hinterland remained passive, Dahomey suffered the infliction of an occasional

---

[1] Ajisafe, op. cit., pp. 120; Johnson, op. cit., pp. 361–3.

[2] C.O. 147/3, Glover to Newcastle, 9 July 1863. See also 147/1, Freeman to Newcastle, 3 July 1862, Minutes by Roger and Newcastle. Hargreaves, *Prelude to the Partition of West Africa*, 1963, pp. 116–20. Newbury, op. cit., pp. 69–70.

[3] C.O. 147/25, see Kimberley's Minute on Leigh Clare to Kimberley, 3 October 1872.

blockade. To the administration in Lagos the general attitude could be expressed as follows:

> Everything pleases,
> Only this man (Gelele) is vile.[1]

In contrast with British policy, the French agents sought a close understanding with Porto Novo and Dahomey. The beginnings can be traced to the period when British anti-slavery measures began to antagonize the two Ewe states. As far back as 1851, the French government had protested against the British blockade of Whydah (Dahomey's port), because French interests, represented by the French commercial house of Régis, were adversely affected. A few years after the abortive Beecroft–Forbes mission to Abomey, Lieutenant Wallon of the French Navy paid two visits to the Dahomian king, to whom he gave two howitzers as a present. Two boys were also taken from the palace to be educated in France.[2] Then when Britain acquired Lagos by force in 1861, a French agent had exploited this high-handed action to ingratiate himself into the favour of Porto Novo. The French in fact alleged that the British were proposing to harass the King of Porto Novo by bombing his town. Faced with this prospect, the King, Sodji, was disposed to accept the support which Dumas, the agent of Régis, offered in the name of France.[3] The French government endorsed the action of Dumas, and a treaty of protection was signed with Porto Novo in February 1863.

Quite apart from the lack of amity between the British official representatives and Dahomey, British merchants did not seem to get on as well as the French merchants did with the local Dahomian representatives at Whydah. For instance, in 1876 the British agent of Messrs F. & A. Swanzy, Turnbull, got himself into difficulties, and was apprehended and bundled off to Abomey, where he was subjected to maltreatment. In view of the indignity inflicted on Turnbull, Hewett, the British

---

[1] C.O. 806/130, Africa, no. 178, Lees to C.O., 28 February 1879.

[2] Ellis, *The Ewe-speaking Peoples*, p. 317.

[3] Hargreaves, op. cit., pp. 116–18 and 201–6. Newbury, op. cit., pp. 103–4.

174

naval commander, was instructed by the British government to demand the excessive compensation of 500 puncheons of palm oil, estimated to be worth £6,000. The demand was, not unexpectedly, rejected outright by Gelele. A British blockade of Whydah followed. The British were apparently ready for more serious action against Dahomey, such as seizing Whydah and preventing all communications between Abomey and the sea.[1] Through the good offices of the French merchants, however, the treaty of Whydah was signed between Captain Sullivan of H.M.S. *Sirius* and the Dahomian governor of Whydah in May 1877. The original compensation of 500 puncheons of oil was reduced to 200. The French company of Régis Aîné undertook to pay the compensation which was theoretically imposed on Dahomey. Gelele probably knew nothing of these proceedings, because it is difficult to see how he would have been willing to bind himself to allow British subjects 'liberty to reside, trade and acquire property in all parts of the kingdom'. In short, the French trading agents, once again, emerged from the episode as Dahomey's friends. In 1878 Gelele ceded to France 'le Territoire de Kotonou'.[2]

The position of Britain and France (or to be more accurate, their official and semi-official representatives), in their relations with Dahomey and Porto Novo, up to the eve of the 'scramble', as seen by a neutral observer, the Swedish traveller Burdo, who visited the Slave Coast and the neighbouring places in 1879, was that

> The English have been wrong in allowing their designs to be seen through of imposing their protection on several points on the Coast, Whydah and the Popos, for example, which are dependents of Dahomey. They have thus, to some extent, alienated Gelele's favour . . . . The mercantile houses in the interior are nearly all in the hands of Frenchmen, agents of Régis Senr and Cyprien Fabre, of Marseilles.[3]

---

[1] C.O. 806/79, West Africa, no. 115—Notes on a possible Embassy to the King of Dahomey, 15 January 1877.

[2] Ellis, *The Ewe-speaking Peoples*, pp. 326–7. Also F.O. 27/2414, Report of the Departmental Committee.

[3] Burdo, *A Voyage up the Niger and Benue*, 1880, pp. 270–2.

The Swede was of course not concerned here with other motives which also inspired British policy, or lack of policy, before the 'scramble'. As regards Porto Novo, the British agents in Lagos sought persistently either to annex the state or to control trade access through it. The British government feared possible complications and therefore refused to endorse the policy advocated by the Lagos agents.[1] If, however, Porto Novo voluntarily surrendered herself to Britain, that was another matter. Up to this time the French had shown no interest in the Yoruba hinterland. The British had a free hand in that area, but the 'strong-arm policy' advocated by Glover with regard to the Yoruba civil war was abandoned. So too was Glover's determination to organize trade routes to the northwest through Ketu. The local British officials were convinced that Ketu was part of Yorubaland, although this conviction bore little relation to the political realities prevailing in that region. For instance, a despatch from Lagos in 1879 fell back on a report by the C.M.S. missionary, Gollmer, who wrote in 1859, in order to prove that

> Ketu is the western province of the Yoruba kingdom . . . the river Opara (Okpara) flowing south from north being the distinctive boundary between the two kingdoms of Yoruba and Dahomey.[2]

The French confirmation in 1883 of the 1863 Porto Novo treaty of protection may be regarded as the first intimation of serious official French interest in the region immediately to the west of Lagos. In the following year Colonel Dorat was appointed the first Military Resident at Porto Novo. He was convinced that

> Our presence in Porto Novo is the one obstacle to the projects of the British Cabinet to render our position untenable or at least useless.[3]

---

[1] F.O. 27/2417, Usher to Hicks-Beach, 27 July 1879; and C.O. to F.O., 22 September 1879.

[2] C.O. 806/141, Africa, no. 192, Lees to C.O., 7 May 1879.

[3] *Etudes Dahoméennes*, pp. 36–40; see Dorat to the Commandant of the Gulf of Guinea, 26 July 1884.

When the tussle between Britain and France began in the region, each side sought to ally herself with the many petty states. Having acquired the 'Ewe' state of Porto Novo, France claimed also the states of Weme, Ipokia, Oke-Odan and Katanu which she alleged were vassals of Porto Novo. Dorat admitted, however, that the vassals had since revolted against the king of Porto Novo. The fact was that the political activities of Porto Novo were much less clear than those of her 'sister' state, Dahomey. When Tofa succeeded to the Porto Novo throne in 1874, he certainly attempted to emulate Gelele of Dahomey. On several occasions he destroyed Weme and Ipokia without annexing them. His adventures earned him the execration of the Lagos administrators, who considered Tofa 'an iniquitous and ever troublesome king'.[1]

In order to counter French claims based on the acquisition of Porto Novo, the governor of Lagos attempted his own reconstruction of the history of the petty states. He came to the conclusion that if there was indeed any suzerain, it was the king of Ijoiyin, who 'is strictly speaking the king of all the Popo (Ewe) and Egbado territory, including Ipokia and Porto Novo'. The situation was however one which called for action, not ancient history. The War Office wisely pointed out that it would be 'very hard to build up a connected history of any particular state'.[2] The governor claimed a protectorate over Katanu, an island state between the Denham Waters and the Porto Novo lagoon. Appa was added. These two 'acquisitions' were accepted by Lord Granville because they formed 'part of the Protectorate of Lagos and I approve of your action in placing them under the jurisdiction of the District of Badagri'.[3] Encouraged, the governor of Lagos reported that Ipokia, Weme, Ado, and Oke-Odan had all renewed their former offers of cession. The British government had serious misgivings about Weme, not because it was useless, but because 'Whemi [Weme] lies inland between Katanu and the territory

---

[1] Ibid., pp. 32–5; also C.S.O. 1/1, 11, Evans to Stanhope, 30 October 1886.

[2] C.O. 806/281, Memorandum already cited.

[3] C.O. 806/262, Confidential, no. 82, Granville to Moloney, 25 June 1886. Also no. 95, Moloney to Granville, 19 June 1886.

of Dahomey, with which it is inadvisable for the settlement of Lagos to be nearer'.[1] The thing to do was to recognize the independence of Weme in order to prevent the French from acquiring that state, although Porto Novo already claimed it as her vassal.

The French were of course not idle while the governor of Lagos was expanding the territory of Lagos.[2] They seized Agege island, which separated the Toche and Zunu creeks. The Zunu creek was cleared and widened so as to ensure a commercially useful link between Agege and Porto Novo. From Porto Novo, the French moved north-eastwards to Ado and Ipokia, and the local French agents advised their government that the French protectorate of Porto Novo could be expanded to include Ado and Ipokia. French action in facilitating access to Porto Novo had an immediate effect on the Lagos trade in palm oil and palm kernels. In addition, a collision between French native soldiers and British Hausa troops occurred in the Agege Creek between Denham Waters and Porto Novo. In order to relieve the local tension, the British and French governments entered into negotiations over what the British Colonial Secretary called 'the Porto Novo difficulty'. A *modus vivendi* was arranged without much acrimony. It was entitled 'Provisional Convention regulating relations between Lagos and Porto Novo'.[3] No specific mention was made of a boundary in the seven articles signed in Lagos in January 1888. The French agreed to withdraw from the Zunu creek while the British were to leave the Agege. The Zunu channel was to be free for use by the subjects of Britain and France. Nothing was said about the frontiers of the petty states of Ipokia, Oke-Odan, Weme and Ado.

The pattern of the colonial boundary foreshadowed by the 1888 Convention was confirmed by the reactions of the British administration in Lagos to the events which took place during 1887 and 1888. Britain was determined to secure Yorubaland.

---

[1] C.O. 806/242, Africa, no. 296, C.O. to F.O., 13 January 1885.

[2] Hargreaves, op. cit., pp. 210–14.

[3] C.O. 806/281, Moloney to Holland, 13 June 1887. C.O. 806/288, Inclosure 1 in no. 71, Moloney to Holland, 2 January 1888. Also Newbury, op. cit., pp. 105–10.

Dahomian attacks on Oke-Odan and the destruction of Ketu were all reported back to London. Refugees from Otta were pouring into Lagos. It was noted with satisfaction in London that Dahomey had not molested Abeokuta. In order to avoid contact with Dahomey, the British Colonial Secretary took shelter in the assumption that Dahomey was under the protection of Portugal. In the event of a Dahomian violation of British territory, the British government could appeal to the Portuguese government for redress.[1] What had actually happened was that one of the descendants of Francisco Da Souza, who had drifted into Whydah from Brazil in 1788 and was given by the king of Dahomey the official title of *Chacha*— to conduct the king's business with visiting vessels—had in 1885, without consulting Gelele, negotiated a treaty with Portugal which purported to hand over the region to Portuguese protection. Gelele had to repudiate the treaty, and Da Souza was seized and taken to Abomey, whence he never returned. The reference to a Portuguese protectorate over Dahomey was therefore quite ridiculous, and the only evidence of Portuguese power in Whydah was 'a padre, a drummer boy, and one man who occasionally walked about the town in a kind of military costume, with four broad red stripes upon his arm'.[2] In April 1888 the Portuguese government formally announced that Portugal had 'given up' the protectorate of Dahomey. Would Britain step in? In December the governor of Lagos dispatched a hysterical telegram to the Colonial Secretary as follows:

> Prince Fasinu, son of Prince Regent of Dahomey, with me. Sent to ask whether Queen of England willing to accept cession country, inclusive of Whydah.[3]

Lord Knutsford consulted Lord Salisbury, the Prime Minister, but the latter, with his characteristic caution, thought it ought

---

[1] C.S.O. 1/1, 12 no. 293, Moloney to Holland, 26 August 1887. C.O. 806/288, C.O. to F.O., 3 October 1887.

[2] Ibid., Admiralty to C.O., 3 April 1888.

[3] C.O. 806/299, Telegraphic, Moloney to Knutsford, 3 December 1888.

to be ascertained first whether the offer had the concurrence of king Gelele of Dahomey, who was at the time incapacitated by illness. The fuss came to nothing, and the western boundary was destined to lie east of Dahomey, and probably east also of the territories Dahomey dominated militarily.

The reaction of the British in Lagos and London to the news of reported French designs on Abeokuta and Oyo was almost electrical. It may be recalled that the British administration in Lagos had always deplored the Yoruba civil war, partly because it retarded Lagos trade and revenue, but partly also because it weakened Yoruba resistance to Dahomian devastations of the western provinces of Oyo. The Alafin of Oyo, whose patrimony was being virtually liquidated by the civil war, had in 1881 appealed to the governor of Lagos. He reminded the governor that 'The Dahomians have taken advantage of this to ruin my kingdom. . . . All my frontier towns are in great panic now, and if I make no stir to protect them they will all scatter'.[1] The Alafin had also appealed to the C.M.S. to urge the Lagos government to intervene and help to restore Yoruba solidarity. He was convinced that 'the whole Yoruba race is a gift from God to me, and hence every loss of life even to an untimely birth is a loss to the Alafin of Oyo'. The efforts of the governor of Lagos to restore amity among the warring groups failed, and when the Governor-General arrived from the Gold Coast in 1882, he thanked the Alafin of Oyo for his faith in the honour of the British government, but informed him at the same time that the Queen of England had no wish to take his country. It was easy to be complacent when the French did not threaten to occupy 'Yorbu proper'.

In 1888 the British government received evidence that Yorubaland was indeed threatened. In April the governor of Lagos reported by telegram to the Colonial Office that a French officer from Porto Novo had gone to Abeokuta via Ado and Ilaro, and had there concluded a treaty which promised a railway from Porto Novo to Abeokuta. The French also in-

---

[1] Johnson, op. cit., Letter signed Adeyemi, King of the Yorubas, to Griffiths, 15 October 1881, p. 463.

tended, according to Moloney's report, to make similar proposals to Oyo.[1] The Liverpool and the Glasgow Chambers of Commerce addressed memorials to the Colonial Office, which asked the Foreign Office to protest to Paris. The Frenchman who caused all the stir was M. Viard, and the French version of the situation was that *'Son voyage devait être purement une investigation commerciale'*. It was quite true that, with the support of the French Catholic missionaries, not of the French government, Viard successfully secured a Treaty of Friendship and Commerce with some leading Egba chiefs. Some French newspapers also upheld the cause of Viard and maintained that the allegation that British territory interposed between Porto Novo and Abeokuta was *'une hérésie géographique'*.[2] The French could have added the word 'political', in view of the political and military uncertainties of the region, thanks largely to Dahomian ravaging activities.

It is against this diplomatic background that the subsequent actions of the governor of Lagos become intelligible. At all costs, the Yoruba hinterland of Lagos must be saved in any demarcation agreement with France. The governor set about doing precisely this, and his proceedings took this form:

> I have informed Messrs George and Leigh that if it is proved in their future dealings with the Egba authorities that the prospect of an annual present, in money or kind, to Abeokuta, to the extent of 400£ . . . would facilitate transactions and bring about their acceptance of the conditions of agreement proposed . . .

This was part of a report in which the governor of Lagos indicated the importance he attached to the urgency of securing Egbaland for Britain.[3] To the Alafin of Oyo, the governor addressed a letter in which he proposed a treaty of protection. In this letter to the 'Head of Yorubaland', the governor

---

[1] C.O. 806/288, Moloney to Knutsford, Tel., 24 April 1888. C.O. 806/299, no. 80, F.O. to C.O., 30 July 1888; Knutsford to Moloney, 18 October 1888; C.O. to F.O., 12 December 1888 and F.O. to C.O., 17 December 1888.

[2] *Le Matin*, 13 August 1888; also C.O. 806/299, no 80, 30 July 1888, and *Etudes Dahoméennes*, Ballot to Gouverneur, 25 April 1888.

[3] C.O. 806/299, Confidential, no. 12, Moloney to Knutsford, 22 May 1888.

reminded him of the solicitude of the Lagos administration for the unity and solidarity of Yorubaland. He asserted that

> Yorubaland was comprised traditionally as regards its corners a few years ago of Yoruba proper, Egba, Ketu and Jebu. Where is Ketu now? And from what direction was it destroyed?[1]

The remarkable thing was that, whilst Moloney acknowledged that if the French secured Dahomey they would undoubtedly claim Ketu as part of Dahomey, he was at the same time reporting that he had signed treaties with refugees from Ketu, which 'is perfectly independent'.[2] The governor's treaty with the Alafin of Oyo claimed that Ketu was a corner of Yorubaland, 'from time immemorial', and the treaty with Ketu affirmed that Ketu 'pays tribute to no other Power'. It must be clear that all these assumptions in the treaties bore no relation to the local political situation.

France, however, repudiated the political clauses in the treaty obtained by Viard from the chiefs of Abeokuta, and Britain realistically declined to ratify Moloney's treaty with Ketu. Even the governor of Lagos himself began to recommend a boundary line between France and Britain somewhere west of the Ado River. He recognized that the confused political status of Ipokia, Ado and Oke-Odan was a tangle which could not easily be unravelled. In the hinterland, all Britain really wanted was 'Yoruba proper'. France, for her part, wanted the territory of Porto Novo and its water systems on which she had spent considerable resources. She certainly had no wish to haggle about territorial rights in Yorubaland, although neither Britain nor France made any attempt to define precisely the western frontiers of that political area. The French had up to 1888 established no official relations in respect of the territory of the Dahomian kingdom, apart, of course, from Cotonou which they had acquired from Dahomey in 1878. The British, who had, were determined to have nothing to do with it. They rather looked forward with glee to French involvement with

---

[1] Hertslet, *Commercial Treaties*, vol. xvii, pp. 192–201.

[2] C.O. 806/299, Moloney to Knutsford, July, August, October 1888. See also Hertslet, *Map of Africa*, vol. i, pp. 106–7; and Declarations, pp. 104–9.

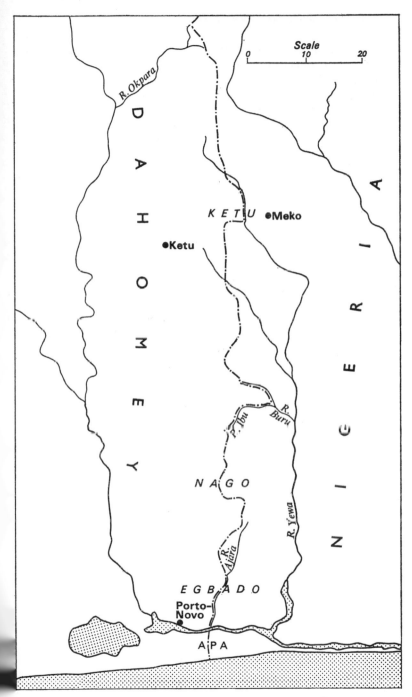

NIGERIA–DAHOMEY BOUNDARY 1906

Dahomey.[1] The desideratum, from the British point of view, was to separate Dahomey from Yorubaland. The French were agreeable.

The actual boundary negotiations produced, as far as this section of the international boundary was concerned, no excitements. Other regions dealt with in the Arrangement signed in Paris in August 1889 included Senegambia, Sierra Leone and the Gold Coast. Article IV concerned the Slave Coast, and defined the spheres of influence of Britain and France in the region as follows:

> On the Slave Coast, the line of demarcation . . . shall be identical with the meridian which intersects the territory of Porto Novo at the Ajarra Creek, leaving Pokrah or Pokea to the English Colony of Lagos. It shall follow the above-mentioned meridian as far as the 9th degree of north latitude, where it shall stop. To the south, it shall terminate on the sea-shore after having passed through the territory of Appah, the capital of which shall continue to belong to England.[2]

The peoples of Katanu and Appa, whom Britain had earlier undertaken to protect, were guaranteed French protection against the king of Porto Novo. Similar rights were vouchsafed the people of Ipokia, now transferred to Lagos. All these peoples in the petty states were at liberty to emigrate within six months to whichever side of the boundary they preferred.

The wording of the boundary arrangement acknowledged the partition of Appa and Porto Novo territories. North of Porto Novo, the boundary was described with a meridian up to the ninth degree of north latitude. It suggested a straight line. Nonetheless, the important consideration is the extent to which the straight line correctly separated the politically organized groups which had hitherto sought to achieve political adjustment among themselves. The realities of the local political situation alone provide criteria for an objective judgement on

---

[1] C.O. 806/299, C.O. to F.O., 12 December 1888; and F.O. to C.O., 17 December 1888.

[2] Hertslet, *Map of Africa*, vol. ii, see no. 226, pp. 729–33. For the actual negotiations see F.O. 84/1950 and 84/1951.

the colonial boundary.[1] This stretch of the colonial boundary is best considered in three sub-divisions—Appa, north of Porto Novo ('Egbado' area), and the Ketu 'buffer'. Appa 'kingdom' was split by the boundary, but no illusions should becloud judgement on the precise nature of the kingdom. Governor Moloney in 1886 estimated its population at 3,255, and came to the conclusion that Appa and Badagry, to the east, were indeed 'a no-man's-land of sparse settlements. . . . Communities are small and of very diverse antecedents with traditions of comparatively recent immigration'.[2] Even as regards the 'dismembered' kingdom of Appa, the colonial boundary provided in Section 2 of Article IV that the inhabitants could move to either side of the boundary. This requirement was of course arbitrary, but was no more serious than what the inhabitants periodically had had to do, rather more precipitately, under the threat of Dahomian or Porto Novo aggression. North of Appa, the boundary intended to separate Porto Novo from Ipokia, Ado and Oke-Odan. These states and many more to the north, usually described as Egbado states, were on the whole mixed Ewe and Yoruba communities. Any boundary here, even if it separated the political frontiers of the multitude of states, was bound to leave linguistic minorities on either side of the boundary. This was exactly what happened. Lagos colony contained 19,122 Ewe and 172,688 Yoruba. Abeokuta province contained 20,239 Ewe and 297,114 Yoruba. These figures are recorded in a survey published in 1951.[3]

North of the 'Egbado' states, the boundary traversed the Ketu region. It is here that the boundary south of the ninth degree of north latitude is most vulnerable to attack. The political fluidity which prevailed in this zone at the time of the boundary arrangement should however be taken into account. There are two ways of looking at the question. A sentimental view would tend to deplore a boundary arrangement which left no possibility of reincarnating the Oyo empire which by

---

[1] See East and Moodie, *The Changing World*, London, 1956, chapter xxxi, pp. 745 f.

[2] R.G.S., vol. xii, 1890, already cited. See also Forde, op. cit., p. 65.

[3] Forde, op. cit., p. 43; see also East and Moodie, op. cit., p. 49.

the end of the nineteenth century had virtually ceased to exist. At the time of the Anglo-French boundary agreement, the Alafin of Oyo no doubt still considered himself the 'Head of Yorubaland, the four corners of which are and have been from time immemorial known as Egba, Ketu, Jebu, and Oyo, embracing within its area that inhabited by all Yoruba speaking peoples . . .'.[1] A supremacy and the traditions of the past were hardly the political reality encountered by the European boundary makers. The governor of Lagos indeed had acknowledged in 1888 that Ketu was lost to Dahomey. He had therefore suggested to the Alafin that Lagos should become the 'fourth corner' of the Oyo kingdom. In recognition of the fact that the Oyo empire had ceased to exist, Moloney attempted to make independent treaties with Oyo, Abeokuta and Ijebu. From 1889 to 1892 successive governors in Lagos were almost completely absorbed in an endeavour to bring to an end the protracted civil war which was in itself a reflection of the political disintegration of the Oyo empire. Ultimately it required the military intervention of the British Lagos administration in 1892 to restore a measure of peace in what was left of Yorubaland. Other evidence of the little power left to the Alafin by the civil war manifested itself during a later Anglo-French crisis in 1897–8. The governor of Lagos attempted to use the Alafin's status in order to secure a few frontier towns in the neighbourhood of south-west Borgu. The governor's disappointment was expressed in his report that 'the Alafin of Oyo has been able to exercise so little authority'.[2] The Egba state, which was the most effective Yoruba state in the boundary zone, had concentrated on expansion south and south-westwards. Westward, it was with extreme difficulty that she maintained the Ogun River as a defensive barrier against Dahomey. The international boundary therefore in no way affected the western frontier of Egbaland, the refugee towns west of the Ogun notwithstanding.

Ketu was undoubtedly the state affected by the colonial

---

[1] C.O. 806/299, Moloney to Knutsford, 21 August 1888.
[2] F.O.C.P. Confidential 7017, Inclosure 1 in 83, C.O. to F.O., 25 October 1897. Also Confidential 7144, McCallum to Chamberlain, 2 December.

boundary. The question here is whether one should consider the territorial Ketu of Yoruba tradition or the political reality represented by Ketu during the closing decades of the nineteenth century. No importance should of course be attached to the claim made in a British treaty with Ketu which claimed that Ketu 'is perfectly independent, and pays tribute to no Power, and territorially is bounded on the north by the country of the Barba, on the east by the territory of the Alafin of Oyo ... on the west by Dahomey ...'. The governor of Lagos however recognized that if the French should acquire Dahomey, 'Ketu . . . will follow—claimed as part of Dahomian territory'.[1] The fact was that, even before the Anglo-French agreement, Ketu was already a disrupted state. The principal Ketu vassal town, Meko, had thrown off the paramountcy of Ketu. After the French occupation of Dahomey in 1893, the principal Ketu ruling house, the Mesha family, already settled in Lagos, was sought out, but it refused to go back to Ketu. The position today is however different.[2] Today, the Alaketu of Ketu in Dahomey continues to visit 'subject' Ketu towns in Nigeria during his enthronement ceremonies. He maintains the view that the boundary separates the English and the French, not the Yoruba. In fact, he has 140 villages in Nigeria, and only twenty in Dahomey. He further complains that his brother Obas in Nigeria would have come to his aid, and lifted his position to more affluent circumstances, but for the colonial boundary. In the meantime, he occupies a small house set in the ruins of what was formerly a large palace.[3]

If Dahomey had organized effectively her eastern frontier, the partition of the state of Ketu might have provoked a situation in which it would have been interesting to study the reaction of a virile indigenous state to the boundary bargain between Britain and France. Unfortunately Dahomey had never organized Ketu as a province of the Dahomian kingdom.

---

[1] C.O. 806/299, Moloney to Knutsford, 31 July 1888. See also C.S.O. 1/1, 10, no. 6, Barrow to Young, 11 January 1885—a proposal to arrange for mass Ketu migration to Lagos was not carried out, but fugitive groups from Ketu continued to arrive there.

[2] Parrinder, op. cit., p. 33 and pp. 66–7.

[3] The facts stated here are the result of field work in Ketu in 1959–60.

She had merely raided and destroyed Ketu towns, and then withdrawn. The intermittent presence of Dahomian forces in and around Ketu did not represent Dahomian recognition that her eastern frontier lay east of Ketu. The death of Gelele at the crucial moment of the international boundary arrangement was another factor. It deprived Dahomey of one of her most dynamic rulers, and a man whom Britain and France feared or respected. His successor, Behanzin, did not possess the political prestige of his father. In 1892 the arbitrary extension of the French protectorate of Porto Novo, to the prejudice of the territorial integrity of Dahomey, precipitated a war between France and Dahomey. The result was that in 1894 Dahomey ceased to exist as an independent African kingdom.[1] With the cessation of the Yoruba civil war, the governor of Lagos was able, between 1892 and 1895, to visit all the border states on the British side of the international boundary. The king of Ipokia assured him that 'there was no trouble in the neighbourhood'. The governor's report on the border zone generally concluded with the remark that everything was 'in a very satisfactory condition'.[2] In the northern portion of the boundary, however, the governor noted that there was evidence of mass Yoruba migration from Shabe across the boundary into Nigeria.

The first Anglo-French survey of the 1889 boundary was begun in 1895. In December, Fuller and Plé set out to traverse the boundary zone and to locate the towns situated in the neighbourhood of the boundary line. It was unfortunate that the survey commissioners were not authorized to ascertain the political allegiance of the towns they visited. All they were required to do was 'to visit all the inhabited villages and to fix their position in relation to the boundary meridian, and determine thereby to which of the two colonies they belong'.[3] In view of the absence of 'natural' boundaries, the commissioners decided to substitute native paths for the meridian, and erect

---

[1] Roberts, *History of French Colonial Policy 1870–1925*, vol. i, p. 295. See also *Etudes Dahoméennes*, ix, section iii; '*Journal Officiel*', 22 June 1894.

[2] C.S.O. 1/1, 13, no. 36, Denham to Ripon, 9 February 1893. See also C.S.O. 1/1, 22, no. 140, McCallum to Chamberlain, 5 May 1898.

[3] Hertslet, *Commercial Treaties*, vol. xxi, p. 365.

pillars where necessary. The rivers Ajara, Idirawan, Amidu, Ibu, Baru, Yewa and Okpara were also accepted as delimiting the Anglo-French possessions, the Okpara forming the boundary for eighty miles up to the ninth parallel of north latitude. This definition of the boundary between Yorubaland and Dahomey was accepted by Britain and France in the convention of 1898. The boundary was more precisely defined in 1906 in order to eliminate ambiguities in the original definition. One important result was the transfer of Idiroko to Nigeria. The final definition was as follows:

> Thence it ascends the thalweg of the river Ajara, its upper course being the Iguidi, as far as the ravine entering the river from the north, immediately west of Idiroko, leaving the town of Idiroko to Lagos. Thence it follows the ravine to its northern end and thence it follows a line drawn to a point on the north side of the shortest road from Ilashe to Ikpaboro on the west bank of the river Igirawan.[1]

This boundary was demarcated in 1911–12 and marked at intervals with low concrete pillars. The local inhabitants do not pretend to understand what the pillars symbolize. The few pillars that can still be found are in fact used by the natives for sharpening their cutlasses.

---

[1] Hertslet, *Map of Africa*, pp. 850–1; *Commercial Treaties*, 1917, pp. 146–65.

6

The Western Boundary—II

Those writers on the partition of Africa who like to over-emphasize the arbitrary nature of African colonial boundaries will undoubtedly find in the evolution of the boundary which traverses Borgu a classic example of colonial boundary making. It is easy for them to point out that the final partition of Borgu was the outcome of protracted diplomatic manoeuvres. The Anglo-French negotiations which accompanied these manoeuvres progressively disregarded the existing indigenous frontiers as well as the treaties which the powers had signed with the African rulers. Anglo-French claims and counter-claims tended in the end to rest almost exclusively on the expediency of safeguarding European peace and concord. There is ample evidence to show that Britain and France originally took the view that Borgu possessed a coherent political framework which should not be dismembered by an arbitrary boundary line. It was this hypothesis which helped to precipitate the celebrated 'race' to Nikki, assumed to be the traditional capital of Borgu. The British commissioners in Paris had then asserted that 'history had clearly proved the unity of the country in the past . . . and . . . the evidence of our own Agents . . . proved its unity at the present time'.[1]

During the final stages of the Anglo-French boundary negotiations the British governor of Lagos forwarded to the

---

[1] F.O.C.P. Confidential 6837, Inclosure 1 in no. 66, Africa, Dufferin to Salisbury, April 1896.

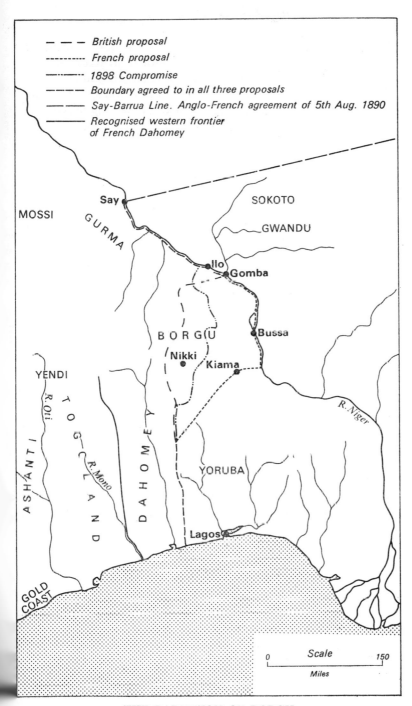

Legend:
- – – – British proposal
- ·········· French proposal
- —·—·— 1898 Compromise
- – — – Boundary agreed to in all three proposals
- — — — Say-Barrua Line. Anglo-French agreement of 5th Aug. 1890
- ——— Recognised western frontier of French Dahomey

MOSSI

GURMA

SOKOTO

GWANDU

Say

Ilo
Gomba

B O R G U

Bussa

Nikki
Kiama

YENDI

R. Ori

A S H A N T I

T O G O L A N D

R. Mono

D A H O M E Y

R. Niger

YORUBA

Lagos

GOLD COAST

Scale

0   150

Miles

THE PARTITION OF BORGU

British commissioners a report from a local Borgu historian which purported to describe the political structure of the territory. According to this local historian, Lamu of Bode, 'Borgu is not divided into independent kingdoms, but all the divisions, including Boussa, are subject to the king of Nikki'.[1] The report was obviously intended by the governor to clinch the argument in favour of regarding the whole of Borgu as a political unit to be taken in its entirety into the British sphere of influence. The French commissioners were not interested in local histories, and it was thus not the desirability of preserving the territorial integrity of Borgu which proved decisive in the Anglo-French boundary agreement which emerged. In this connection, it is relevant to recall that as far back as 1893 the British Ambassador in Paris had written to the British government about the sentiments of 'unmitigated and bitter dislike' which animated the French people towards the British over the boundary controversy. The reaction of the British Prime Minister, Lord Rosebery, to the Ambassador's warning expressed itself in the observation that it would be unwise 'to fan a French flame'. The next British Prime Minister, Lord Salisbury, made it clear after his assumption of office that he would not go to war with France in order to preserve Borgu, 'a malarious African desert'. In these circumstances, a *modus vivendi* was found which appeared to satisfy national honour and repute, but at the expense of the Borgawa.[2]

Later historical references to Borgu continued to postulate that Borgu was 'a kingdom of great antiquity'.[3] These then afford the orthodox background against which the Borgu boundary agreement is usually criticized. The verdict that the colonial boundary is therefore arbitrary is hardly surprising. Nevertheless this judgement is oversimplified because it is

---

[1] Ibid. Confidential 7297, Inclosure in no. 24, C.O. to F.O., 15 April 1898.

[2] Gooch and Temperley, *British Documents on the Origins of the War*, vol. ii, F.O., France, 3121, no. 450, Dufferin to Rosebery, 3 November 1893. *The History of The Times*, 1884–1912, p. 249.

[3] Lady Lugard, *A Tropical Dependency*, 1905, p. 106. Orr, *The Making of Nigeria*, see footnote, p. 72.

made without an objective assessment of the local political situation which prevailed during the nineteenth century. The assumption that Borgu was a state with anything remotely approaching a comprehensive political organization is inconsistent with the facts. It is also easy to exaggerate the inflamed national temper which the Borgu crisis in the end provoked. The negotiations began as far back as 1892 in an atmosphere of reasonableness. At that time the issue was simply the nature of the kingdom of Borgu.

The present chapter is therefore concerned primarily with two things: to investigate the political conditions which prevailed in Borgu, and to estimate the influence of these conditions on the course of the European negotiations which ultimately demarcated the region. It must be noted that the Borgawa are today one of the least known of the peoples of Nigeria. This unenviable obscurity is reflected in the scarcity of material available for the study of the people, their language, and their country.[1] Everything about Borgu, except its location, seems shrouded in mystery. Even today a visitor to Borgu is acutely aware of a kind of indefinable strangeness in the air and in the people. The new men, usually Moslems, who as a result of British intervention now dominate the political life of Borgu can hardly be said to represent the people known in

---

[1] A scrutiny of the National Archives records reveals very few, and probably out-of-date, studies of the Borgawa. These are included in a collection described as Special List of Records Related to Historical Anthropology and Social Studies among Provincial Administration Record Groups in Kaduna. The most important of the records in the groups is undoubtedly the *Gazetteer of Ilorin Province*, revised and supplemented by a succession of British Administrative Officers. Then there is what the authors describe as the Language and Ethnography of Borgu Division in two volumes. In addition to these, there are also assessment reports and notes which have little of historical importance. Lugard referred to the people as 'this strange people'; see R.G.S., vol. vi, September 1895. Murdock, in his *Africa, its Peoples and their Culture History*, 1959, pp. 77–87, says little about the Borgawa apart from a reference to what he calls the Borgawa cluster and the Bussa intrusive elements. It was not without cause that Hanotaux described the diplomatic wrangling about the political structure of Borgu as *'une situation à la vérité assez confuse'*. See Hanotaux and Martineau, *Histoire des Colonies Françaises*, vol. iv, p. 306.

history as the Borgawa. It has however been claimed, and rightly so, that 'pride of tradition is one of the characteristics of the Borgawa', and the impressive record of this tradition in the Gazetteer fully corroborates this view. Thus it is to the tradition cherished by the true Borgawa that one must turn in an attempt to reconstruct the early history of the people. For the nineteenth century, European records are available and throw considerable light on the posture of political affairs during the period immediately before the scramble for and dismemberment of the territory which the Borgawa call 'our country'. These people variously called Borgawa (by the Hausa) and Bariba (by the Yoruba), but who call themselves 'Barba' and their language 'Bargu', occupy a territory enclosed by the ninth and twelfth parallels of latitude and the first and fourth meridians of east longitude, comprising an area of about 40,000 square miles.

The Borgawa were not members of a single linguistic or ethnic group. The aboriginal inhabitants were the Zanna (in the Nikki district), the Boko (in the Aliyara district), the Bokoberu (in the Kaiama district), the Kamberri and the Laru (in the Bussa and Wawa districts). It is interesting to note that as late as the nineteenth century the king of Bussa informed Clapperton that the aborigines were the Cambrie (presumably Clapperton's spelling of Kamberri). All the aborigines became the peasantry of later immigrant groups—the followers of Kisra whom the ruling houses in Borgu still cherish as their ancestors. Therefore the origin of Borgu as a political community known to tradition is bound up with the famous Kisra migration. Everybody of any consequence found in or around the emirate court of Bussa or Kaiama is ready with a version of the Kisra legend. The Yoruba, Bornu and the Jukun have their tradition of the Kisra migration, and it is hardly surprising that the much propagated legend is not very helpful to the problem of ascertaining earlier linguistic and ethnic connections between the Borgawa and their immediate and remote neighbours. In any case, the most generally held tradition in Bussa maintains that the ruling families of Borgu, Bornu and the Yoruba were members of the same migration, and therefore postulates a common ancestry. What is said to

194

have happened is briefly as follows.[1] The first group of people to be led out of the Arabian peninsula westward finally settled in Bornu. Then the second group, the Yoruba, found a leader in Lamurudu when Kisra refused to accompany it. Lastly, Kisra himself decided to move with the Borgawa group. They sojourned in Bornu, then crossed the Niger at Illo, and finally settled in Borgu.

The possibility of a close affinity between the groups mentioned above is not supported by any reliable or conclusive evidence. The king of Bussa informed Clapperton that his family ancestors were descended from the sultans of Bornu and that they paid tribute to Bornu 'until recently'. An old Mallam informed Duff that the tribute from Borgu to Bornu amounted annually to 100 sickles, 100 choppers, 100 bundles of 'apples' for horse medicine, and 100 bundles of firewood. In return, the ruler of Bornu sent to Borgu 100 camels, 100 horses and 100 suits of cloth. This story lends itself to fascinating speculations. The articles enumerated above could be mere items of trade between a semi-desert people and a people living in a forest environment. It is also well known that during the early thirteenth century the political and military expansion of Kanem-Bornu had carried the influence of that state to the Niger in the west. The nearness of so powerful a neighbour would no doubt generate a desire on the part of the rulers of Borgu to formulate a basis of friendship and association with Bornu. Prestige and expediency might have provided ample justification for the claim that the rulers of Borgu came originally from Bornu. Much has indeed been made of the names Bariba and Beri-beri which are names also applied to Borgu and Bornu respectively. Governor Moloney of Lagos claimed that the language of Borgu had a close affinity to that of Bornu, and proceeded by way of proof to select Borgu and Bornu words for *one, two, three, four, body, child, dog* and *rain*.[2] The

---

[1] Hermon-Hodge, *Gazetteer of Ilorin Province*, 1939, pp. 115 f. Duff, *Gazetteer of Kontagora Province*, 1920, p. 23. Clapperton, *Journal of a Second Expedition*, pp. 102–3.

[2] R.G.S., vol. xii, 1890, p. 610. According to Murdock, op. cit., pp. 77–80, Bargu, unlike Kanuri, belongs to the Voltaic sub-family of the Nigritic stock.

correspondence is intriguing but hardly conclusive. It would appear too that the Borgawa were intimately connected with the foundation of Katunga, the old capital of the Oyo empire. According to Borgu tradition, Oranyan, one of the legendary heroes of the early Yoruba, met with the king of the Bariba and consulted with him over a suitable site for a permanent capital. The Bariba king reportedly put a charm round the neck of a python and told Oranyan to follow wherever the python might lead. Oranyan did as he was advised, and at a site where the python stopped for seven days and then disappeared, the Yoruba leader construed the python's behaviour to indicate that the site was the one approved by the gods for the foundation of Old Oyo. This tradition suggests the probability of close relations between the Borgawa and the Yoruba after the foundation of their respective states. This association, whatever its antiquity, was to find dramatic expression in the military alliance of the third decade of the nineteenth century.

The impression may have been created, by the allusions so far made to Borgu tradition, that there existed sometime in the past a Borgu nation under one ruler. This tempting conclusion is negatived by the details of the Kisra legend. When Kisra arrived in Borgu, after crossing the Niger at Illo, he decided to settle in Bussa, and allowed his brothers to set up their own seats of authority in Illo and Nikki. The three chief Borgu towns—Bussa, Nikki and Illo—have variants of the tradition explaining the activities of Kisra and his brothers. Each town indeed claims that it was Kisra and not his brothers who founded it. The lack of unanimity is part of the difficulty of determining which of the states could claim spiritual hegemony in Borgu.[1] Nothing, moreover, is revealed in Borgu tradition about the precise structure of authority in each of the Borgawa states. The occupation of the Borgu hinterland was inspired from Nikki. Adventuring members of the house of Nikki led their followers and founded the towns in southern Borgu— Kaiama, Banara, Yashikera, Okuta and Ilesha. The last two were originally Yoruba outposts over which Nikki princes

---

[1] Hogben, *The Mohammedan Emirates of Nigeria*, 1930, pp. 164 f. Duff, op. cit., pp. 23–5.

installed themselves. The southward expansion of the Borgawa is enshrined in a Borgu tradition which claims a spectacular victory over the Yoruba. The Borgu hero was a son of the king of Nikki, called Sabi Agba, who with a few bowmen and fifty horses is said to have routed an invading horde of Yoruba warriors from Gwanara. Therefore the pioneering activities of Kisra and his brothers, and the subsequent emigration into southern Borgu of scions of the Nikki ruling house, led to the foundation of small states in Borgu, independent of each other, but variously claiming Nikki or Bussa or Illo as traditional overlord. This dispersion of authority in Borgu, with the consequent absence of one focus of comprehensive Borgawa political loyalty was an inherent weakness in the political organization of Borgu. The view which was ultimately accepted by the first British administrators was that

> Sarkin Bussa and Sarkin Nikki have always been regarded as blood relations, and from a religious point of view, however, Nikki was held to be the leader for many years before our advent, since the chiefs of Nikki were in a much stronger position both as regards size of territory and number of followers.[1]

Until the nineteenth century there was apparently no clash over the respective spheres of authority between Bussa and Nikki. In fact there is abundant evidence that they co-operated fully when the territorial integrity of Borgu was threatened from outside. Nevertheless the absence of comprehensive political integration embracing all Borgu exposed that territory to the subtle intrigues of European agents who for their selfish reasons undertook to interpret the political structure of Borgu.

Apart from the confusion caused by the break-up of the Kisra ruling clan, another element of difficulty in an attempt to identify the Borgawa is the fact that the conquering Bisagwe clan seem not to have preserved their distinctive language. Each Kisra group assimilated the language of the aboriginal inhabitants over whom it imposed its political authority. Thus at Bussa and Wawa the language spoken is described in Hausa

---

[1] Duff, op. cit., p. 25.

as Bussanchi, which, according to Murdock, belongs to the
Mande sub-family.[1] West of Bussa, the language spoken in
Nikki and Kaiama is Borganchi or Bargu, the language of the
'aboriginal' Zana.[2] It should be observed, however, that the
apparent absence of linguistic uniformity coupled with the
absence of political unity became the excuse for a French
insinuation that the Boko, the Zana and the Bariba and so
forth were different nationalities.[3] Politically and linguistically
united or not, Borgu was from its undefined 'ancient' beginnings a distinct political area the integrity of which the
Borgawa were determined to defend with their blood. The
Borgawa proudly claim, with justice, that until the partition of
their country by the Europeans they had never yielded to alien
domination. No precise details are available of the heroic
struggle against the territorial ambitions of the Askias of
Songhay. Borgu remained on the periphery of the Songhay
empire, and was never subjugated by the Askias.[4] With the
break-up of the empire, a constant and direct threat to the
independence of Borgu was removed.

There is abundant evidence to show that during the opening
decades of the nineteenth century the indomitable spirit and
sturdy independence of the Borgawa remained undiminished.
When Clapperton traversed the region and encountered the
messengers of the king of Dahomey, he was informed by the
messengers that Borgu and Dahomey were good neighbours
who treated each other with courtesy and respect. The people
of Borgu received all their rum and European goods from
Dahomey. The latter obtained slaves in exchange.[5] The two
other neighbours of Borgu were Fulani-dominated Hausaland
and the Yoruba. Before the political upheavals precipitated by
the Fulani jihad, the Habe rulers of the north had good reasons
to respect the independence of Borgu. About 1750, the con-

---

[1] Murdock, op. cit., p. 80.

[2] Hermon-Hodge, op. cit., pp. 39 f.

[3] F.O.C.P. Confidential 6697, no. 224, Africa, Howard to Salisbury,
22 August 1895. Also *Politique Coloniale*, 17 and 20 August 1895.

[4] Lady Lugard, op. cit., p. 197. Barth, *Travels and Discoveries*, vol. iv,
pp. 410 f.

[5] Clapperton, op. cit., pp. 83–4; Hermon-Hodge, op. cit., p. 27.

stant plundering of Hausa trade caravans and the enslavement of their personnel forced the Habe rulers to organize a punitive expedition against Borgu. The reception accorded the Hausa invaders, thanks largely to virulent poison on the Borgawa arrows, was hardly what the Habe rulers anticipated. The invaders withdrew in confusion, and the Borgawa were left to their own devices by succeeding Habe rulers. Sultan Bello's description of the Borgawa is interesting:

> The inhabitants are Sudanese . . . . Now these people are devils and of a stubborn nature.[1]

There were two possible reasons for the Fulani ruler's condemnation. Successive Fulani invasions of Borgu had usually ended in the complete discomfiture of the Fulani horde. There is also the possibility that Bello was thinking of the fact that attempts to convert the ruling houses of Borgu to Islam persisted in by Mallams produced no results. The Borgu rulers showed great contempt for the elaborate rituals of Islam, and liked to believe that it was their duty to keep up the 'ancient challenge' to the Prophet.

Fulani invasions began with an attack launched from Nupe in 1820. Led by Mallam Magaji, the elder son of Mallam Dendo, the first Emir of Nupe, an invading army crossed into Borgu from Bojibo on the Niger. The Fulani first invested Wawa, a district of Bussa. Then, quite unexpectedly, the jubilant Fulani found themselves overwhelmed by Borgawa forces who poured in from all directions. The Fulani army broke up, one contingent fleeing precipitately across the Niger, another in considerable disarray moving towards Kaiama, only to be more decisively routed by one of the sons of the king of Nikki. Gwandu, the suzerain of Nupe, decided to join forces with Nupe in order to avenge the defeat sustained by Fulani troops. According to the Fulani version of what followed, Gwandu troops crossed the Niger at Gaya and completely overran the northernmost Borgu state of Illo. Borgawa tradition denies this but concedes that there was Fulani occupation—

---

[1] Bello, *Infanku 'l Maisuri*; paraphrase by Arnett, pp. 17 f.

only temporary—of Illo. The Borgu ruling family shortly afterwards regained the full independence of Illo.[1]

The next encounter with the Fulani was to prove an unprecedented calamity for the Borgawa. The Ilorin, or the Eleduwe, war c. 1830 was not brought about by a direct Fulani threat to Borgu. It was indeed one directed against the Yoruba ruler, the Alafin of Oyo. The Borgu rulers probably realized that the defeat of the Yoruba would enable the Fulani to outflank rather dangerously the southern regions of Borgu. It was therefore partly self-interest which inspired the military alliance between Borgu princes and the Alafin of Oyo.[2] The Borgawa–Yoruba allies accepted the supreme leadership of the king of Nikki, Eleduwe, and military contingents came from Bussa and Kaiama. The Fulani of Ilorin were supported by a strong force from Gwandu. The encounter which ensued ended disastrously for the anti-Fulani allies. The Borgawa claim that their own forces fought very bravely but were let down by their allies, 'a pusillanimous, contemptible, cowardly and treacherous rabble'. It is only fair to point out that Yoruba tradition explains the defeat of the allies by referring to the greed and rapacity of the Borgawa. The Yoruba apparently feared the Borgawa more than they feared the Fulani. For Borgu, however, the war was an unparalleled disaster from which Nikki did not recover for many decades.[3] The kings of Nikki, Kaiama and Wawa lost their lives. The king of Bussa, who sent only a deputy to lead his contingent in the Elewude war, and whose life was therefore spared in the colossal disaster to Borgu forces, began from this time to regard himself as the overlord of the whole of Borgu.

The alliance of Borgu with the Yoruba and their overwhelming defeat naturally provided an excellent opportunity for the chastisement of the obstinate Borgawa by the Sultan of Gwandu. In 1835 Gwandu forces invaded Borgu but achieved surprisingly little. Gombe on the north-west outskirts of the

---

[1] Ibid., p. 91. Hermon-Hodge, op. cit., pp. 122 f.

[2] For an earlier Yoruba–Borgawa alliance against Nupe, see Ajayi and Smith, *Yoruba Warfare*, p. 3.

[3] Hermon-Hodge, op. cit., pp. 122 f. Also Johnson, *History of the Yorubas*, pp. 260–8.

Bussa principality was captured by the Fulani. This small Fulani enclave in Borguland would perhaps explain Barth's mistake in including Borgu as one of the provinces subject to Gwandu.[1] Hostilities between Borgu, or a Borgu principality, and Gwandu occurred intermittently in the second half of the nineteenth century. Indeed, at one stage king Gazere of Bussa formed a short-lived military alliance with Sarkin Kebbi, the redoubtable Habe opponent of Sultan Aliu of Gwandu. Another restless Bussa king, Dan Toro, attempted the invasion of an outlying province of Gwandu. Ultimately, the Sultan condescended to issue a letter of appeal to the Bussa king in order to secure relief from the harassments organized from Bussa.

For the purpose of understanding the structure of Borgu, it is to be noted that in the wars of offence and defence fought by the Borgawa in the nineteenth century the rulers of Nikki, Bussa and Kaiama co-operated fully in the face of 'national' danger. There is however no evidence that there existed an organized national military machine controlled from one Borgu centre. The Eleduwe war no doubt emphasized Nikki leadership, and no one in Borgu questioned the assumption of the powers of commander-in-chief of the Borgu forces by the king of Nikki. To what extent this outcome was due to the personality of the then king or to traditional practice it is difficult to say. In any case, the war cost the lives of the rulers of Nikki and Kaiama, but not that of the king of Bussa. It is therefore hardly surprising that European records usually spoke of the primacy of Bussa in Borguland. This is indeed not to say that Bussa was not important before the disastrous Eleduwe war. Before the war, when Clapperton arrived in Wawa, he was told that he ought to visit the Bussa king on the ground that 'all this part of the country is nominally under him. The sultan of Nikki is next to him, and equal to him in power'.[2] Then in Bussa itself Clapperton was given to understand that the king of Bussa could, next to the Hausa, raise more horses than any other

---

[1] Barth, op. cit., vol. iv, pp. 203 f. Also R.G.S., vol. viii, 1896; see Wallace, p. 219.

[2] Clapperton, *A Journal*, pp. 88–90.

prince between the Hausa country and the sea. He could take the Yoruba country any time he wanted it. Clapperton was obviously impressed with what he was told, and came to the conclusion that

> The kingdom [of Borgu] is divided into the petty states of Nikki, Kiama, Wawa, and Boussa, of which Boussa is considered the head . . . . These states sometimes make war upon one another, when the sultan of Boussa interferes, and makes both parties pay.[1]

Clapperton was of course unaware of the fact that Bussa and its nearest Borgu neighbour, Wawa, were themselves often at war with each other.

The Landers' expedition probably took place after the Eleduwe war, and the surviving Borgu ruler, Kitoro of Bussa, delivered himself of a speech in the presence of the Lander brothers which revealed the king's new claim to an enhanced political status in Borgu. The Landers' comment illustrates the point.

> If such a comparison may be ventured on, the commencement of his speech was in its nature not much unlike that delivered on the opening of parliament by the Majesty of England. The king of Boosa [Bussa] began by assuring his people of the internal tranquillity of the empire, and of the friendly disposition of foreign powers towards him . . .[2]

It is unfortunate that the king of Bussa did not elaborate on his claims, and no one can pretend to know what the king meant by 'foreign powers'. Although the speech did not define the Bussa empire, it was clear to the Landers, as a result of private discussions, that the king had Borgu in mind. However, the reality of the status of the Bussa king was soon put to a test. It appeared that a caravan which included Bussa men was plundered in the heart of Borgu. It was suspected that the chiefs of Nikki and Kaiama shared the booty between them. In anger the Bussa king sent a peremptory order to Nikki for the restoration of the horses and property lost by the Bussa traders.

---

[1] Ibid., pp. 102–3 and p. 117.
[2] Lander, R. and J., *Narrative of an Expedition*, vol. ii, p. 13.

According to the Landers, the Nikki chief treated the message with contemptuous indifference. What happened next certainly throws much light on the hollowness of the claim to political dominance advanced by the king of Bussa.

> [The king] assembled the priests of the ancient religion of the country of which he is head, and by their joint assistance, it is said, he made a powerful enchantment by which the legs and arms of his enemy became entirely useless.[1]

It was Bussa's charms, not its political or military supremacy, which accomplished the submission of Nikki. The king of the latter place sought the forgiveness of the Bussa king, and dispatched messengers and presents to Bussa. All this of course reveals little of value to an attempt to reconstruct the new relationship developing in the nineteenth century between the principal centres of power in Borgu. The Landers' records, usually more discriminating than Clapperton's, leave no clear picture of the alignment of political forces within Borgu. There is no way of knowing how much irony the Landers implied in their final account of the restitution of peace throughout the Bussa empire.

> Ever since the arrival of the Borgoo [Nikki] messengers, nothing else is heard in the city but music, which is continued from sunrise to sunset; and the long Arab trumpets are likewise sounded constantly in the middle of the night, the king taking this whimsical method of displaying his consequence and grandeur to the foreigner.[2]

The death of Kitoro in 1835 plunged Bussa into a civil war in which the heirs to the throne fought it out. Wawa, Nikki and Kaiama gave their support to opposing candidates. In the circumstances it is permissible to assume that if Bussa enjoyed primacy in Borgu at the time of the visit of the Landers, the

---

[1] Ibid., pp. 30–32. According to Hermon-Hodge, it was Kitoro who reigned in Bussa from 1793 to 1835, and was presented by Mungo Park with a silver medallion. Park's gesture could well explain the king's reference to foreign powers.

[2] Ibid., p. 35.

civil war progressively eroded this hegemony. The independence of Borgu as a whole owed much to the increasing preoccupation of the Ilorin Fulani with Yorubaland in the period after 1835. There were indeed occasions when Fulani incursions thrust into northern Borgu from Yauri and Nupe, but these were not sustained efforts at territorial conquest.[1] Two energetic rulers emerged in Bussa in the persons of Gazere and Dan Toro, who were in a position to carry the war into Gwandu provincial territory. The activities of these kings naturally tended to emphasize the prestige of Bussa in spite of intermittent internal upheavals. Nikki, on the other hand, was shrouded in obscurity. Before Lugard's journey into the hinterland of Borgu in 1894, no European successfully penetrated the region. Wolf, Duncan, Hess and Kling either lost their lives or were forced back. These years were from a historical point of view blank ones for Nikki. The position of Bussa on the Niger conferred special advantages which were denied Nikki or Kaiama. Reference has already been made to Bussa's role in the protracted war with the Fulani northern neighbours, including a military alliance with the celebrated Habe ruler of Argungu against Aliu. The latter development had indeed been a recognition of Bussa's political standing. Bussa also enjoyed the benefits of an excellent strategic position commercially. The trade between the Fulani states of the central Sudan, on the one hand, and Dahomey and neighbouring forest states, on the other, crossed the Niger at Illo, Gaya and Bussa. Bussa bordered the Niger at the navigable portion of that river and so controlled the trade between Kano, Salaga and Yendi. As Lugard explained, 'there is no fixed duty for the merchants to pay, but the chief takes just as much as can be squeezed from them.[2] It was of course not a matter of squeezing but one of proper diplomatic relations between Bussa and the states whose nationals wished to pass through Bussa.

It is therefore true that Bussa enjoyed both prestige and commercial importance. The latter meant material wealth.

---

[1] *Gazetteer* (Ilorin), pp. 125–31; *Gazetteer* (Kontagora), p. 27. Rofia Island (on the Niger) was ceded to Bussa by Yauri, a vassal of Gwandu.

[2] F.O.C.P. Confidential 6894, see Inclosure in no. 143, Howard to Salisbury, 5 August 1896.

Prestige and effective political power were however two different things. Bussa's political influence in the neighbouring Borgu principalities of Wawa and Illo was at best nominal. Wawa indeed periodically challenged the pretensions of Bussa. The relations between the two were further complicated by intermittent civil wars in which contending candidates sought support from the factions into which both states were split. It may be noted by way of anticipation that during the crucial period of the Anglo–French controversy over the political structure of Borgu, Bussa was itself paralysed by anarchy. The Bussa king who in 1890 concluded the famous Lister Treaty died and bequeathed Bussa a disputed succession. Ikki, the late king's brother, faced a competitor who drew support from Wawa, theoretically a dependency of Bussa. In the end it was French assistance that enabled Ikki to secure the Bussa throne and subdue neighbouring Wawa.[1] In view however of the position of Bussa on the Niger, it is not surprising that official relations established between European agents and Borgu were based on the assumption that Bussa was the pre-eminent state of Borgu and enjoyed a paramount status. For instance, the first treaty between Borgu and Goldie's company was signed by Bussa in November 1885. The political implications of the treaty were admittedly vague. In January 1890 a more specific treaty was signed, again with Bussa, in which

> We, the Emir and chiefs of Bussa (or Borgu), in council assembled (representing our country, its dependencies and tributaries on both sides of the River Niger, and as far back as our dominion extends)[2]

agreed to transfer the whole of Borgu to the political and commercial control of the British company. In spite of what the company chose to believe, my contention is that the activities of the various Borgu states during the nineteenth century did not contribute to the emergence of Borgu as a coherently organized political community. In times of external danger the

---

[1] Ibid. Confidential 7017, Memorandum on the Local Situation in Borgu, 11 October 1897.
[2] Hertslet, *Map of Africa*, vol. i, p. 128.

rulers in the various centres of political power in Borgu rallied to the support of one another. For the rest, they went their separate ways. That these rulers called themselves 'brothers' could not have had much political significance. In the second half of the century, Borgu, with the exception of Bussa, had become a land of mystery.

The earliest boundary negotiations regarding the Borgu region recognized that Borgu was a political unit under the paramountcy of Bussa. For instance, the first stretch of the western boundary between Lagos and Porto Novo, which came into being in 1889, stopped at the ninth parallel 'because the Intelligence Division [of the British War Office] suggested that to carry the line beyond would cut off a portion of Borgu with which the Royal Niger Company had treaties'.[1] As mentioned already, the Royal Niger Company did have a vague treaty with Bussa in 1885. The views secretly conveyed to the Foreign Office by the company reveal a lack of certainty on the part of the company as to the precise political situation in Borgu. In a dispatch of 17 June 1889 the company asserted that Borgu lay within the empire of Gwandu. Then after the 1890 Lister treaty with Bussa, the company put forward a diametrically opposite interpretation of the political status of Borgu. It now recalled that

> [The native ruler of Borgu] is a powerful Ruler, who has proved himself more than a match for the Sokoto Empire, so far as the defence of his own territories is concerned.[2]

The conflicting views of the Royal Niger Company were inspired by considerations which had nothing to do with an honest attempt to investigate the true state of affairs in Borgu. In the light of prospective French or German encroachment, the important thing was indeed to secure Bussa, situated near the Bussa Fall. If Britain controlled Bussa, she could deny France the right to sail up the Niger without coming under the conditions which the Royal Niger Company mercilessly enforced. But so far there was no serious threat to the British

---

[1] F.O.C.P. Confidential 6572, no. 25, C.O. to F.O., 27 February 1894.
[2] Ibid. Confidential 6164, R.N.C. to F.O., no. 8, 9 February 1891.

position in Borgu. The occasion for the confused declarations of the Royal Niger Company was the obscure activities of a German, Captain Kling. French agents had not as yet appeared on the scene.

The French colonial expansionists who advocated colonial projects encompassing the Sahara and the central Sudan were just getting off the mark. French activities which stemmed from Senegal had not yet reached Timbuktu. The French position in Porto Novo was apparently circumscribed territorially by the presence in the hinterland of the powerful kingdom of Dahomey. In spite of these obvious handicaps for the French, one of the officials of the British Foreign Office had the foresight to warn the Royal Niger Company that a prospective Anglo–French struggle over Borgu lay ahead. He therefore urged that the British position on 'the Central Niger and the rear of Lagos' should be safeguarded.[1] French unpreparedness explains their willingness to sign the 1890 Anglo–French Declaration which apparently denied them freedom of access to Borgu. As the declaration was badly worded, the French were to find ample excuse for invading Borgu.

The negotiations between Britain and France for a boundary in respect of the territory of Borgu passed through three phases. During the first phase France was on the defensive because she had not as yet achieved complete political control over Dahomey. Britain was on the other hand well armed, not only with Lister's Bussa treaty of 1890 but also with the Anglo–French Say–Barrua Line Declaration. She could therefore insist with complacency on the importance of maintaining the territorial integrity of Borgu. In the second phase France, after the conquest of Dahomey, progressively abandoned her defensive attitude, and advanced claims based partly on the theory of the hinterland of Dahomey and partly on the hypothesis that Borgu was not a coherent political entity for the acquisition of which a treaty with Bussa could be considered adequate. There was a comical German interlude. This interlude, though intrinsically unimportant, reveals growing appre-

---

[1] F.O. 84/1951, see minute by Anderson on no. 88, Africa, 27 June 1889. Also F.O.C.P. Confidential 6352, Hatzfeldt to Rosebery, 1 December 1892.

hension on the part of Britain. Was Borgu worth a struggle and could Britain not repeat the Anglo–German diplomatic master-stroke which shut the French out from Adamawa in 1893 ? The last phase in the Anglo–French controversy was one of extreme bitterness, in which rising tempers almost completely obscured the original question of whether Borgu was a nation or an incoherent agglomeration of separate states. A place for France on the navigable portion of the Niger, the security of Britain's claims east of the Niger, in Egypt and the Anglo–Egyptian Sudan, the hinterland of the Gold Coast and so forth became issues of contention. In these circumstances, it was inevitable that the unity of Borgu should recede into the background.[1] The documentary material on the Anglo–French negotiations is invaluable because it reveals the various ways in which the political structure of Borgu was interpreted. It was diplomatically convenient for Britain to uphold, sincerely or not, the assumption that Borgu was a nation centrally controlled from Bussa or Nikki, or from both. Since Britain argued from second-hand information provided by the trading agents of the Royal Niger Company, France was not disposed to accept the validity of the data forwarded by a company the legality of whose actions she questioned. Strangely enough, it was the dangerous 'game' of effective occupation which began in 1895 that revealed the stark realities of politics in Borgu.

The British position up to 1892 was therefore based on the Anglo–French 1890 Declaration, reinforced as regards Borgu by the Lister treaty with Bussa. Not only had France signed an engagement of self-denial south of the Say–Barrua line, but Britain indeed felt herself free to extend her influence in the direction of the Upper Niger. The Berlin West African Conference which awarded Britain and France exclusive control over the Lower and Upper Niger, respectively, had not fixed any point of demarcation on the Niger. As the French had not advanced beyond Timbuktu from Senegal, nor conquered Dahomey, the thing for Britain to do was to anticipate the French by the conclusion of treaties 'in those territories'.[2] It

---

[1] See *Politique Coloniale*, 3 September 1895.

[2] F.O.C.P. Confidential 6364, F.O. to C.O., no. 77, 24 March 1892.

was against the background of these ugly possibilities that Hanotaux and Haussmann opened boundary negotiations with Cross and Phipps in Paris in the spring of 1892. Hanotaux proposed a direct line from Say, west of the Niger, to Bonduku, a place situated at latitude 8° on the western boundary of the Gold Coast. The proposed line would have secured for Britain the 'whole hinterland of the Gold Coast Colony, Ashanti and Dahomey'. All Britain would then have lost was the north-west corner of Gurma. The British boundary commissioners were delighted. So too were the officials of the British Foreign Office. Unfortunately Lord Salisbury thought that after the exhaustion of French energy which was bound to result from the Dahomian war, which was then just beginning, the French would be ready with more concessions to Britain. Salisbury indeed believed that the French would be 'very tired of West African negotiations'.[1] One must bear in mind the complacency with which the British government approached these preliminary negotiations. At the time of the Hanotaux proposal, the Royal Niger Company claimed, falsely, that it had treaty relations with Gurma. There was nothing to prevent the British from playing for higher stakes, including a position on the Niger at Timbuktu.

The utter lack of realism in the British attitude was revealed in a despatch from Lord Knutsford:

> The interests of the Colonies of the Gold Coast and Lagos would be fully assured if such a line were to be drawn due west from Say as far as the meridian 0° of Greenwich, then along that meridian to about 10° 30′ north of latitude, and then in a south-westerly direction until . . . 9th parallel of latitude.

In the event of France subsequently conquering Dahomey—and this she was not expected to achieve—she should not seek to extend her influence into the interior behind that country, or Porto Novo, beyond the eighth parallel of latitude.[2] The Colonial Office proposal apparently assumed that France had

---

[1] F.O. 84/2208, Dufferin to Salisbury, 13 May 1892 and minutes by Anderson, Lowther and Salisbury.

[2] F.O.C.P. Confidential 6364, C.O. to F.O., no. 147, 7 June 1892. (The Intelligence Division of the War Office, too, approved the C.O. plan.)

forgotten that the 1889 Lagos–Porto Novo agreement extended as far as the ninth parallel of latitude. The proposal was quite fantastic, and France naturally rejected it. Hanotaux withdrew his earlier proposal, and gave as his reasons the fact that

> The sacrifice we have made for the [Dahomian] war, and the arrangements we shall have to make at its conclusion, will probably force us to insist on more territory in the rear of that country.[1]

Between 1892 and 1894 France was in fact involved in an expensive war with Dahomey. The treaty which France had earlier signed with the Dahomian king, Behanzin, was couched in the hypocritical terms typical of European dealings with African potentates during the period. As soon as France was ready with troops and munitions, it was an easy enough matter to find a *casus belli*. The outcome was that in 1892 French forces under the command of Colonel Dodds overran Dahomey and proclaimed a protectorate. Then in 1894 M. Ballot was appointed governor of French Dahomey.[2] The stage was thus set for the second stage of the boundary negotiations between Britain and France in regard to Borgu, now a crucial hinterland.

There was at least one realist in the British Foreign Office, and this was Anderson of the African Department. He revived the fears he first entertained in 1889 regarding the integrity of Borgu. In a confidential letter he hinted at the possibility of French action between the Gold Coast and the Niger, and urged the Royal Niger Company to take steps to forestall French ambitions to the north of Borgu in the direction of Say. The company complacently argued that the possibility of French expansion to the east, after passing the ninth parallel, was out of the question, 'as the Company is fully protected by its Treaties'.[3] The treaty which safeguarded Borgu was no doubt the 1890 Agreement in which the king of Bussa had spoken of his 'dominions'. Between 1890 and 1894, no agent of

---

[1] Africa, 38, see Phipps, Private to Anderson, 23 October 1892. Also Confidential 6697, no. 65, Memorandum by Anderson.

[2] Hanotaux and Martineau, *Histoire*, p. 295.

[3] F.O.C.P. Confidential 6572, see nos. 45 and 51, March 1894. Also Anderson to R.N.C., no. 79, 10 April 1894.

the Royal Niger Company attempted to penetrate the hinterland of Borgu, which was assumed to be under the protection of Great Britain. The British government accepted the company's assurances, and proceeded to inform the French government that France ought to know that

> Under Treaties with Borgu or Barba, the whole of the territory comprised in and dependent on that Sultanate has been for a considerable time within the British sphere. The 'Hinterland' of Dahomey is thus closed.[1]

It is impossible not to admire the subtlety with which Hanotaux approached the impending boundary negotiations. After the conquest of Dahomey, Hanotaux did not immediately press the issue of a hinterland for Dahomey and thus challenge the position of Britain in Borgu. He also refrained from questioning the additional British assumption that the Say–Barrua line fully protected the integrity of Borgu's political frontiers. In his private conversations with Phipps, of the British Niger Commission, Hanotaux asked for no more than a communicating corridor between Dahomey and the Niger somewhere on the right bank, south of Say.[2] In view of the aggressive form which French colonial activities had assumed in the central Sudan, the British government was disposed to accept the French request for a corridor as a very reasonable one, provided France recognized the general British position east of the Niger and south of the Say–Barrua line. The immediate result was that for the second time Hanotaux proposed a boundary line. This proposed boundary, subsequently to be referred to as the Hanotaux Line, was 'the line drawn from the coast east of Dahomey to be prolonged due northwards to Gomba on the Niger, the line thence to follow the Niger (western bank) as far as Say'.[3] A glance at the map will show that a direct extension northward of the eastern boundary between Lagos and Dahomey would cut off Nikki from Borgu.

---

[1] Ibid., no. 300A, Kimberley to Dufferin, 14 August 1894.

[2] Ibid., no. 232, Africa Confidential, Phipps to Kimberley, 13 September 1894.

[3] Ibid., no. 260, Africa Most Confidential, Phipps to Kimberley, 4 October 1894. Also D.D.F. xi, p. 204, Hanotaux to Dufferin, 9 June 1894.

For this reason the Hanotaux Line was unacceptable to Britain. Up to this time, England continued to insist that the political rights of Bussa comprehended all Borgu. The next phase of the Anglo–French controversy materialized when the French raised the basic issue of the validity of the British contention that the king of Bussa ruled all Borgu. How did the British know, since on their own admission, no agent of the Royal Niger Company had dared to visit the towns in Borgu other than Bussa? Hanotaux went on to assert, also without any proof, that no single chief had authority which was comprehensive enough to embrace the territories of Borgu. For the first time, the French suggested that if indeed any one Borgu chief was paramount, then it was the chief of Nikki. The British had no answer, and so the Anglo–French negotiations lapsed.

One imperative, however, emerged from the abortive negotiations. The mysterious chief of Nikki must be traced. The French had apparently drawn the same conclusion. The upshot was a comical phase of European activity in this part of West Africa admirably described as 'a veritable steeplechase'.[1] Those engaged in the race for Nikki did not however regard their proceedings as a burlesque. Lugard, in the employ of the Royal Niger Company, set out on the Lower Niger with over 200 porters and forty soldiers. According to him,

> No man could force his way through the unknown of such a country as Borgu unless he were buoyed up by a sense of the nobility and high importance of his mission.[2]

Decœur, who acted for France, left Dahomey for Borgu with over one hundred Senegalese soldiers. Lugard beat Decœur by sixteen days, although this was not known in Europe. The latter point and also the fact that Lugard made no contact with the chief of Nikki personally were to add complications to the Anglo–French controversy. Lugard's expedition to Borgu was in a way a historically useful inquiry into the political

---

[1] *Politique Coloniale*, see Article on the Decœur expedition, 19 January 1895.
[2] Perham, *Lugard*, quotation from Lugard's diary, p. 508.

structure of Borgu. Lugard was a shrewd observer, and his private diary provides extremely useful material on Borgu.

Lugard visited Bussa, Kaiama, Nikki and Kishi—the centres of political power in Borgu. The question he set out to investigate was which of the Borgu states exercised some kind of overlordship over the whole territory. He apparently attached little reliability to the earlier pronouncements by his employers on Borgu, and thought, like his friend Willcocks, that 'the history of Borgu has surely yet to be written'.[1] The first Borgu potentate Lugard visited was the chief of Bussa, whom the Royal Niger Company had begun to style 'Sultan of Borgu'. Lugard considered his mission to Bussa an 'abasement before these petty African chieflets'. He conceded, however, that 'the King is a gentleman of much local importance . . . [whose] theory seemed to be that there were many white men, but only one Bussa'. Lugard's interview with the Bussa chief was held 'in a hovel in the company of a couple of goats'. As already mentioned, Lugard spoke scathingly on the appearance and demeanour of his Bussa host.[2] As regards Bussa's political status in Borgu, Lugard thought that the Royal Niger Company was wrong in the belief that the chief of Bussa was a paramount ruler. The chief had power on the Niger frontage only. He claimed no tribute from Kaiama or Nikki, but was looked up to as 'father'.

The reference to Bussa as 'father' might have been useful if the story from Kaiama had confirmed the nominal primacy of Bussa. According to the chief of Kaiama, the king of Nikki (not Bussa) was his senior brother. He spoke of Nikki with reverence, but concluded that the chiefs of Bussa, Kaiama and Nikki were all independent kings, and the only kings of Borgu. Another chief whom Lugard encountered at Ilesha, a Borgu town, informed Lugard that if the king of Nikki asked him (the chief of Ilesha) to eat sand, he would do so. Lugard heard enough to impel him towards Nikki, and there is little wonder that his arrival there left him with a feeling of anti-climax. At Nikki, he 'found' the king to be very old and blind. The real power at

---

[1] See Willcocks, *From Kabul to Kumasi*, 1904, p. 190.
[2] Perham, op. cit., quoted p. 501. R.G.S., vol. vi, September 1895.

court was a Moslem missionary, Abdulla, with whom Lugard concluded the all-important treaty.[1] Apart from the uncertainties surrounding the status of the Borgu chiefs, Lugard's experience during his Borgu expedition and the information vouchsafed by the chief of Kaiama, who regarded himself as Lugard's friend, tended to confirm the picture of Borgu which Clapperton conveyed in his Journal more than sixty years back. One Borgu town could plunder another, and no protection appeared to be afforded by any ruler. About to depart from Kaiama, Lugard was warned by the chief that 'a robber chief with 600 warriors had planned to attack us'. The attack did in fact materialize and Lugard had to fight his way out with his 'rawest of recruits, undisciplined and untrained'.[2]

After Lugard's departure, the French agent, Decœur, arrived at Nikki and signed his treaty with the chief of the place. France now possessed '*un Traité, en bonne et due forme, avec le Roi de Nikki, capitale du Borgou*'. But when the French realized that Lugard arrived at Nikki before their agent, they began to question not only the validity of Lugard's treaty but also the claim that Nikki was paramount in Borgu. For instance, the *Politique Coloniale* explained the status of the chief of Nikki as follows:

> The king of Nikki, it is true, styles himself king of Borgu because he resides in the ancient capital of Borgu, but he is far from having any power. Nikki probably from the ruins still existing was formerly a great centre. At present it is only an agglomeration of small and miserable villages, of which the king, covered with dirty rags, was lodged in a poor straw hut, has not even sufficient authority to make his will respected by his immediate attendants. His power is as chimerical as his budget.[3]

The assumption that Borgu was a nation under a paramount

---

[1] F.O. 2/167, no. 194, Treaty with Nikki, 10 November 1894 (full text).

[2] Hermon-Hodge, op. cit., quotes Lugard's address, pp. 20 f. Perham, op. cit., p. 504.

[3] F.O.C.P. Confidential 6697, no. 224, Africa, Howard to Salisbury, 22 August 1895. Enclosed articles from the *Politique Coloniale* of 17 and 20 August 1895.

ruler was gradually abandoned although, without really believing it, the British boundary commissioners continued up to April 1896 to speak of the unity of Borgu. The French, on the other hand, never again gave up their contention that Borgu was at best an agglomeration of independent miserably poor states. Since the original British position had been undermined, the French launched in 1895 a remarkable number of treaty-collecting expeditions into Borgu. The governor of Dahomey, Ballot, made his way to Nikki and made the chief of that place confirm that he had entered into no agreement with an English representative. From Nikki, Ballot traversed northern Borgu and began to explore the Niger frontage of Borgu. Another Frenchman, Toutée, reached Kaiama and obtained a treaty with the chief. The French were indeed entrenching themselves not only in Borgu but along the Niger between Say and Bussa. At Bajibo, work was begun in the construction of a French fortress named Fort d'Arenberg, after a French patriot who poured money into French colonial designs.[1] Kishi, Kaiama, Bussa, Fada Ngurma, Say, Illo and a host of other 'states' entered into treaty relations with France.

The position of the British government in regard to Borgu was not a happy one during the months of 1895. The Royal Niger Company could reply to the activities of the French only by pouring in unrealistic reports about conditions in Borgu. For instance, the Agent-General's report insinuated that 'the Kiama and Boussas are all on the alert, and if a chance offers at all they will attack the French'.[2] The Borgu chiefs were wiser than the Royal Niger Company would have had the British government believe.

The British government had no illusions about the growing intransigence of the French government in respect of Borgu. In March 1895 Lord Kimberley held private conversations with the French Ambassador, de Courcel, on the Borgu situation. According to the Ambassador, there was nothing to

---

[1] See Toutée in *L'Estafette*, 5 June 1895, and Presidential Decree, 1 August 1895, ratifying the French Treaties.

[2] F.O.C.P. Confidential 6697, see Inclosure 1 and 3 in no. 265, R.N.C. to F.O., 26 June 1895.

show that France had ever recognized the jurisdiction of the Royal Niger Company, on whose activities the British case rested. Nevertheless he believed that a *modus vivendi* could be found, and he therefore proposed that the 'rapids' near Bussa should make a natural division between the Upper and Lower Niger, a division vaguely suggested by the Berlin Conference in 1884–5. The Ambassador asked why the 'rapids' should not form an excellent boundary terminus for an extension of the Lagos–Dahomey line.[1] It was at this juncture that the British government turned with understandable relief to resurrect the unrealistic boundary negotiations which had dragged out a miserable and mocking existence since 1891.

No official of the British Foreign Office was as nervous as Goldie of the Royal Niger Company over the Anglo–French impasse in Borgu. His company had apparently let down the British cause because it could not implement the suggestions offered from the Foreign Office in 1889 and 1894. Even the reported success of its latest agent, Lugard, had left inconvenient loop-holes for the French to exploit. It is no wonder then that it was Goldie who turned to his German friend Vohsen in the hopes of repeating the Anglo–German 1893 'miracle' in Adamawa. In regard to Borgu the auspices for an Anglo–German diplomatic master-stroke seemed even better. Borgu was an important hinterland for German Togoland, and so the Germans were as interested in Borgu as anybody else. The German newspaper *Kolnische Zeitung* had in 1894 suggested that Lagos, Dahomey and Togoland should all extend their hinterland to the navigable Niger below the Bussa 'rapids'.[2] Where, in 1893, the German government had had no agent who had set foot in Northern Adamawa, in 1894 two German agents were somewhere in the neighbourhood of Borgu. The Germans apparently attached great importance to these activities. The occupation of the territories lying to the north and north-east of Togoland and, if possible, an advance to the Niger, became 'the most important problem for German

---

[1] Ibid., no. 111A, Africa, Kimberley to Dufferin, 28 March 1895. D.D.F., xl, p. 650, Courcel to Hanotaux, 2 April 1895.
[2] F.O.C.P., 6783, Memo by Anderson, no. 65, 31 August 1895.

Colonial policy'.[1] At first the reaction of the Royal Niger Company to suspected German activities had been to admonish the British government that no portion of the dominion of the native ruler of Borgu should be handed over to a German protectorate.

In 1895 the French threat appeared more menacing than the activities of two obscure Germans, Herr von Pawlikowski and Dr Gruner. The latter's expedition took him to Say and then to Gwandu. As far as Borgu was concerned, his report did nothing to clarify the local political geography. From Say to Bussa, Gruner 'discovered' from eleven to twelve different chieftains on the Niger 'who acknowledge no suzerain, and who live for the most part by fighting each other'.[2] These inconvenient details notwithstanding, Goldie believed that if the Germans were ready to acknowledge the territorial integrity of Borgu, negotiations should be easy. His private conversations with Vohsen were at this stage referred to their respective governments. The British boundary proposal to the German government was quite simple, but it completely ignored the French position in Dahomey. A line prolonged northwards to the Niger between Lagos and Port Novo from the ninth degree of north latitude should be deflected in such a way as to leave in the British sphere the territory 'properly belonging to Nikki'. West of the line but east of the 'legitimate' hinterland of the Gold Coast, the Germans could deal with the French as they thought fit. The intelligence division of the British War Office indeed deplored what it called a generous line, because it was prejudicial to the continuity of British territory between the Gold Coast, Lagos and the Royal Niger Company's 'possessions'.[3]

It turned out that the German government was as anxious

---

[1] Ibid. Confidential 6572, see no. 103, 149 and 195, Malet to Kimberley. Also Inclosure, 5 October 1894, and Confidential 6164, no. 8, R.N.C. to F.O., 8 February 1895.

[2] Ibid. Confidential 6697, no. 79, Gosselin to Kimberley, 27 June 1895. See also F.O. 64/1372, Goldie to F.O., 11 January 1895 and enclosure.

[3] F.O.C.P. Confidential 6697, see Memorandum of Bases for an Arrangement, 16 March 1895; no. 175 Intelligence Division to F.O., 24 April 1895; and F.O. 64/1367, Kimberley to Hatzfeldt, 14 June 1895.

as the French for a navigable portion of the Niger. In addition, Germany sought compensation for 'giving up' the territory of Nikki, although she could produce no evidence that any German had yet set foot on the soil of that state. The Germans believed that Britain knew as little of the Borgu country as Germany, and so both Powers were in fact engaged in partitioning a no-man's-land. Anderson of the British Foreign Office and the German Ambassador, Count Hatzfeldt, met in November 1895 to resume negotiations for an Anglo–German boundary through Borgu. Britain would now not insist on including Gurma and the right bank of the Niger as far as Gombe as parts of Borgu. The clever German Ambassador realized that Britain was primarily trying to use Germany against France, in a year, besides, in which the Germans and the French had no colonial quarrel. Germany could therefore consider seriously any British offer if it included a navigable portion of the Niger, whether it split Borgu territory or not. The Anglo–German talks produced nothing, but a new note of compromise could be detected in the British position.[1]

The spirit of compromise with which Britain approached the renewed boundary negotiations with France is admirably revealed in a memorandum which ran as follows:

> With regard to the delimitation of the west of the Lower Niger ... the Commissioners should bear in mind that the desire of Her Majesty's Government is to secure an equitable settlement which shall give to the British and French possessions alike such access to the markets of the interior as will enable them to pursue their legitimate development without hindrance.[2]

In the open, however, both British and French commissioners continued to argue about the treaties with the Borgu chieftains, but more and more with an air of unreality. Then the French developed what the British negotiators described as the 'new theory' that, in respect of all parts of Africa, the question of indigenous suzerainty was one which they (the French) thought

---

[1] F.O. 83/1386, Anderson's Memorandum on the Negotiations, 28 November 1895. F.O. 83/1359, Memo by Gosselin, 16 December 1895.

[2] F.O. 27/3277, Telegram, Salisbury to Dufferin, 31 January 1896, and F.O. 27/3273, Salisbury to Dufferin, 7 February 1896.

was hardly worth taking into consideration. They therefore proceeded to base their rights to Borgu on the theory that a claim to African territory should rest only on 'effective occupation'.[1] In any case, the rights of two great Powers should not be determined 'merely by the speed shown by explorers who carry the flags of each country'.

In spite of these disconcerting beginnings, the British commissioners proposed a boundary almost identical with the one put before Germany in the previous year. The only difference was that Nikki could now go to France if the boundary line ran from the north-eastern limit of the frontier of Dahomey direct to a point 10 kilometres north of Gomba. The spirit of compromise manifest in the British proposal was obviously not appreciated by the French, because the latter raised other territorial issues in and around the frontiers under discussion—the Say–Argungu–Gomba triangle, Yola and Bornu. For sacrificing the above regions, the French expected adequate compensation to the west of the Niger. In other words, the British should surrender a substantial portion of Borgu in order to safeguard their claims to the region east of the Lower Niger.[2] From this time on, Borgu was not considered apart from the problem of the northern boundary, but in the interest of clarity it is intended to deal with Borgu separately from the northern zones and concentrate on the proceedings which culminated in the mutilation of Borgu.

As regards this territory, the French boundary commissioners invariably talked in terms of the independent states of Bussa, Nikki, and Kaiama (spelt Koma in the French texts). The Royal Niger Company's treaty with Bussa the French rejected on grounds which they did not reveal. Lugard's treaty with Kaiama contained a name which was not the king's true name. In Nikki, Lugard had not, in the first instance, treated with the king. The French could not accept the action of a materialistically-minded Moslem non-Bariba as representing that of the king of Nikki. Although the British commissioners

---

[1] Lebon, *La Politique de la France en Afrique, 1896–8*, pp. 58–66. See also Confidential 6837, no. 45, Dufferin to Salisbury, 6 March 1896.

[2] Ibid. See reported interview between Dufferin and French Foreign Minister, M. Berthelot, in no. 22.

could not find an appropriate answer to the French contentions, they continued to argue as follows:

> We could not abandon the principle of suzerainty. This principle was recognized in all international negotiations and we held that, in treating with a suzerain, the rights conferred . . . extended to the whole of the territory under his dominion.[1]

Which suzerain in Borgu? asked the French. Faced with another breakdown in the negotiations, the British government authorized the commissioners to propose a new line for the partition of Borgu. This new line was described as

> a boundary eastwards, from the intersection of the 9th parallel with the meridian forming the eastern boundary of Dahomey, along the 9th parallel as far as . . . (3° 30' east of Greenwich) and then northward along the meridian until its intersection with a line drawn direct from Say to Barrua.

The fall of the French Government in the spring of 1896 held up negotiations for a time, but the re-emergence of Hanotaux as French Foreign Minister did not materially affect the French attitude to the issues concerning the structure of Borgu. In fact, Hanotaux's own attitude to British colonial claims had hardened into one of undisguised hostility. The Anglo–French Declaration of 1890 was a betrayal of French colonial interests, and such betrayal should never again be permitted.[2] Borgu provided France with another opportunity to uphold her 'legitimate' rights.

It is therefore hardly surprising that when Hanotaux personally intervened in the work of the Niger commissioners a breakdown in the talks was inevitable. His counter-proposal to the boundary which Salisbury had authorized involved the complete surrender of the stakes for which Britain played. Hanotaux demanded that

> [A line] starting from the eastern frontier of Dahomey at its intersection with the 8th degree of north latitude should follow that

---

[1] Ibid. Inclosure 1 in no. 66, Dufferin to Salisbury, April 1896.
[2] Hanotaux, *Fachoda*, 1909, pp. 487–8. Hanotaux and Martineau, *Histoire*, pp. 306–8.

parallel eastward to the Niger, and then that river up to Say, the right bank falling to France and the left bank to Great Britain.[1]

Ironically, Hanotaux's proposed line almost perfectly respected the territorial integrity of Borgu, a principle on which the British delegates had also insisted. In this case, however, Britain would be the loser of Borgu, and France would also obtain some control of the navigable portion of the Lower Niger. Salisbury rejected the French proposal as wholly unacceptable, but both sides began in greater earnest to speak of compromises. The compromises progressively ignored the earlier British contention that Borgu was one nation. The need to soothe ruffled national feelings and reconcile imperial interests became, in the view of the Powers, more important than the territorial integrity of Borgu. Britain's chief apprehension was admirably summarized as follows:

> To give the French access to the navigable portion of the Niger . . . would be disastrous.[2]

The second British boundary commissioner, Everett, thought Britain ought to sacrifice Borgu in order to guarantee the security of Sokoto and Bornu south of the fourteenth parallel of latitude. Goldie, however, had his own ideas, and he did not mince his words in conveying these ideas to the British government. 'If ever the French get a port on the Niger I will sell up the whole business and clear out.'[3] The Anglo–French talks broke down, and events in Borgu moved to a climax.

Before the formal breakdown of the Borgu boundary negotiations, the French Chamber of Deputies held a debate on the colonial estimates. The debate afforded the French Colonial Minister an opportunity to reply to the criticisms of the colonial

---

[1] F.O.C.P. Confidential 6837, Inclosure in no. 75, Dufferin to Salisbury, 8 May 1896. See also Salisbury to Dufferin, 12 May 1896.

[2] F.O. 27/3276, Howard to Salisbury, 5 August 1896. See also Memorandum by Howard.

[3] F.O. 27/3301, Everett to Hill, 31 December 1896. See no. 149, Intelligence Division to F.O. on Goldie's views.

group respecting French inactivity in the hinterland of Dahomey.

'I have instructed the Governor, M. Ballot, to return to his post in Dahomey, and I have placed at his disposal three Chiefs of Missions who are empowered to delimit the northern "Hinterland" of this possession, in order to consolidate our existing rights in this region,' declared the Colonial Minister, to the shouts of 'Hear! Hear!' by the Deputies.[1] The crisis which began to develop in 1897 and reached its climax in 1898 presents a fascinating paradox. Whereas Borgu was the scene of menacing military activities, the core of the arguments in London and Paris was concerned with the interpretations of the frontiers of the Sokoto empire and the meaning of the Say–Barrua Line. Then when the whole diplomatic situation became a tangle, personalities, national honour, colonial ambitions in other regions, and so forth all added to the manner in which the original issue of the political structure of Borgu was reduced to complete obscurity. It must be conceded that the behaviour of the Borgu princelings during the crisis contributed nothing to support the assumption that an organized indigenous state was being occupied by alien Powers preparatory to its partition.

True to his word, the French Colonial Minister, M. Lebon, initiated dramatic movements of French missions into the region known as the 'Boucle du Niger'. The French excuse was the military action which the Royal Niger Company was taking against Nupe and Ilorin. In the French view the company's action was a prelude to effective occupation. Bretonet moved into Borgu and, after passing through Saki and Kishi, installed himself in Bussa as French Resident. M. Baud moved into Gurma. Captain Voulet occupied Mossi, more to the west. Lastly, Major Valet established himself at Say. These were proceedings which were in conformity with the colonial temper of France. There were material compensations in prospect. For instance,

France will have a trade route . . . from Dahomey via Ketu,

---

[1] F.O.C.P. Confidential 6894, no. 218, Monson to Salisbury, 8 December 1896.

Tchaki [Saki], and Kishi—passing through a peaceful and industrious population already devoted to the French cause.[1]

The British government at first began by merely protesting against what it called 'aggressions into British territory'. At Bussa, where Bretonet made himself Resident, the French found no evidence of British authority. In fact the new Bussa chief, Ikki, solicited the assistance of French troops in order to subdue the vassal district of Wawa, which supported a rival candidate to the throne of Bussa. To counter this obvious French advantage, Goldie forwarded a report from his lieutenant in the region, which claimed that another Borgu state, Kaiama, had rallied to the support of Ikki of Bussa. Consequently, 'the people of Kiama, who wish to serve the Company, took alarm and seized the king. Whether they beheaded him or not before the arrival of the French is uncertain.' The Kaiama king was in fact not beheaded by anybody, because he appeared before Willcocks and the French Commander in 1898 to announce that 'I love France'.[2] In January 1898 the British Colonial Office reported that the French had captured the king of Nikki, and the Colonial Secretary deplored the inability of the British government to afford the king of Nikki the protection which he was alleged to have sought. The French view, however, was that the king welcomed their arrival. These events which took place in Bussa, Kaiama and Nikki revealed nothing remotely suggestive of any feeling of political solidarity among the Borgu chiefs, who witnessed strange activities disturbing to the 'peace' of their territory.

A great deal has rightly been written in commendation of the spirit of assertiveness which Chamberlain as Colonial Secretary brought to the British position in the Anglo–French negotiations which were resumed in Paris. Joseph Chamberlain condemned what he called the 'ingrained inclination for . . .

---

[1] *Journal des Débats*, 22 March 1897. *La Politique Coloniale,* 30 March 1897. F.O.C.P. Confidential 7000, Memorandum by the Intelligence Division, October 1897. Lebon, *La Politique de la France en Afrique, 1896–8,* p. 66.

[2] F.O.C.P. Confidential 7017, Memorandum on the Local Situation in Borgu by Goldie, 11 October 1897; see also Willcocks, op. cit., p. 191.

compromise' on the part of the British commissioners and, perhaps too, on the part of the British government. As far back as June 1897, he feared that,

> While the Company are relying upon their Treaties to secure the evacuation of the places which the French have occupied on the right bank of the Niger, they are running the risk of French interference on the left bank.[1]

Deploring French action was not enough. He decided therefore to establish a West African Frontier Force of 2,000 or 3,000 men at the expense of the Imperial Exchequer. Lugard was selected as commandant of the force in September 1897. The resulting situation in Borgu was that British and French troops faced each other in several Borgu villages. It was a miracle that war was not triggered off.

The readiness of the French government to reopen boundary discussions and their readiness for compromise perhaps justify the claim that the W.A.F.F. organized by Chamberlain successfully demonstrated to the French that the 'occupation policy . . . was futile'. On the other hand, it must be remembered that Salisbury, the British Prime Minister, had always wanted a peaceful solution in an area to which he attached little importance. There is indeed no evidence that he would have permitted a shooting war with the French there. Thus at the first opportunity he wrote to Gosselin in Paris that the time had come to express the views of the British government 'as to the lines on which a compromise might possibly be arrived at between the respective claims of Great Britain and France'. Salisbury concluded by indicating that he was prepared to renounce part of Borgu and give to the French access to the Niger between Leaba and Bajibo, from the neighbourhood of Nikki, the line of communication passing between Kaiama and Bussa.[2] Colonel Binger, for the French, reacted favourably,

---

[1] See Garvin, *Life of Chamberlain*, vol. iii, pp. 208–19. Perham, *Lugard*, pp. 631–41 and 676–95. C.O. 147/124, C.O. to F.O., 14 August 1897; C.O. 147/116, C.O. to W.O., 17 August 1897.

[2] C.O. 537/14, see Memorandum dated 25 January 1898. Gooch and Temperley, *British Documents*, vol. i, no. 438, Africa, Salisbury to Gosselin, 30 December 1897.

and observed that further examination of rights and treaties would serve no useful purpose. All that was indeed necessary was for both parties to make up their minds as to what territory they must keep and what they could concede with a view to reaching an amicable settlement. At this stage of the exercise in mutual compromise, Chamberlain listed the regions which England was prepared to barter. These included: I Borgu outside Bussa, Kaiama, Ilesha and Kishi, places situated in the direct Lagos hinterland; II Nikki; III Gurma; IV Asben; V the Argungu triangle, etc.[1] The present boundary discussion concerns numbers I and II.

In spite of the preponderance of extraneous factors it is remarkable how the renewed negotiations invariably went back to the question of the political structure of Borgu. The latest interpretation of this structure put forward by the British commissioners was that the kings of Bussa and Nikki were descendants of one family, the elder branch ruling the eastern states with Bussa at the head, and the younger branch the western states with Nikki at the head. The French agreed, although the British did not indicate the source of their information. The French indeed produced a map which purported to trace the limits of the frontiers of the various states of Bussa, Kaiama and Nikki.[2] The map ignored the districts of Illo and Ashigere, but Goldie's agent was soon to inform the commissioners that he 'discovered' 'Bussa's half-brother' ruling at Illo. There was no reason why the commissioners should be unduly preoccupied with the indigenous frontiers. As regards the frontier between Kaiama and Nikki, Lugard was ready with the information that 'the western boundary of Kiama is vague, little populated and is swept by robber bands'.[3]

In view of these circumstances, it was not long before the outlines of the manner in which Borgu would be partitioned

---

[1] F.O.C.P. Confidential 7017, Memorandum by Chamberlain, Inclosure in no. 239, C.O. to F.O., 2 December 1897.

[2] Ibid., no. 393, Monson to Salisbury, 27 November 1897. Also Inclosure in no. 465, Gosselin to Salisbury, 31 December 1897. C.O. 96/306, Goldie to Chamberlain, 19 July 1897.

[3] F.O.C.P. Confidential 7144, C.O. to F.O., no. 35, 12 January 1898. See Inclosure 1, Memorandum by Lugard.

gradually emerged. The only obstacle to a boundary agreement satisfactory to both Powers was the French request for a corridor, thirty-five miles wide, from Nikki to the Niger. Salisbury would not compromise on this issue, and a peremptory telegram informed the British commissioners in Paris that it has been 'decided by the Cabinet that no sovereignty or territory on the banks of the Niger shall be transferred to the French'.[1] Once again the British determination to hold on to the navigable portion of the Niger, as they had done in the case of the Benue, guaranteed a solid block of territory for Nigeria. The final diplomatic manoeuvres included Hanotaux's '*Projet de Convention*' and Salisbury's scheme. The difference between the two concerned issues outside the territory of Borgu. Before the end of June the Powers settled all their differences. Article II of the Anglo–French Convention of 1898 described the Borgu boundary as follows:

> The line of demarcation shall start from the extremity of the present frontier on the 9th degree of north latitude and shall be drawn northwards so as to include in the British sphere the territories of Bere and Okuta, together with the towns of Ashigere and Bete. It will follow generally the direction of the meridian 3° 2′ east of Greenwich, thus leaving Nikki and the surrounding district within the French sphere, but will be deflected so as to touch the Niger at a point ten miles to the north of the town of Illo, leaving within the British sphere all territory belonging to the Province of Boussa and the district of Gomba.[2]

The Protocol was signed in Paris on 14 June 1898.

The arrangement which thus determined a portion of the western boundary of Nigeria, involving as it does the partition of Borgu, was a compromise which was deplored by the 'colonial groups' of both France and Britain on the ground of loss of territory, not on the ground that an indigenous 'state' was dismembered. For instance, Chamberlain feelingly spoke

---

[1] Ibid., no. 3, Africa, Telegraphic, Salisbury to Monson, 29 January 1898. See also Memorandum by Monson, Gosselin and Everett, 20 January 1898.

[2] Ibid. Confidential 7297, Inclosure in Monson to Salisbury, no. 212, 15 June 1898.

of the British sacrifice of 100 miles from Illo to Say. The underlying assumption was that the Lagos–Dahomey boundary of
1889 should have been continued northwards, west of Nikki,
to strike the Niger at a point near Say. The French group, led
by Etienne, deplored the fact that the boundary had not more
arbitrarily turned north-eastwards through Kaiama in order
to give the French a portion of the Niger frontage south of the
'rapids'.[1] Not a word was said in commiseration of the
Borgawa whose territory was 'permanently' split by two alien
but powerful European nations.

There was no immediate reaction on the part of the Borgu
princelings to the partition of their country probably because
they were individually involved in the problems associated
with the imposition of alien rule over them. Between 1898 and
1902 British Borgu was under military rule, and British garri-
sons were stationed at Bussa, Kaiama, Ilesha, Okuta and
Yashikera. The king of Bussa, Kisaru Dogo, who, from the
British standpoint, had compromised his position by having
consorted with the French, was for the time being forgiven.
He was recognized by the British as chief over Bussa and the
outlying districts of Illo, Aliyara and Wawa. All was well,
apparently. After the death of Kisaru Dogo in 1902, Kitoro II
was installed chief with the grade of first class by a British
Resident. In 1905 the British administration arbitrarily
decided to transfer Illo and the northern division of Bussa's
principality to the Sultan of Gwandu who, thanks to the
exigencies of British diplomacy, had lost part of his territory to
France. This mutilation of Bussa territory produced an immediate reaction. It was 'an exceedingly bitter pill for Sarkin
Bussa to swallow'.[2] In Kaiama, after the British occupation,
the king, Mora Tasude, emerged from hiding. His former
declaration that 'I love France' was explained away. How, he
asked, was he to know beforehand whether France or Britain
would win? 'He knelt at Willcocks' feet and asked him for his
foregiveness'.[3] Willcocks and Lugard, the king's former

---

[1] F.O. 27/3413, Monson to Salisbury, 24 June 1898. F.O. 27/3145, see
Monson's extracts from the Parisian press, no. 204, 4 August 1898.

[2] Hermon-Hodge, op. cit., pp. 134–5.

[3] Willcocks, op. cit., pp. 207–8. Perham, *Lugard*, p. 709.

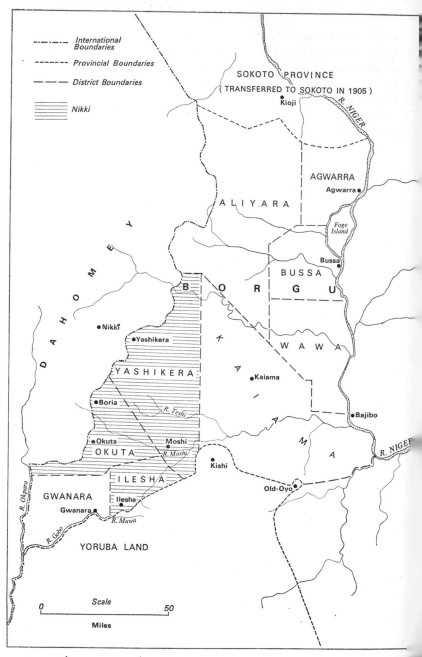

'friend', felt quite sorry for him. He was therefore recognized by the British as chief not only of Kaiama but also of the several Nikki districts which lay on the British side of Borgu. The chief of Kaiama thus attained a status equal to that of the chief of Bussa.

In the French portion of Borgu, Nikki indeed suffered the most grievous political dismemberment from the Anglo–French partition of Borgu. The towns originally founded by the members of the Nikki ruling house—Tabira, Okuta, Boria, Yashikera, and even Kaiama—were now lost to Nikki. The king of Nikki had died at the time the Anglo–French Convention was being signed. His eldest son, Ojo (also called Woru Yoru), was then the chief of Yashikera, and he expected to succeed to the throne of Nikki, as was the custom. The French who were in control of Nikki refused to accept a candidate to the throne of Nikki who came from the British sphere. An adventurer called Sabi Erima, who had no connection with the ruling house of Nikki, was recognized by the French as ruler of Nikki.[1] Ojo was consequently degraded to the status of a district head under Kaiama. It is therefore hardly surprising that when in 1900 the Delimitation Commissioners arrived in Yashikera, they noted that

> [Ojo] claims to be king of the whole country, without regard to the Anglo-French frontier, and begged me to take him to Nikki and turn out the French. The political state of Borgu is, consequently, somewhat unsettled.[2]

In 1903 Ojo became so dissatisfied with his status that he rallied his followers and returned to Nikki to settle as a private citizen of Dahomey. There was for him a happy ending, for in 1917 the French appointed him Emir of Nikki to rule over his reduced patrimony. His colleagues on the British side fared worse. British Borgu was in 1907 amalgamated with the Northern Nigeria Province of Kontagora and was then

---

[1] F.O.C.P. Confidential 7297, Inclosure in no. 24, C.O. to F.O., 15 April 1898.

[2] Ibid. Confidential 8976, no. 16, C.O. to F.O., 2 July 1901 (Report of Lieutenant-Colonel Lang on the Anglo-French Commission on Borgu, 1900).

administered from Yelwa. British-appointed Fulani political agents from Yelwa soon flooded Borgu and progressively drove the indigenous rulers of Borgu to desperation. British administrators accepted the insinuations of their hand-picked agents to the effect that the Borgawa were 'truculent . . . savages and ready to a man to rise and fight' the British. A revolt did in fact occur, but as a result of the banishment of the chief of Bussa. The revolt spread to many parts of Borgu, but here again the Borgawa did not rise as one united people. Each princeling rallied the forces of his own centre of power to face the British punitive expedition which inevitably followed. A Fulani from Gwandu named Jibrim was appointed Emir of British Borgu. The political confusion arising out of the British proceedings led to the exodus southwards and westwards of a large number of Borgawa. The predominantly westward movement of the fleeing Borgawa was not accidental, and the British administrators noted that 'the western half of [British] Borgu still turns to Nikki . . . instinctively . . ., an instinct which no artificial boundary can kill'.[1]

The need to survey the boundary on the spot had led in 1900 to the appointment of an Anglo–French Borgu Commission. The commissioners had considerable trouble in identifying the starting point described as the intersection of the Okpara River and the 9° north parallel. A cross cut into a tree by the Lagos–Dahomey Commission could not last for ever. The Borgu commissioners selected another starting point, and proceeded to map out the 216 miles of boundary between the 9° north latitude and the River Niger, comprising arcs around villages, the thalweg of the river Wan, lines parallel to roads, and arbitrary straight lines. The commissioners were convinced that something concrete should be done to impress on the minds of the Borgawa that an Anglo–French boundary ran through their country. They even set about doing this by placing 'marks at intervals of about 500 metres, along the roads in cases where the line runs parallel to roads. These marks consist of trees blazed then cut down alternately'.[2] By

[1] Hermon-Hodge, op. cit., pp. 153–60.
[2] Hertslet, op. cit., vol. ii, p. 799.

1912 the marked boundary had disappeared, and farmers were clearing the bush on whichever side of the boundary they liked for their crops. The disputes which the British Residents anticipated did not materialize.[1]

It has been claimed that pride of tradition is one of the characteristics of the Borgawa. It is however difficult to say what political importance they attach to the tradition which they proudly proclaim—that Borgu was founded by a national leader, Kisra. More realistically, they also recall that in the old days the kings of Nikki, Bussa, Kaiama and Illo performed coronation ceremonies for one another. The idea that a Borgu nation was dismembered by the action of Britain and France is not likely ever to be abandoned by intelligent and very imaginative Borgu Mallams. One of them put this patriotic view in what amounts to this: 'Borgu was the only "pagan" state able to resist the Fulani invasion, but with two European nations waiting at its gates, what could the Borgawa do? It is all very sad', he concluded.[2]

The exact manner in which the Anglo–French boundary affected the realities of Borgu political life and institutions is another matter. The objective situation at the time of the boundary arrangement was one clearly inconsistent with the assumption that Borgu was a coherent nation. The political life of the Borgawa revolved around the three capitals, Nikki, Bussa and Kaiama. Illo was very much on the periphery. The chiefs of these places were independent of one another, and paid no tribute to anyone. Generally speaking, Bussa politically dominated the districts of Illo and Wawa, and these were adjacent to the River Niger. Kaiama lay dormant in the heart of Borgu. The ruling princes of Nikki were in control of western Borgu, including Yashikera, Okuta, Ilesha and Banara.[3] It was therefore Nikki as overlord of western Borgu which was politically dismembered by the international boundary. Invariably the chief of Ashigere (or Yashikera) was the eldest son of the king of Nikki. The boundary sundered this

---

[1] C.S.O. 8/6/10, 4215/1912, Resident of Gando to the Resident of Sokoto, 1 July 1912.

[2] See also Temple, O., *Notes on the Tribes*, 1922, pp. 494 f.

[3] C.S.O. 1/1, 22, no. 140, McCallum to Chamberlain, 5 May 1898.

relationship and separated from Nikki the other vassal districts enumerated above. But times have changed. Today the Borgu traditional chieftaincies in both Nigeria and Dahomey have degenerated into almost complete anonymity. Borgawa pride in their ancestry, in their unconquered record, and in their prowess in arms have become a thing of the past. Is there any hope then of an irredentist movement among 'these strange people'?

7

The Northern Boundary

The region traversed by the northern international boundary is that known as the Central Sudan. It embraces an area stretching from the Middle Niger to the eastern environs of Lake Chad. The northern portion of the region is extremely arid and justifies this description:

> There is a belt of barren land which starts about five miles south of Zinder and continues northwards. . . . It was drearily bare country, undulating in places with low rounded rises, sandy or covered with withered grass, and often with rough outcrops of gravel and boulders and rock, while, in patches, there was some scrappy bush and an odd tree.[1]

Buchanan was of course speaking only in respect of the region which lies roughly north of a line drawn through Katsina, Kano and the Chad. In the southerly sections of the Central Sudan, particularly along the river courses, excellent grass and tree growths abound for a considerable part of the year. The most noticeable geographical feature throughout the boundary zone is its lack of natural barriers, and it was this that laid the region open to cultural waves from the north and north-east. Invader after invader arrived to absorb or conquer existing ethnic groups to form 'bastard peoples of ill-defined racial types'. It has indeed been claimed that the mingling of diverse ethnic groups here has no parallel in Africa.

It is usual to divide the vast region of the Central Sudan into

---

[1] Buchanan, *Out of the World North of Nigeria*, 1921, pp. 84–5.

THE CENTRAL SUDAN

Scale

0   150   300

Miles

--- Kanem circa 1300

.... Bornu circa 1800

three broad linguistic zones—the Songhay, the Hausa, and the Kanuri, going from west to east.[1] This simplified classification is convenient, but it has no reference whatsoever to the ethnic differentiation of the inhabitants. The groups which were probably the aborigines and are found today in isolated and naturally protected hill-tops and swamps were themselves also largely exposed to considerable intermingling with immigrant groups, as will be illustrated with examples in due course.

Taking the Songhay linguistic zone first, it is to be noted that three 'distinct' peoples known as the Zaberma, the Songhay, and the Dendi are involved.[2] The term 'Songhay' is usually applied to the region, although the majority of the inhabitants described here as Zaberma had spoken and used the Hausa language for centuries. The name Songhay has persisted because the cradle of the Songhay empire was the banks of the Niger from the present Nigerian boundary upstream to the Middle Niger. This was an ideal meeting point for Negro cultivators and Berber nomads. What emerged from the fifteenth century as the Songhay empire was not an empire which embraced a homogeneous group. The overthrow of the empire by Moroccan forces and the subsequent period of spoliation and anarchy led to the flight of the 'indigenous' Songhay dynasty to Dendi. Into this region the Tuareg and the Fulani later infiltrated. The people we call the Songhay are a nation of about 330,000 which exercised political dominion in the region.

The Hausa-speaking groups have been described as 'a hotch-potch of peoples of various origin . . . recruited indiscriminately from neighbouring tribes'.[3] The term 'Hausa' does not represent a single race or stock but rather an intermingling of diverse elements including Saharan nomads, Nilotic Sudan groups and later immigrants associated with the Abayajidda legend. The language is virtually the 'lingua franca' of the Sudan, and a large proportion of the peoples

---

[1] See Tilho, *Documents Scientifiques de la Mission*, 1914, vol. ii, map facing p. 308.

[2] Murdock, *Africa, its Peoples*, p. 138.

[3] Seligman, *The Races of Africa*, London, 1957, pp. 79–80.

ostensibly embraced by the Songhay and Kanuri zones spoke and still speak Hausa. Hausaland indeed originally stretched farther north than we realize today. For many centuries it embraced the regions of Air and Damergu, to the north and north-east. The history of perhaps the largest linguistic group in the Sudan is bound up with the fortunes of a number of city-states which came to be known as the Hausa states. It would serve no purpose in this study to enter into a discussion of the myth which seeks to explain the foundation of the Hausa states, which included Daura, Biram, Katsina, Zegzeg (Zaria), Kano, Rano, Gobir, Kebbi and Zanfara.[1] The structure of Hausa politics is however important. It helps to explain the ease with which the states were overthrown by the Fulani.

The Hausa political unit was the walled village surrounded by an area of open fields for cultivation and a collection of open hamlets. The state came into existence when the walled village was acknowledged by the surrounding hamlets as suzerain. The fortified town afforded security to the cultivators of the soil in time of danger. In due course an elaborate system of court ceremonial and a hierarchy of chiefs emerged. The few historical documents which exist show no evidence of political unity among the states. One state would occasionally achieve a sort of hegemony over the others, but on the whole a state of chronic internecine war prevailed. Throughout their history, most Hausa men were apparently indifferent to the ups and downs of politics which brought about the fluctuations of the fortunes of the Hausa states. They were born traders, and this avocation they pursued in the midst of the most violent political and religious upheavals. Islam spread to Hausaland in the second half of the fourteenth century, primarily because it was the religion of traders who were settled in special quarters in the states and familiarized the Hausa people with its tenets and characteristics. Lack of political unity did not prevent the Hausa states from thriving on the prosperous desert trade for many centuries. Kano and Katsina came to be recognized as celebrated emporia of the

---

[1] Barth, *Travels and Discoveries*, vol. ii, pp. 71–2; Bello, *Infanku 'l Maisuri*, pp. 17–18. Palmer, *Sudanese Memoirs*, 1928, vol. iii, pp. 132 f.

Sudan, and Katsina also achieved eminence as a centre of Islamic learning.

Three Hausa states—Katsina, Gobir and Kebbi—deserve special mention in view of the part their leaders were destined to play in the course of the nineteenth century events which transformed the political configuration of Hausaland. The Kano chronicle claims that Katsina was the place where many Fulani settled when they arrived from the west. As Katsina apparently welcomed Islamic scholars, it became a refuge in a land that was predominantly pagan. The destruction of the Songhay empire was to the advantage of Katsina. In addition to the 'old quarter' of the capital, 'stranger quarters' came to form an important part of Katsina. The stranger quarters included sections reserved for people from Bornu, for Arabs and for the different industries and trades which flourished. Katsina was both prosperous and well organized.[1] It refused to yield to the ambitions of Bornu, and it was destined not to yield to the Fulani in the nineteenth century.

The eighteenth century witnessed the rise of Gobir to ascendancy in Hausaland. The state originally possessed territories which stretched as far north as the region of Air, but the Hausa were forced down to the present location of Gobir by wave after wave of Saharan tribesmen.[2] Having been long involved in a life and death struggle with the fierce Tuareg, the Gobirawa deservedly achieved a reputation for military prowess. They soon began to demonstrate their military talents in Hausaland. Having subjugated Zanfara, they sought to dominate Katsina and Kano. It was Gobir, as the leading Hausa state, that was first confronted with the Fulani menace. The rulers of the proud state of Gobir persisted in their refusal to submit to the Fulani 'upstarts'.

Kebbi was the most westerly of the Hausa states. According to Bello, the Fulani historian, the people of Kebbi were the descendants of a Katsina mother and a Songhay father.[3] This claim probably arose out of the fact that the rulers of Kebbi

---

[1] Lugard (Lady), *A Tropical Dependency*, 1964, pp. 262–3.
[2] Trimingham, *A History of Islam in West Africa*, 1962, p. 128.
[3] Bello, op. cit., see pp. 6–17.

were for at least a century closely associated with the great Askias of Songhay. The Kanta of Kebbi was at one time one of the greatest generals of Songhay, and played a celebrated part in the Songhay victories over Katsina and Air. A quarrel later erupted, and the Kebbi ruler decided to proclaim and to maintain the independence of Kebbi. In fact he successfully incorporated into the Kebbi empire the eastern tip of Songhay including Zerma. Like Katsina and Gobir, Kebbi possessed traditions of bravery and independence which stood their rulers in good stead during the trying decades of the nineteenth century. The frontier fluidity produced by the intransigence of the Habe rulers was brilliantly described by Dr Barth, as will be noted later.

With the arrival of the Fulani (Fula, Filani, Fellata, Fulbe) a new element was introduced into the Niger Sudan. The Fulani, first located in the neighbourhood of the Senegal River, had begun an eastward movement as far back as the thirteenth or fourteenth century. It was not however a mass movement, although by the eighteenth century the Fulani already formed a considerable element in the population of the Niger Sudan, including regions as far east as the land that was later called Adamawa. Many Fulani clerics were distinguished scholars and by reason of this distinction they insinuated themselves into prominent positions as high priests, councillors and teachers. Three things should however be noted in regard to the presence of the Fulani who permeated Hausaland and Bornu. Firstly, the Fulani did not form themselves into a massive group possessing political homogeneity. They were broken up into clans. It was the Torobe groups which settled in Gobir that produced the man, Usuman dan Fodio, whose career transformed Hausaland. In the second place, the dark-skinned Torobe, just mentioned, left pockets of settlements along the Niger in their original progress eastwards from the Senegal.[1] There persisted a bond of sympathy between the Fulani groups in the Middle Niger and the main Torobe clan in Hausaland. This sentimental bond was to be a

---

[1] See El-Masri, 'The Life of Shehu Usuman dan Fodio' (*J.H.S.N.*, vol. ii, no. 4, 1963, p. 435).

source of much political confusion in the attempts to establish the westward extent of the empire of dan Fodio during the nineteenth century.[1] Until the nineteenth century however, the Fulani settled peacefully among the existing Sudan states and did very little to attract attention to themselves generally. Lastly, there was the Fulani group popularly known as the Cow Fulani. This group took no interest in the religious and political upheavals which convulsed the Central Sudan. They were pastoralists and moved from place to place in search of good pasture. Political frontiers and alliances meant nothing to them. They therefore remained a political enigma in their encampments in Zaberma, Konni, Gobir, Kano, Katsina, Damagarim and Bornu.[2]

Another 'racial' group which contributed to the ethnic heterogeneity of the Central Sudan was the Tuareg, 'the people of the Veil'. The Tuareg constituted for centuries the terror of the caravan routes of the Sahara. When they moved into the centre of the Sahara, under the pressure of the Arabs, they partly absorbed the Hausa-speaking Gobirawa and drove the remainder south to the region now partly occupied by Sokoto.[3] The Tuareg, also called the Asbenawa (i.e. the people of Asben, or Air), were too warlike to lend themselves to a coherent political system, although at one time the groups recognized the suzerainty of the Sultan of Agades. It became traditional, however, to speak of Asben or Air as the proper country of the Tuareg. It should be mentioned that the term 'Tuareg' has no ethnic significance. In fact it is a term of opprobrium, and it is not known what precise ethnic groups originally made up the people who achieved notoriety in the Sudan. If the Tuareg had remained in their country in Air, they might not have become a source of ethnic and political confusion in the region traversed by the northern boundary. They had to live, and so Tuareg groups moved periodically south to settle, to trade or to plunder. In explanation of the

---

[1] Bovill, *Caravans of the Old Sahara*, 1933, pp. 223 f. Murdock, op. cit.; see p. 414 for the major Fulani concentrations.

[2] Hopen, *The Pastoral Fulbe Family in Gwandu*, 1958, pp. 2–3 and p. 15.

[3] Arnett, *Gazetteer of Sokoto Province*, 1920, p. 10. Rodd, *People of the Veil*, 1926, pp. 403–8.

Tuareg struggle for existence, it has been observed with substantial truth that

> There is a line beyond which the struggle for existence is too hard ... this is the condition of the Tuareg(s) of the south—a life of misery and frequent and always possible starvation; at best a diet of milk and such grasses as exist in the sand.[1]

In the circumstances of desert existence, it is easy to understand why the Tuareg could not confine themselves to Air. Thus in addition to occupying the region north of Sokoto, many Tuareg groups also settled temporarily or permanently in the Hausa states of Katsina and Kano. It will also be recalled that it was the Tuareg who made assault after assault against the Moroccan governors installed in Timbuktu and Gao on the Middle Niger. But it was in the Hausa states that large settlements of Tuareg came into existence. In Katsina, for example, the Tuareg called themselves the Kel Katchena (the people of Katsina). In any case, the wide dispersion of the Tuareg, like that of the Cow Fulani, completely ruled out the likelihood of the existence of specific political allegiance based on 'race' or on a precise territorial framework. The role played by the Tuareg in the political life of the Niger Sudan was admirably reflected in Dr Barth's description of the Tuareg as 'those inveterate enemies of well-organized communities'.[2]

The Kanuri linguistic zone lay to the east of Hausaland. The term 'Kanuri' does not describe the people of any particular state. The Kanuri originally comprised a clan of black Saharan nomads. The latter have also been described as Negroid Kushites. These nomads intermingled with the settled So peoples and thus gave rise to hybrid groups known as the Kanembu. In due course many Kanembu moved into the region south of Lake Chad, where many more So peoples were further absorbed to produce the people traditionally referred to as the Kanuri.[3] The Kanuri language gradually provided a basis for a measure of cultural unity embracing the

---

[1] R.G.S., vol. xxviii, 1906; see pp. 280 f. Also Rodd, op. cit., p. 39.

[2] Barth, op. cit., vol. ii, Appendix, pp. 660 f; also vol. iii, p. 10.

[3] Palmer, *Sudanese Memoirs*, vol. ii, p. 64. Palmer, *Gazetteer of Bornu Province*, pp. 9–12. *Harvard African Studies*, vol. x, 1932, pp. 14–15.

original Kanuri and the So peoples who accepted Kanuri. There were many So groups which retained their original language and were protected by marshes and rivers from being absorbed into the Kanuri complex like their kin located immediately north, south and west of Lake Chad. The Kotoko, the Buduma (Yedima) and the Musgu afford good examples of non-Kanuri groups which retained their separate identity. Even in the predominantly Kanuri zone of the Chad region, there were other indigenous groups which were not assimilated by the Kanuri, for instance, the Bedde and the Manga. It is clear therefore that the Chad formed an important centre of ethnic and cultural diffusion. The geographical position of the Chad and the lack of natural barriers which characterizes the region allowed the easy influx of peoples from the north and the east. The Shuwa Arabs provided a new 'racial' element in the population of the Kanuri linguistic zone. There were mixed populations of Kanuri, Shuwa Arab and Fulani in some places. The Arabs later played a great part in the slaving activities of Bornu and achieved wealth for themselves, and also influence in Bornu affairs. There were many occasions when they provided for the Bornu rulers much-needed military leadership. But did the Arabs regard themselves as organic members of the state? Dr Barth referred to them as 'a crowd of faithless Shuwa', and went on to show how at a critical moment in a war against Wadai, the Shuwa went over to the enemy and helped in the slaughter of the Kanuri.[1] None of the states which emerged in this zone possessed either ethnic or cultural homogeneity. No state contained a clearly defined unified people.

The So people, who occupied the region originally and had evolved a remarkable civilization of their own, did not found states. Apparently the So civilization was one that throve within the framework of walled towns.[2] It was therefore left to the immigrant desert nomads to lay the foundations for the states of Kanem, Bornu, Bulala, Bagirmi and Wadai which

---

[1] Palmer, *Gazetteer of Bornu Province;* see Introduction and pp. 19–22. Barth, op. cit., vol. ii, pp. 666–70.

[2] Lebeuf and Detourbet, *La Civilisation du Tchad*, 1950, pp. 176–80.

emerged in the region under consideration.[1] For the purposes of the present study, the important states were Kanem and Bornu. Kanem was founded when the nomad chieftaincy was transformed into a cohesive nucleus for the government of immigrant nomads and the settled So cultivators. Its expansion coincided with the increasing control of the eastern Saharan trade routes by the ruling Kanembu. While Kanem was flourishing, many Kanembu groups were drifting towards the fertile banks of the Yobe river and into the region which came to be known as Bornu. Then, in the fourteenth century, the Kanem ruling dynasty, tired of constant dynastic quarrels and the unending incursions of the Bulala,[2] transferred its seat of government from N'jimi to Bornu. In the latter place the foundations of an extensive empire were laid by a succession of remarkable rulers. Under ibn Dunama (1476–1503) the capital N'gazargama was built, and an effective administrative system emerged. Bornu influence and authority were increasingly extended westwards to Hausaland, and a number of Hausa states, including Kano, submitted to the necessity of paying tribute to Bornu. The most celebrated of the early rulers of Bornu was undoubtedly Idris Alooma (1570–1602). Under him, Bornu arms were carried triumphantly in all directions. Walled So towns were subdued. The Tuareg were crushingly defeated in a series of fierce battles. The Bulala menace to Kanem was temporarily checked. Islam became the state religion, and the first brick mosques made their appearance in many Bornu centres. The reign of Alooma was the period when the Bornu empire attained its widest territorial extent and its greatest prosperity and fame.[3] Administratively the Mai (the king), the Queen Mother and a supreme council of twelve were in control. Recipients of titles were kept in the capital, and were not allowed personally to administer the provinces and districts to which their titles theoretically assigned to them. Freedmen and eunuchs under the Mai

---

[1] Trimingham, op. cit., pp. 110 f.

[2] The Kanembu and the Bulala were related but rival lineages. See Trimingham, op. cit., p. 108.

[3] Lady Lugard, op. cit., pp. 279–81.

wielded effective power. The political organization was based on the characteristic feudal structure involving two basic categories of people. There were those of the Bornu region including vassal groups over which the Mai oppointed governors. There were also vassal peoples who retained their own rulers, language and culture. Thus, as in the western Sudan, Bornu had no strict frontiers. The empire was the type of dominion which left ample room for a fluid political situation. A great deal therefore depended on the dynamism of the Mai and his officials.

None of the successors of Idris Alooma appears to have had the ability to keep the frontiers of Bornu from fluctuating to the prejudice of the empire. Kanem was virtually surrendered to the Bulala. The Tuareg renewed their attacks on the northern regions of Bornu. From the south the Jukun carried their raids into Bornu territory. More and more Hausa states reasserted their complete independence and repudiated the payment of tribute to Bornu. The eastern states of Bagirmi and Wadai became increasingly insolent in their relations with Bornu. Within Bornu itself, the Bedde, who were under the direct control of the Galadima,[1] began a sort of pan-Bedde confederation which sought to re-establish the independence of the Bedde people. Towards the end of the eighteenth century Bornu had already declined considerably and had almost reached a stage of stagnation. It was during the reign of Mai Ahmad (1791–1808) that reference was made to the gathering political storm in verses which were translated by Palmer:[2]

> 'Verily a cloud has settled upon God's earth, a cloud
> so dense that escape from it is impossible
> . . . .
> as though it were time to set the world in order by
> preaching
> Alas! that I know all about the tongue of the fox.'

The storm forecast in the verses quoted above materialized in the convulsions which engulfed Hausaland and Bornu in the

---

[1] Governor of the western provinces.
[2] Palmer, *The Bornu Sahara and Sudan*, 1936, p. 52.

opening years of the nineteenth century. The resulting transformation in the political scene cannot but be a source of controversy for a long time. This study is concerned primarily with
a historical account of the rise and expansion of the Fulani
empire. It will serve no useful purpose to embark on inconclusive speculations about distinctions between religious and
political suzerainty. A brief examination of the structural
weaknesses will help, however, to explain the fluctuations
which characterized the empire as the nineteenth century slid
by. It is generally accepted that the Fulani jihad attained its
greatest prestige, religious and military, under dan Fodio and
his son Bello. Under the latter something like a territorial
framework became clearer. The best approach to the task of
establishing the extent of the empire seems to require firstly an
account of the political achievements of dan Fodio, his son,
and his brother; secondly, it is necessary to follow the subsequent fluctuations of the frontiers which were in part the
results of the internal structural weaknesses. The manner in
which the European agents who engaged in the boundary
controversy jumped to conclusions about the size of the Fulani
empire justifies the more discriminating study of the fortunes
of the empire attempted here. One example will suffice to
illustrate the point. Lugard claimed in 1904 that

> The influence of Sokoto extends from Bornu in the east to
> Timbuctu in the west, and as far as Agades in the Sahara.
> Throughout this vast area he [the Sokoto Sultan] is considered
> the religious and temporal chief, and no king is made and no war
> waged without his consent.[1]

This kind of assessment ignores completely the historical
realities of the Central Sudan during the nineteenth century.

Usuman dan Fodio belonged to the dark-skinned Torobe
who settled in the Hausa state of Gobir. Usuman was born in
1754, and after his studies he began as a roving preacher,
condemning the tendency of many Fulani Moslems to compromise with 'pagan' practices. He denounced also the 'unsuffer-
able' manner in which Fulani clerics were treated by 'pagan'

---

[1] R.G.S., vol. xxiii, 1904, p. 25.

Habe rulers. It was quite clear from his teaching that, like many other clerics before him, he was animated by a desire to establish a purified religion within the framework of a régime of Allah.[1] There were other clerics in Hausaland who thought the same way, and the news of successful jihads in the Western Sudan was not lost on them. Usuman's religious enthusiasm and his reputation as a scholar and teacher made it easy for him to gather disciples around himself. His town, Degel, became a sort of local 'Mecca' for Islam enthusiasts, Fulani and Hausa alike.

The first Hausa ruler to recognize the implications of the teaching and the peregrinations of Usuman dan Fodio in Gobir, Kebbi and Zanfara was the young Gobir king called Yunfa, who had been a pupil of Usuman. In Gobir, Usuman was beginning to behave like an 'over-mighty' subject, con-demning the enslavement of Moslems and even attempting to rescue them. Yunfa was determined to remain master in his own house. The king dispatched troops to arrest dan Fodio in Degel. The flight of the Fulani leader from the town on 21 February 1804 provided the local 'Hegira'.[2] It should also have been a warning to the Hausa rulers that the time had come for a co-ordinated effort to eliminate the Fulani menace. But true to their historical antecedents, the Hausa states went their separate ways. The king of Gobir indeed sent messages to the rulers of Katsina, Kano, Zegzeg and Daura to convey the warning that he, Yunfa, 'had neglected a small fire in his country until it had spread beyond his power to control. Having failed to extinguish it it had now burnt him.'[3] Although it was the slogan 'Islam in danger' which launched the Fulani jihad, Usuman dan Fodio's appeal to his followers had political and racial as well as religious implications. There is evidence to show that the Hausa rulers criminally under-rated the significance of the 'flight' from Degel.

The initial but crucial Gobir operations against the fanatical followers of the religious leader were haphazard and, in any case, hopelessly mismanaged. Meanwhile other Fulani leaders

---

[1] Trimingham, op. cit., pp. 195 f.   [2] Bovill, *Caravans*, pp. 223 f.
[3] Bello, op. cit., quoted p. 131.

among the scattered clans in the Niger Sudan, motivated partly by religious zeal and partly by political ambitions, sought and received the 'authorization' and the blessing of dan Fodio to embark on the overthrow of the 'pagan' rulers and to extend the religious movement. The result was that while Usuman and his brother, Abdullahi, were carving Sokoto and Gwandu out of the Hausa states of Gobir and Kebbi, other Fulani 'flag-bearers' were creating Fulani-dominated emirates on the ruins of former Hausa states and the western frontiers of Bornu. The original 'flag-bearers', of whom there are records, included: Umaru (Katsina), Suleiman (Kano), Mallam Musa (Zaria), Sambo (Hadeija), Adama (Adamawa), Dendo (Nupe), Abdu Alimi (Ilorin), Muhaman (Bagirmi), Gwoni (Bornu), Isiaku (Daura), Yakubu (Bauchi), Yero (Gombe), Zaki (Katagum).[1] In the early years of the jihad, however, everything depended on the outcome of the contest in the immediate neighbourhood of Gobir and Kebbi, where the Fulani were confronted by the combined forces of the Gobirawa, the Kebbawa and the Tuareg.

The battle for Alkalawa, the capital of Gobir, which occurred in 1805, was indeed the decisive event in the Fulani uprising. Yunfa and his allies were routed and the Gobir capital was razed to the ground. The news of the Fulani success against the most powerful Hausa state travelled like wildfire through the open country of the Central Sudan. Fulani leaders were almost everywhere carried into power on the crest of the resulting religious fervour and military prestige. The impact of the outcome of the battle of Alkalawa was admirably summarized by Bello:

> The Moslems in every part of the country were waiting to hear the result of the war with Alkalawa . . . the heathens were downcast, and their backbone broken.[2]

Sokoto, built for dan Fodio in 1809, became the capital of a

---

[1] Temple, O., *Notes on the Tribes*, 1922, pp. 549–50.
[2] Bello, op. cit., pp. 94–95.

Fulani empire which embraced new Fulani emirates super-
imposed on the former states. Some Hausa states disappeared,
for instance, Zanfara. As each Fulani leader attempted to
carve out his own emirate, new units appeared. Bauchi,
Gombe, Katagum, Missau, Keffi, Nasarawa, Lafia and so
forth were examples. On the whole the new leaders adopted
the Hausa state structure, already described, with its hierarchy of dignitaries and titles.

It would be wrong to imagine that the Fulani empire
embraced the whole of Hausaland or that it broke the backbone of all the Hausa dynasties. The northerly Hausa states of
Gobir, Kebbi and Katsina lost their capitals to the Fulani. At
first, too, they lost the greater part of their domains, but the
dynasties continued to exist. The latter founded new capitals
from which they carried on the war (intermittently, of course)
against the Fulani capitals of Sokoto, Gwandu and Katsina.
The second capital of Gobir was originally founded with the
blessing of Sokoto by a defecting cousin of the fugitive Habe
king of Gobir. The Gobirawa rallied under their legitimate
king and seized Sabon 'Birni, which then became the capital of
a dismembered Gobir state. Kebbi, the ancient Hausa stronghold against the ambitions of the Songhay rulers, lost its
capital Bernin 'Kebbi to the Fulani early in the jihad. The
Kebbi king moved west with many of his subjects to organize
a war of attrition against the Fulani capital of Gwandu. A new
and formidable Kebbawa capital emerged in Argungu which
remained intact until the arrival of the British imperialists.
The unsettled situation in the region north and west of the twin
Fulani capitals was fully acknowledged by Bello when he
wrote as follows:

In truth the Mallams of the Sudanese and Tuareg people who
followed their way of life assisted them in their hostile operations
against us. We had no supporters among the chiefs of these
countries because they stood in together and declared themselves against us, and made a mutual undertaking of their
intention to destroy us.[1]

---

[1] Ibid., p. 50; also see Arnett, op. cit., Introduction and pp. 5–12.

The ruling house of Hausa Katsina, like those of Gobir and Kebbi, refusing to submit to the Fulani, put up a determined struggle for the preservation of the independence of Katsina. The Fulani, however, had an able leader in Umaru Dallaji, who successfully established himself as the Emir of Katsina. The Hausa ruler of Katsina fled northwards to Dankama with as many as 39,000 Katsinawa, including all the nobility. The Habe ruler, Halidu, vowed to regain his ancestral capital from the Fulani. If he failed, he would take his life. According to Katsina traditions, Halidu did indeed fall into a well in 1807 after an abortive attempt to recapture Katsina.[1] His successors founded a new state called Maradi, the inhabitants of which 'could countenance nothing but war with the Fulani'. For the purpose of assessing the frontiers of the Fulani empire, two conclusions should be drawn from the foregoing. Habe rulers continued without interruption to reign over their reduced domains up to the arrival of Europeans. Their states were as well organized as the normal Sudanese states, and some of them acquired vassal states.

There was a clear distinction between the intransigent Hausa states and those which accepted the new order symbolized by Fulani rule. The Fulani emirates became fiefs. Apart from recognizing the spiritual leadership of Sokoto, the emirs paid annual tribute of slaves and produce to Sokoto. It may also be assumed that, at first, Sokoto also expected an occasional levy of soldiers from the emirates. She also had a say in the selection of successors to the emirates, usually from among the families of the first fief-holders. Usuman dan Fodio was more interested in religious reforms than in the political organization of the empire his leadership won for the Fulani. He retired from politics and, before his death, divided his empire between his son and his brother. Bello ruled from Sokoto the eastern provinces which included Kano, Daura, Zaria, Bauchi and other areas. Abdullahi controlled from Gwandu the western provinces of the empire, including Nupe, Yauri and Ilorin. The empire was loosely organized and there was therefore

---

[1] Palmer, *Sudanese Memoirs*, vol. iii, pp. 79–82. See also Hogben, *The Muhammadan Emirates of Nigeria*, 1930, footnote 1, p. 95.

considerable decentralization of government. Each province was ruled by an emir. Whether any of the emirs seriously recognized the existence of a central government is an open question. For example, the Emir of Nupe interpreted his relationship with Gwandu as follows:

> The Sultan of Stanboul is Head of the Mohammedan religion . . . After him was the Sultan of Sokoto. . . . Next to him, though nearly equal, was the Sultan of Gwandu, and after him the Emir of Nupe.[1]

It can be contended that, everything considered, a Fulani empire based on Sokoto and Gwandu continued to function after the death of Usuman dan Fodio. There were more or less recognizable ties, partly religious and partly political, which bound the provinces to the central governments. It must also be accepted that the empire did not include the whole of Gobir, Maradi and Kebbi. The latter states were not merely 'foci of rebellion',[2] but were indeed remnants of Hausa states which continued to be well organized and to have fluctuating frontiers with the Fulani empire.

There was no doubt that the Fulani effectively entrenched themselves in the heart of Hausaland. The northern and western extent of the empire alone became a subject of controversy, and in this respect Lugard's undiscriminating estimate of the empire should be borne in mind. The relations of the first Fulani rulers with the Tuareg rulers lent themselves to the subsequent exaggeration of the northern extent of the Fulani empire. The misinterpretation arose chiefly from ascribing political significance to the undoubted religious prestige which Sokoto enjoyed during the early decades of the nineteenth century. As regards the Tuareg, it will be recalled that the Tuareg population of Adar and their ruler had, in alliance with the Hausa of Gobir and Kebbi, fought the battles of Alwassa and Alkalawa against the Fulani. But in 1808 the Sultan of Tuareg Agades paid his famous visit to Usuman dan Fodio 'to receive his blessing and become his disciple. He did

---

[1] Confidential 5913, Report by Macdonald, p. 18.
[2] R.G.S., vol. xxiv, 1904, pp. 636 f. Trimingham, op. cit., pp. 202 f.

homage to Shehu . . . and acknowledged the truth of his mission'.[1] The only political result of the visit of the Agades Sultan, Mohammadu Bakiri, was an attempt to partition Adar, theoretically a vassal of Asben, into Sokoto and Agades spheres of influence. Before this arrangement could mean anything concrete, the Shehu of Sokoto advised the Agades Sultan to admonish the Adarawa to depose their Sarki (king). The people of Adar indeed complied, but within a year, they also deposed another ruler appointed from Agades. Mustafa, the Agades-sponsored ruler, lost his precarious hold on the Adarawa because the latter wished above everything else to continue their alliance with Gobir and Kebbi. Another Sultan of Agades, Kanna, followed his predecessor's example in admiring the Shehu of Sokoto. He promised that 'If you call for me and my followers to make a holy war upon those who quarrel with you, we will answer your call and come and help you'.[2] The Sultan of Agades proceeded to assume the new title of Sarkin Musulimi Kanna. These proceedings would suggest Sokoto suzerainty over Air.

During Bello's reign in Sokoto, the Sarkin Air found himself beset with domestic turmoil. He naturally appealed to Bello, and the latter's reply should certainly dispose of any assumption that Sokoto had political pretensions to that Tuareg region:

> It is your duty . . . both yours and that of your followers to command your people to act in accordance with the Book . . . . If, indeed, you have any power over the people, you should drive them out from among you. If you have not any power then you should rise up and flee and leave their towns, and go to those towns which are Mohammedan . . . you know best your own affairs, since you know more about them than we do. The master of the house knows what is in his house.[3]

Bello did not claim that Sokoto was the master of Asben or Air. The relations between Sokoto and the Tuareg of Air remained

---

[1] Bello, op. cit., pp. 95–7. [2] Ibid., p. 120.
[3] Ibid., pp. 120–1.

indeed friendly, and no official support was given by Air to the relentless war waged by Kebbi, Gobir and Maradi. Friendship was one thing, the feudal subordination of Air to Sokoto was quite another.[1]

Another region of considerable confusion for an attempt to establish the extent of the Sokoto–Gwandu empire was the Middle Niger neighbourhood. As we have seen, many sections of the Fulani Torobe clans were settled along this portion of the river. The news of the triumph of Shehu Usuman in Hausaland inspired the local Fulani to rally round local leaders. The best known of the latter was Ahmadu Labo (or Mohammed Lebo), who organized a local jihad near Segu. The outcome was the overthrow of the 'pagan' dynasty of Māsina and the establishment of a Fulani theocracy. It was not long before the city of Timbuktu fell to the Māsina Fulani leader. It was for a long time assumed that Lebo was one of the 'flag-bearers' of Usuman dan Fodio, and that the Fulani conquests in the Middle Niger region, including Timbuktu, formed a feudal part of the Fulani empire in Hausaland.[2] All that took place by way of association between dan Fodio and Ahmadu was an exchange of letters in which they congratulated each other on their successes. The next formidable ruler of the Māsina region, al-hajj 'Umar, established a kind of dynastic link by marrying a daughter of Sultan Bello. For the rest, 'Umar carried on his own campaigns, which reduced that part of the Sudan to a state of virtual anarchy. 'Umar was killed before he had had time to organize his conquests into a coherent state.[3] His successors, who had to deal with French encroachments, fought and died without seeking or receiving aid from Sokoto or Gwandu. Even before the arrival of the French, Timbuktu often changed hands between the Fulani and the Tuareg, and it was not for nothing that Dr Barth described Timbuktu as 'politically unstable'. Any suggestion,

---

[1] Palmer, *Notes on Some Asben Records*, pp. 397–400. See also Tilho, op. cit., vol. ii, p. 480.

[2] See Fage, *Introduction to the History of West Africa*, map, p. 145. Murdock, op. cit., see map, p. 414. Bovill, *The Golden Trade of the Moors*, 1958, pp. 228–31.

[3] Trimingham, op. cit., pp. 162–5.

therefore, that Sokoto influence, let alone authority, extended to Timbuktu during the nineteenth century lacks historical validity.

The region immediately west of the famous trading centre of Jega on the Sokoto River, including Illo, Gaya, Say and Gurma, was presumably part of the empire of Gwandu. Dr Barth's enumeration of the provinces subject to Gwandu certainly included this region. The first ruler of Gwandu, Abdullahi, was undoubtedly a resolute warrior, and early in the jihad he led or organized Fulani thrusts not only into Dendi but also into Zerma. Gomba in Borgu territory was seized by Gwandu. Illo was for a time under Fulani control. The activities of the Fulani in the Songhay provinces of Dendi and Gurma were a story of mingled success and failure.[1] The capital of Dendi, Yelu, was captured in 1808, plundered, and then abandoned. Gaya, the trade entrepôt, was permanently controlled by Gwandu. The subsequent efforts of the Dendi chief, Fodi, to liberate the whole of Dendi were directed against the main target, Gaya, which was strategically situated to control the Dallol Foga and Dallol Mauri. The important centres of Gurma, including Liptako, Botu and Dore, had always been centres of Fulani and Hausa concentration because they were important trading stations. 'Fada-n-Gurma', which Dr Barth visited, was in fact the Hausa name for the Gurma capital. The region of Gurma was a politically fluid one. When the Fulani seized centres which lay on the trade routes it would be wrong to assume that they thereby added a province to the Gwandu empire. In any case, the prestige enjoyed by the Fulani during the opening years of the jihad, which cowed the local rulers into acquiescence, soon evaporated. The Gurma and Dendi chiefs recovered from their temporary stupefaction and made a determined effort to reduce the Fulani strongholds in their territories to miserable enclaves. Dr Barth's description of the state of affairs in Dore represents reasonably accurately the general situation west of Gaya throughout the nineteenth century.

The political state of the country was at the present moment

---

[1] Trimingham, op. cit., p. 202 and footnote.

worse than its material condition. The disorder and anarchy were
such as to make it appear as if there were no government at all.[1]

Other observers attributed the political confusion prevailing
in the region to the Fulani '. . . that infamous tribe of robbers
and traders in human flesh, who after laying waste the Sudan,
had, under pretext of a holy war, brought desolation, famine,
slavery and death to the peaceful if somewhat degraded races
of the Niger basin'.[2] Whoever were to blame for the state of
affairs, the point that should be borne in mind is the extreme
difficulty of determining the political frontier of the Sokoto–
Gwandu empire in the region.

The situation within the traditional frontiers of Hausaland,
where it might be expected that the Fulani could stabilize the
new political frontiers, presents its own problems. Bello, who
succeeded Usuman dan Fodio to rule the eastern empire of
Sokoto, was interested in the political consolidation of the
empire. Only Usuman and a few of his original followers were
animated by genuine religious fervour which had injected an
element of fanaticism in battle. Then the fruits of victory began
to undermine the religious conviction which had produced
success in many directions. The jihad degenerated into mere
slave-raiding, which in its turn produced destructive wars.
Thus when Clapperton visited Sokoto in 1821–2 and again in
1825–6, he noted the loss of military ardour on the part of the
Fulani rulers.[3] It was this loss of martial and religious zeal
which laid the empire open to ruin within and assault from
without. The effects of the latter are of importance in assessing
the effective northern and north-western frontiers of the
Fulani empire centred on Sokoto.

The Fulani neighbours whose political relations with Sokoto
are relevant to this study included, from east to west, Maradi,
Gobir, Konni and Adar. As regards the frontiers of Gwandu,

---

[1] Barth, op. cit., vol. iv, pp. 215–7; vol. v, Appendix, p. 538. Also the
Deutsche Kolonial Zeitung, 29 June 1895 (Report by Lieut. Von Karnap).
And *Politique Colonial*, 15 June 1895.

[2] Bell (Translation), *French Enterprise in Africa*, 1898, p. 421.

[3] Denham and Clapperton, *Narrative of Travels*, 1928, vol. ii, p. 378; see
also Appendix no. xii, p. 451. Bovill, *Caravans*, p. 231.

Kebbi and her vassals Arewa and Zaberma are important. Just before the arrival of Dr Barth in the Central Sudan, the independent Katsinawa were ruled by Umaru dan Mari (called Damonari by Tilho). He was succeeded by Binoni (1848–53) and dan Mahedi (1853–7). Thus during and after Dr Barth's visit, the Habe in Maradi were not a disorganized rabble. They were ably led by kings set on recovering their ancient capital, now in Fulani hands. The defence of the frontiers of Fulani Katsina was left entirely to the local emir because the suzerain in Sokoto was himself up to his neck in trouble with his own frontiers. Barth, with his characteristic shrewdness and objectivity, noted that the region of Gazawa was important in the struggle between Habe Katsina and Fulani Katsina. The region between Gazawa and the Katsina Fulani capital was also disputed territory, 'no one being responsible'.[1] The region around Katsina was itself exposed to regular and unchecked incursions from Maradi. No assistance came to Fulani Katsina from Fulani Kano. Writing scathingly about the Fulani in Kano, Dr Barth observed that

> The Fulbe . . . by obtaining possession of wealth and comfort, their warlike character has been greatly impaired, and the Fellani-n-Kano have become notorious for their cowardice throughout the whole of Negroland.[2]

In such a state of affairs, the northern frontier of Fulani Katsina would appear to have lain not far from the very gates of the capital.

The frontier between Sokoto and Habe Gobir was in a worse condition than that between Katsina and Maradi. It was with special reference to the northern frontier of Sokoto that Barth spoke of 'the lamentable condition in which I found this . . . kingdom'.[3] Aliu Baba, who was one of the sons of Bello and reigned from 1842 to 1859, had none of his father's warlike qualities. Under him, the provincial emirs enjoyed unlimited powers and he could not enforce any of the rights

---

[1] Barth, op. cit., vol. ii, pp. 84–146.   [2] Ibid.
[3] Ibid., vol. iv, pp. 154–67; vol. v, pp. 337–42.

which traditionally belonged to the suzerain. The Gobirawa and the Tuareg dominated the trade routes leading to the capital. On the whole Aliu could do no more than keep the Gobirawa from overrunning his second seat, Wurno. The king of Gobir, Yacubu, was during his reign from 1836 to 1858 on the offensive against Sokoto. He raided in all directions into Sokoto from his capital Sabon 'Birni. Barth noted the dread which the Fulani had for the warlike king of Gobir and could not help referring to the Fulani leaders as 'these effeminate conquerors'. The frontier between Gobir and Sokoto was therefore at best a no-man's-land politically.

The situation to the north-west and west of Sokoto was a rather complicated one. The Kebbawa had built a new capital in Argungu, a place situated between Sokoto and Gwandu (the twin capitals of the Fulani empire). The Habe king of Kebbi, Yakubu Nabame (1849–54), maintained the Habe tradition of fighting the Fulani.[1] His allies were the Songhay vassals inherited by Kebbi, Arewa and Zaberma. The latter had reasons to regard the Fulani as the common enemy. The king of Argungu and his allies carried on a war of destruction and not of political consolidation. Their objectives seem not to have included the possibility of recovering Kebbi territory seized by the Fulani in the early years of the jihad. The Sultan of Gwandu, Haliru, seemed quite incapable of any military action. Barth felt really sorry for the state of affairs in Gwandu. The irony of Barth's observations was that he enumerated what he considered to be the wealthy provinces of Gwandu to include the eastern half of Kebbi, Mauri, Zaberma, Dendina and so forth, and then concluded that

> As for the town of Gando (Gwandu) itself . . . the insecurity of the neighbourhood was so great that it was not possible, at least in a northerly direction, to proceed many yards from the wall. Several times during my stay the alarm was given that the enemy was approaching . . . the enemy being established in several strong places at scarcely half a day's journey distance.[2]

---

[1] Hogben, *Emirates*, pp. 105 f. Arnett, *Gazetteer of Sokoto Province*, p. 9.
[2] Barth, op. cit., vol. iv, pp. 201–3; vol. v, p. 328.

On the basis of the clear evidence provided by Dr Barth, it is reasonable to suggest that the frontiers of the Sokoto–Gwandu empire to the north and to the west did not lie far from the Fulani strongholds of Katsina, Wurno and Gwandu. There was therefore no historical justification for Lugard's assessment of the extent of the empire, although one should bear in mind that Lugard had diplomatic reasons for the assessment he made in 1904.

The picture, as left in Barth's accounts, of the political situation which prevailed in respect of the frontiers of Sokoto and Gwandu has been emphasized for two reasons. In the first place, it was the most objective available during the nineteenth century. Towards the end of that century, the Sudan swarmed with European visitors who interpreted the local state of affairs in a manner that suited the diplomatic requirements of their different countries. In the second place, the situation seen by Barth remained more or less unchanged from 1855 to the end of the century. It is true that Sokoto and Gwandu produced one or two energetic rulers who assumed the offensive against their restless neighbours. For instance, Haliru of Gwandu was killed in 1859 fighting a coalition of the Kebbawa, Arewana and Zaberawa. This disaster was followed by the famous treaty between Gwandu and the ruler of Argungu, Toga. The treaty included the remarkable stipulation that the Kebbawa should keep the towns held by them at the time the treaty was signed in 1866. Some of the towns, although originally belonging to Kebbi, were menacingly near Gwandu. The peace, however, lasted only eight years.[1] In the 1880s, Gwandu and Sokoto co-operated militarily and carried out very extensive expeditions. To the north of Sokoto, Umaru, the Sultan of Sokoto from 1881 to 1891, led his army into Konni, but he was routed later when he attempted to assault the Gobir capital, Sabon 'Birni. It can be said therefore that the frontiers remained fluid during the last decade of the nineteenth century. The Middle Niger was completely dominated by the Tuareg. The independent Gobir, Kebbi and Maradi Habe rulers harassed the frontiers with impunity. Kano was indeed often

---

[1] Arnett, op. cit., p. 17; Hogben, op. cit., pp. 105 f.

subjected to raids by Zinder. The end of the century indeed saw the almost complete decadence of the Fulani empire.[1] When European agents arrived, they found Samma ruling at Argungu, Nassara at Gobir, and dan Kata at Maradi.[2]

It is now time to turn to the north-eastern section of the international zone in order to see how the events of the nineteenth century affected the indigenous frontiers of Bornu, a state of great antiquity in the region south of Lake Chad. Until the Fulani threat in the first decade of the nineteenth century, Bornu with its widespread system of vassal states lacked energy, but there prevailed relative stability and peace within the borders. The ruling clans and the Arabs had grown rich by raiding and enslaving Negro populations which surrounded them. These slaves supplied the needs of 'an indolent aristocracy in an arid country'.[3] The rigours of Islam had long been replaced by a veneer of conformity. Under the indolent Mai Ahmed, an unworthy descendant of Idris of the sixteenth century, Bornu temporarily succumbed under the impact of the Fulani jihad. The Fulani in Bornu were stirred up. In the western province of Bornu they carved out the Emirate of Hadeija, and then embarked on a full-blooded invasion of Bornu. In 1808 the Bornu capital N'gazargamu was captured, and the king was in full flight. Fortunately for Bornu, the Fulani victory was not driven home because many of the Fulani contingents were more interested in booty than in laying the foundations for a régime of clerics. In Bornu's extremity a saviour appeared in the person of a Kanembu cleric named El Kanemi, who could rally Kanembu as well as Shuwa Arabs to the defence of Bornu. In 1811 the Bornu capital was again captured by the Fulani and the Mai fled eastwards. Once again El Kanemi came to the rescue, but this time he stayed to found both a new dynasty and a new Bornu capital.[4] The Fulani never again seriously

---

[1] Trimingham, op. cit., p. 205.

[2] Tilho, op. cit., vol. ii, pp. 472–80; pp. 456 f. Hopen, op. cit., pp. 15–16; Lugard, *Annual Report*, Northern Nigeria, 1902.

[3] Palmer, *Gazetteer of Bornu Province*, pp. 19–20.

[4] Bello, op. cit., pp. 79–87; Palmer, *The Bornu Sahara*, pp. 258–68.

menaced Bornu, being apparently content with the additional emirate of Katagum carved out of Bornu's western vassal states.

The new capital built by El Kanemi was Kukawa, from which he wielded effective authority, leaving court ceremonial to the native Mai. The supersession of the Sef dynasty by El Kanemi inevitably weakened the hold of the upstart dynasty over the Bornu ruling clans that had formerly been associated with the rulers of Bornu. The Mai did not for his part accept his empty and mocking status without protest. He sought alliances with Wadai and Bagirmi in order to retrieve his former position. His intrigues ultimately embroiled El Kanemi in a protracted quarrel with the rulers of Wadai and Bagirmi. El Kanemi's energy was at first occupied in reorganizing the Bornu state. This exercise was in no way revolutionary. Although he made himself absolute ruler and appointed as his lieutenants men who were dependent on him for their elevation, Bornu retained its feudal features. There was a portion of Bornu, Bilād Kukawa, ruled directly by El Kanemi's men, and there were the vassal states which paid tribute. The vassal states to the west and north of Bornu included Bedde, Munio, Manga, Gummel, Damagarin (Zinder) and Kanem. To the south of Lake Chad were the petty native chieftaincies of Logon, Kuseri, N'gala, Mandara and so forth which were no more than a Bornu preserve for slave-hunting. To the east of the Chad lay the states of Bagirmi and Wadai, which acknowledged a vague sort of subservience to Bornu.[1] It is the history of these peripheral states that is extremely important in determining the effective frontiers of Bornu under El Kanemi and his successors.

The direct western frontier with the Fulani may, for the purposes of this study, be ignored. It may however be mentioned that Bornu never recovered Hadeija and Katagum from the Fulani. The relations between Bornu and her eastern neighbours were marked by the ups and downs of military success and defeat. Denham in 1824 watched one of these wars

---

[1] See Trimingham, op. cit., pp. 212 f. And Benton, *The Sultanate of Bornu*, 1913, p. 40 and attached map for the appanages of Bornu.

in the famous battle of Ngala.[1] El Kanemi had too many other preoccupations to concentrate effort in the east. Bornu virtually lost Wadai. In Bagirmi the curious situation developed in which Bagirmi paid tribute to both Bornu and Wadai. Shortly after the assertion of independence by Wadai, Kanem was also wrested from Bornu by the Tuareg. In the north-west, however, El Kanemi was able to chastise rebellious Zinder and Manga. There is evidence of a fascinating example of boundary making in a letter written by El Kanemi to Bello of Sokoto:

> We profess the same religion, and it is not fitting that our subjects should make war on each other. Between our two kingdoms are the 'pagan' Bedde tribes, on whom it is permissible to levy contribution: let us respect this limit: what lies to the east of their country shall be ours: what lies to the west shall be yours. As for Muniyo, Damagaram and Daura, they will continue to be vassals of the Sultan of Bornu, who in return will surrender to you all his claims to Gobir and Katsina.[2]

Umar succeeded his father, El Kanemi, in 1835 and reigned till 1880. He was visited by many European travellers, Barth, Vogel, Rohlfs and Nachtigal. They all left on record their impressions of the state of affairs in Bornu. We gather from these writings that Umar had a standing army of 1000 foot and 1000 cavalry, armed with guns, and about 3000 men armed with spears and bows. He could also count on levies provided by the provinces and by the Shuwa Arabs. It is however to Barth's shrewd observations that we must turn for the posture of affairs during the middle years of the nineteenth century. There were specific officials appointed to guard the frontiers of Bornu. For instance, the governor of the Yobe River had the special responsibility of holding down the Tuareg from the north. During Barth's visit he noted that the towns bordering on Lake Chad to the north-west, including Barrua, bought peace by paying tribute to Tuareg freebooters. He conferred

---

[1] Denham and Clapperton, op. cit., vol. i, pp. 207 and 222–3. Barth, op. cit., vol. iii, p. 7.
[2] Palmer, *The Bornu Sahara*, quoted p. 269; also Tilho, op. cit. vol. ii, quoted pp. 362–3.

on the region in the neighbourhood of Barrua and north of the Yobe the peculiar designation of a 'political quarantine station'.[1] It was therefore not for nothing that Barth found himself 'plunged into sad reflections on the fate of this once splendid empire of Kanem'. The civil war which involved Umar and his brother on the one hand, and Umar and the surviving member of the Sef dynasty on the other, did not help to arrest the shrinking of the frontiers of Bornu. Under Umar the tendency on the part of vassal Zinder to assert its independence and even to dominate the outlying principalities of Munio, Gummel and Machena gathered momentum. Bornu found less and less energy to cope with the rebellious vassals of the north-west. Barth concluded his reflections on Bornu with an observation which was destined to prove a true prophesy: 'Time will show whether Bornu is again to flourish under this dynasty or whether it has to undergo another revolution'.[2] During the closing years of Umar's reign Bornu was in decline. Umar more and more confined himself to religious speculations and allowed pleasure-loving favourites to exercise ineffective authority. There was no disposition to safeguard the integrity of Kanuri Bornu, let alone to rally forces to assert Bornu authority over the frontier provinces. Kanem fell under the suzerainty of Wadai. Zinder and the north-western vassal state practically ceased to have any political relations with Kukawa.[3]

The successors of Umar—Abu Bakr (1880–84), Ibrahim (1884–5), Hashim (1885–93)—were utterly incompetent. The evidence of the records of Rohlfs (1866), Nachtigal (1870) and Monteil (1892) indicates that when, in 1893, Rabeh[4] arrived from the eastern Sudan, Bornu was ripe for dissolution. There

---

[1] Barth, op. cit., vol. iii, pp. 36–47.

[2] Ibid., vol. ii, p. 671; see also Nachtigal, *Sahara und Sudan 1879–1881*, vol. ii, pp. 712–26.

[3] Trimingham, op. cit., p. 210.

[4] Rabeh, the son of a slave woman, rose in the army of Zubeir Pasha from a mere recruit to one of the Pasha's chief lieutenants. In 1878 he left the eastern Sudan with an armed following and began a life of adventure which took him to Bornu in 1893. (See C.O. 537/11, Inclosure 1 in I.D.W.O. to F.O., 21 December 1898.)

is a description of Bornu and her people at the close of the nineteenth century which is worth quoting because it helps to explain why an empire of antiquity and former splendour became leaderless and incapable of defending any frontiers. Jackson writes as follows:

> The people of Bornu are cheerful, indolent, fond of food and clothes, and not very keen about their religion. They like military display, martial music, and waving of spears, but it is doubtful if there is much good fighting stuff among them.[1]

The state religion, which had animated the political activities of El Kanemi, and to a smaller extent those of Umar, became by the end of the century a mere formality. Bornu was convulsed with internal problems which undermined the peace and stability of the empire. The Galadima behaved more and more as an independent ruler. The situation was not unlike that of the mid-eighteenth century summarized by Urvoy.[2] A worse fate indeed was to come. The hollow edifice of the Bornu empire collapsed, and the last independent Shehu of Bornu, Kiari, was executed by Rabeh in 1893. Kukawa, the once proud queen of the Central Sudan, was reduced to a melancholy heap of ruins. Zinder, the remaining important vassal of Bornu, did not come to the aid of the Shehu. As a matter of fact, she now confirmed her independence and tightened her hold on two other vassal states—Gummel and Machena. The disruption which overtook Bornu naturally complicates the problem of assessing the effects of the colonial boundary on the indigenous political order.

The foregoing will have shown that during the nineteenth century the Central Sudan was not tidily divided into the Fulani and Bornu empires. There were indeed other states, some of which enjoyed a status of quasi-independence. None of the states was ethnically homogeneous, primarily because a region which lacked natural barriers lent itself to extreme ethnic and cultural diffusion. There are in addition three other

---

[1] R.G.S., vol. xxvi, 1905; see Jackson, 'The Anglo-German Boundary Expedition in Nigeria, 1903'.

[2] Urvoy, *Histoire de l'Empire du Bornou*, Paris, 1949, p. 86.

considerations which bedevil any attempt to demarcate the frontiers of the states discussed in this chapter, quite apart from the frontier fluctuations resulting from internal weakness or external pressure. These considerations, which include trade, slave-raiding and religion, will also show the unwisdom of any excessive tendency to attach to the indigenous frontiers the conception of separation or reverence which properly belongs to modern boundaries. In the first place, the structural same-ness of the Central Sudan, which was partly responsible for the ill-defined ethnic frontiers and hardly contributed to political stability, was nonetheless conducive to trade. It is quite difficult today to realize how important the desert routes were, as arteries of trade and cultural diffusion, before the first decade of the twentieth century. The celebrated caravan routes from North Africa to the Sudan made the Sahara desert a close human link rather than the human 'divide' it appears to be today.[1] When Barth described Kano as 'the garden of Central Africa', he had in mind the commercial importance of Kano to all and sundry, whether they were Hausa or Tuareg or Kanuri. It has been claimed that it was the determination of the Kano Hausa not to ruin or prejudice their trade which explains the easy submission of Kano to the Fulani. The Hausa cared little who their masters were and were utterly indifferent to political frontiers as long as they were allowed peacefully to manufacture and peddle their trade goods.[2] The Hausa were ubiquitous traders.

No state in the Niger Sudan was economically self-sufficient. The more extreme the desert or semi-desert conditions, the thinner was the line between starvation and plenty. The Tuareg had to be on the move all the time, and as Bovill put it,

The necessity for trade, which transcended all considerations of race and creed and politics, had to be satisfied and it seems that

---

[1] *Les Grandes Voies Maritimes dans le Monde, XV–XIX Siècles*, Paris, 1965. See Anene, *Liaison and Competition between Sea and Land Routes . . . The Central Sudan and North Africa*, pp. 191–207.

[2] Barth, op. cit., vol. ii, p. 104 and p. 126. See also Bovill, *The Golden Trade*, pp. 220–3.

the twelfth parallel afforded exceptionally favourable advantages for the growth of the necessary entrepôts.[1]

Several examples can be given to show how completely the peoples of the Central Sudan divorced trade from politics. The caravan through the famous Bilma salt region was under the political control of the negroid Tebu of Jibesti, the bitter enemies of the Tuareg of Air. Raids and counter-raids characterized their political relations. Yet, in spite of mutual political hostility, the annual salt caravan to and from Bilma, followed by the famous journey into Hausaland, appeared to be the most regularized aspect of life among the Tuareg of Air. In Hausaland the Tuareg traders disposed of their salt and dates, engaged in transport work for many months, invested their earnings in grain, cotton cloth, sugar, snuff, Kola nuts and so forth, and returned to Asben when the rains came. Back home they had barely three months to take advantage of the fresh pasture before making preparations for the following year's routine.[2] At the height of the jihad, Tuareg and Hausa traders were welcome to Hausaland, whether or not the Fulani were at war with the Tuareg and with the intransigent Habe states. The trade routes were not of course always safe, and it was not an uncommon event for caravans to comprise Tuareg, Fulani, Hausa and Arab merchants who, technically, belonged to states of war with one another. The local rulers were as anxious as the merchants themselves that the entrepôts, often the capitals of states or provinces, should remain centres of peaceful and lively trade. The local chief afforded security, and for this service the merchants paid a tax which was often wrongly described as tribute. The payment of a trade tax has therefore been a source of confusion in interpreting the political relationships of the Central Sudan states.

When Joseph Thomson paid his historic visit to Sokoto in 1885, his sojourn at Jega, an important trade centre, revealed to him a 'novel' picture of Hausaland. He noted the 'throbbing rush of commercial life, [which] burst upon them with all the

---

[1] Bovill, *Caravans*, p. 255. Lugard (Lady), op. cit., p. 263.
[2] Barth, op. cit., vol. i, p. 339; Rodd, op. cit., pp. 382–93; *Colonial Reports—Annual*, no. 409, Northern Nigeria, 1902; Bovill, *Caravans*, p. 238.

astonishing effect of a transformation scene'. He also noted articles of trade from Tripoli, Morocco, Senegal, Sierra Leone, Lagos and so forth. Continuing his observations, Thomson attempted to identify the traders:

> The travellers, by the way, were no less interesting—the warlike Mohammedan Fellani, the vivacious and more simply clothed Hausa, the fierce-looking, spear-armed Tuareg Bedouins from the Sahara, with other types mingling and passing in bewildering variety.[1]

It was natural enough for Thomson to conclude that Sokoto politically dominated the Tuareg and everybody else. He probably would have found the same type of assembly in Kanuri or Songhay trade centres. There were, as was to be expected, many occasions when local rulers seized enemy traders and confiscated their merchandise. These confiscations were as much a matter of royal whim as of state policy. War conditions also periodically disrupted trade routes and paralysed the economic life of the trade centres. The point, however, is that in the Central Sudan, merchants tended to be internationalists, indifferent to the political fortunes of states and apparently unaware of any special obligations to the states that happened to be their own. It is of interest to recall that when the Sultan of Agades visited Sokoto to seek the Shehu's blessings, Bello, the heir to the Sokoto throne, made a special point of asking the guest to 'throw open for us the roads'.[2] It is probable that it was the Fulani control of the trade centres of the Niger bend that partly contributed to the wrong assumption that the Sokoto–Gwandu empire was extensive in that direction.

Slave-raiding, even more than trade, was disruptive of political allegiance and frontier stability in the Niger Sudan. It should be borne in mind that here trade, tribute, and even domestic establishments were inextricably bound up with slavery and slave-hunting. There was no region of equal size in Africa, or indeed in the world, where the slave trade during the

---

[1] Rev. J. B. Thomson, *Joseph Thomson (African Explorer)*, 1896, p. 155.
[2] Bello, op. cit., pp. 120–1; Arnett, op. cit., p. 29.

nineteenth century flourished so fully. Local traditions suggest that Katsina sent 1000 slaves, Adamawa 10,000 slaves annually to Sokoto as tribute. Barth recorded that Bagirmi paid an annual tribute of '100 ordinary male slaves, 30 handsome female slaves' to Wadai, and 100 slaves to Bornu.[1] Bornu claimed the Logon and Musgu petty states as vassals, because they provided slaves, not because Bornu was interested in establishing and maintaining the south-eastern frontiers of her empire. Her objection to Adamawa encroachments on Mandara was primarily because the Fulani from Adamawa also raided for slaves and so depleted Bornu supplies. In such a situation it would have been impossible to indicate a frontier between Bornu and Adamawa. The distinguished clerics of Sokoto and Bornu appear to have attached more importance to slavery than to the need for defining more precisely their frontiers. El Kanemi's letter to Bello, already quoted, suggested the whole Bedde country as a frontier in which both sides could raid for slaves at will. When the Fulani jihad deteriorated, Fulani military activities were thinly disguised slaving expeditions, often against 'pagan' and Hausa towns situated within the Fulani frontiers and others which lay between Fulani strongholds. The Bornu and the Fulani political areas were as a consequence subject to nearly 'all the evils of a perpetual civil war'.[2] It is difficult to imagine that the Bedde, the Musgu and the other 'pagans' within and on the periphery of the Sudan states regarded themselves as patriotic members of any of the organized states.

The confusion caused by language, 'race', trade, slave-raiding, and most important, physical monotony, helped to produce what has been called 'the vagaries of desert politics'. Here would appear a justification for the hardly complimentary observation by a German traveller that the

[The] Negro is entirely deficient in public spirit and other political virtues. In the same degree as the idea of the state is

---

[1] Barth, op. cit., vol. iii, pp. 281–305 and pp. 436–43. Lugard, see R.G.S., vol. xxiii, 1904, p. 7. Robinson, *Hausaland*, 1896, p. 128.

[2] R.G.S., vol. viii, 1896; Robinson, 'The Hausa Territories', pp. 207–8.

foreign to him, he lacks also the sense of patriotism and loyalty to a dynasty.[1]

The prejudiced German should have sought explanation in the conditions under which political life operated in the Niger Sudan during the nineteenth century. Language was not a factor in differentiating political allegiance. Islamized Hausa and Islamized 'pagan', in alliance with the 'town' Fulani, fought 'pagan' Hausa. The 'Cow' Fulani settled where they could find peace and pasture, irrespective of political frontiers. The Tuareg traded and settled with, or plundered, political allies and enemy alike. The Shuwa Arabs in Bornu fought for or against Bornu dynasties according as the situation appeared to open possibilities of wealth and plunder. Moslem Fulani fought Moslem Kanuri. States wedged in between powerful neighbours often paid tribute to both. The situation was one of unparalleled complexity. Yet, in spite of the prevailing confusion, trade caravans of Arab, Kanuri, Fulani and Hausa went on doing what their forefathers had always done— buying and selling their wares in such centres as Kuka, Zinder, Kano, Katsina, Gaya and Jega, when the routes were not too dangerous. Divergent linguistic, ethnic and religious groups were united under the political systems which functioned in the Niger Sudan, but not because the groups felt themselves one and wished to be one.[2] Then as the rulers became progressively degenerate, the artificial political structures they ruled as states or empires tended to dissolve. Vassal units hived off when they could. The inevitable result of all the factors discussed above was the perpetual fluctuation or fluidity (and often the non-existence) of 'indigenous' political frontiers in the boundary zone being considered in the present chapter.[3] As *The Obligations of Princes* shrewdly observed, 'Times of alarm are not like times of safety'.[4] When Denham

---

[1] Benton, op. cit., quotes Herr Lippert in Appendix V.

[2] Westermann, *The Africa of Today*, 1934, p. 160. Vandeleur, *Campaigning*; see Introduction by Goldie, xxi.

[3] East and Moodie, *The Changing World*, pp. 46–47.

[4] Sheikh Muhammad al Maghili, *The Obligations of Princes*, written between 1492 and 1503. See also Kumm, *The Sudan*, 1907, p. 34.

graphically described the Central Sudan as 'in a sense a new world . . . where semi-Arabized potentates went a-warring with mail-clad knights, and powerful Barons brought their contingent of retainers to assist their liege lord in his campaign of plunder and conquest',[1] he painted a picture which mocked the political paralysis encountered by Europeans at the end of the nineteenth century.

The British and the French governments began the business of partitioning the Niger Sudan in 1890. A provisional international boundary came into existence when, in August, Britain and France made an arrangement generally described as the Say–Barrua Line. A straight line was not intended since it was to be 'drawn in such manner as to comprise in the sphere of action of the Niger Company all that fairly belongs to the Kingdom of Sokoto'. The arrangement had seemed clear to all concerned. The leading French newspapers accepted the view expressed by *République Française* that 'the line . . . places the kingdoms of . . . Sokoto and Bornu, the richest and most populous parts of the Soudan, within the spheres of the British possessions'.[2] Under normal circumstances, the final boundary agreement should have provoked no controversy. Events decreed otherwise. To understand what appear, in retrospect, as senseless and extraordinary arguments, it must be realized that the simple 1890 Declaration bore in its very naïvety seeds of dissension. There were also other factors, most extraneous, which helped to determine the nature of the Anglo–French controversy and influenced the final result. In the first place, the French and the British governments presupposed the existence of an ascertainable frontier in a region where peripheral zones of varying width, now occupied and now deserted, were the only frontiers that separated warring and not particularly distinct states. The extent of the Sokoto empire had to be interpreted and be mutually acceptable to the two Powers in order to effect the stipulated deviation of the Say-Barrua Line.

---

[1] Morel, *Affairs of West Africa*, 1902, quotes Denham, p. 44.
[2] See *The Times*, 9 August 1890. Parl. Pap., C. 6130, *Africa*, no. 9 (1890), lxxxi, pp. 512–13.

Joseph Thomson, who secured the famous 1885 treaty with the Sultans of the twin capitals of the Fulani empire, initiated what may be called the official British assessment of the extent of that empire. During his visit, Thomson had watched in fascination a throng of Mohammedan Fulani, Hausa, Tuareg, and Bedouin transacting a lively trade. He came to the misguided conclusion that the nationalities represented were subject to Sokoto and Gwandu. As regards the latter, its Sultan's 'rule extends over the main river from Lokoja to near Timbuktu'.[1] The exaggerated estimates of the Fulani empire were reaffirmed in the treaties secured by the Agent-General of the Royal Niger Company in 1894. In article 7, the Sultan of Sokoto asserted that 'Asben, Adamawa . . . are included in my dominion.' The Sultan of Gwandu claimed that 'The country of Gurma is included in my dominions—the latter extending to Libtako.'[2] Wallace, the author of these treaties, undertook to tour the neighbourhood of Sokoto and Katsina. He noted the political confusion which prevailed in the region immediately north of Sokoto—a region increasingly dominated by independent Gobir and Maradi—but dismissed the evidence of his eyes with almost criminal levity. The region he traversed was to him merely 'a retreat [of] marauding tribes . . . under the rule of Sokoto'.[3] It is hardly to be wondered at that the French refused to accept what they regarded as fanciful and indeed fraudulent interpretations of the Fulani empire, especially after their own agents had been to see for themselves and collect data on the local political situation.

In the second place, the Say–Barrua Line touched on Bornu territory, with the ruler of which neither Britain nor France had any treaty relations. The agents of both Powers, Wallace for Britain and Monteil for France, had undertaken diplomatic missions for that purpose and failed. When Britain and Germany rather precipitately partitioned the region south of Lake Chad, Britain's basic objective was to keep France out of the regions dangerously near the Nile Valley. The Anglo–German

---

[1] Thomson, op. cit., pp. 160 f. See also F.O.C.P. 5610, R.N.C. to Pauncefote, 11 January 1887.

[2] See *The Times*, 12 November 1897.

[3] R.G.S., vol. viii, 1896; see Wallace, 'Notes on a Journey', pp. 211–18.

1893 Agreement did not achieve the British objective. In the following year Britain tried again to shut out the French, this time by entering into a most peculiar arrangement with Leopold of the Congo Free State. The British Foreign Office 'expert' on colonial questions confessed that 'to keep France entirely off the Nile would be a triumph for British diplomacy and might justify a surrender elsewhere'.[1] This surrender might conceivably include the Chad region. On the whole, the British position in respect of Bornu was very vulnerable, the Say–Burrua Line notwithstanding.

Another factor which influenced the Anglo–French negotiations for the northern boundary was the overlapping of the negotiations for the regions west and east of the River Niger. For Britain, particularly, this overlapping tended to reduce the negotiations to a choice between the exclusive control of the Lower Niger and what the British assumed to be the more northerly zones of the Fulani empire. The dilemma expressed itself in the conflict of priorities upheld by the two most outspoken advocates of the British cause. Chamberlain was prepared to make concessions to France on the right bank of the Niger down to Leaba, as a price for securing the inclusiveness of all that belonged to Sokoto. Goldie thought otherwise. He would rather surrender the whole of Sokoto and Bornu than give the French a place on the navigable portion of the Lower Niger.[2] There were two other complicating circumstances bound up with the negotiations which need only be mentioned in passing. The Germans intruded into the Anglo–French negotiations by claiming treaty rights with Gwandu. This arose from the activities of Dr Gruner, who passed through the region in 1895. Lastly, Salisbury's reference to the Sahara as having what agriculturists might call 'light soil' was to be often recalled by the French negotiators. Lord Salisbury's outburst in an unguarded moment naturally depreciated the

---

[1] F.O. 27/3209, see Minute by Anderson, 12 October 1894. Taylor, 'Prelude to Fashoda' in *The English Review*, vol. lxv, 1950. Hansard, iv, 31, 782; and 32, 388–406. *The Cologne Gazette*, 16 June 1894. Langer, *The Diplomacy of Imperialism*, pp. 127–37.

[2] F.O.C.P. Confidential 7002, see Inclosure 3 in no. 236, C.O. to F.O., 26 June 1897. Also no. 32, R.N.C. to F.O., 27 July 1897.

value of the northern part of the Niger Sudan for purposes of diplomatic bargaining.

Before the formal opening of negotiations by France and Britain for a more specific definition of the northern boundary, the spectacular journey of Monteil from the Senegal to Lake Chad not only created a sensation but indeed precipitated a preliminary kind of controversy. Monteil's mission embraced the sensitive portions of the Niger Sudan, including Say, Kebbi, Zaberma, Mauri, Sokoto and Kuka. The Frenchman claimed, to the jubilation of French newspapers, that he had secured treaties of protection from the rulers of Say, Kebbi and Sokoto. The French therefore drew the conclusion summarized by *La Politique Coloniale* that:

> *Aussi bien au Sokoto qu'au Bornou, l'Angleterre n'avait ni établissement, ni influence, nitraité.*[1]

Monteil also informed his countrymen that Kebbi, Mauri and Zaberma were independent of Sokoto. The fanatical manner in which the French press and geographical societies championed the claims of Monteil was the more serious because most French colonial enthusiasts had always thought that the French government were guilty of stupidity when they accepted the 1890 declaration because at that time, they argued, the British had no better-founded pretensions than the French to the protectorate of the natives peopling 'a problematical hinterland'. The British government called upon the Royal Niger Company to produce appropriate replies to the French contentions. The position of the company was quite simple, in spite of all the fuss. The company called attention to the Say–Barrua Line and rested its case there. As for the territories which the French alleged were independent of Sokoto, the company explained, without producing any evidence, that Kebbi was subject to Gwandu and, through Gwandu, to Sokoto. Conveniently, no mention was made of Zaberma, Mauri, Gobir and so forth.[2]

---

[1] *La Politique Coloniale*, 18 February 1893; *Revue Française*, 15 February 1893. Monteil, *De Saint-Louis à Tripoli par le Lac Tchad*, 1895, p. 253.

[2] F.O.C.P. Confidential 6471, R.N.C. to Rosebery, 8 March 1893. See also no. 153 Intelligence Division to F.O., 10 July 1893.

It was at this point that the Royal Niger Company decided to dispatch its Agent-General on a mission to Sokoto and Gwandu, and to obtain new treaties in which the native potentates would state categorically the extent of their dominions, northwards and westwards. It was unfortunate that William Wallace was not another Dr Barth. He appears to have made up his mind as to the extent of the Sokoto–Gwandu empire even before he set out. Wallace probably believed his own findings, but the French did not.[1] Thus, when the formal negotiations began, the first enquiry which Phipps, one of the British boundary commissioners, made of the British government was to clarify the 'equitable limits' of the kingdom of Sokoto. This issue of 'equitable limits' was the core of the controversy throughout the protracted negotiations. The complicated state of European diplomacy in 1894 was projected on to the local situation. France and Germany made a separate agreement about the eastern and southern shores of Lake Chad. In March, Hanotaux expressed the view that the Say–Barrua Line was intended to be for Britain (but not for France) a self-denying declaration. France might penetrate into regions south of the line, but Britain could not operate north of the line. In any case, concluded Hanotaux, Bornu was outside the sphere of Sokoto and had not been mentioned in the 1890 Declaration.[2] The breakdown of the negotiations in 1894 was caused by the deadlock over Borgu and not by the conflicting interpretations of the extent of the Sokoto empire. As regards the latter, Rosebery made the only honest remark which emanated from the statesmen engaged in carving up Africa: 'To talk of delimiting the frontiers of Sokoto in Europe is absurd.'

Bewildering events were in the meantime taking place in the neighbourhood of the eastern end of the Say–Barrua Line. By 1894 Rabeh, an adventurer from the eastern Sudan, had not only overrun Bornu but was threatening the Sokoto empire itself. The Royal Niger Company watched these developments

---

[1] Ibid., no. 349, R.N.C. to F.O., 28 December 1893.
[2] Ibid. Confidential 6572, see Inclosure in no. 29, Dufferin to Rosebery, 4 March 1894; and Rosebery to Dufferin, 11 March 1894.

with mingled interest and trepidation, but it was prepared 'to interveneso as to bring about an amicable arrangement between Rabeh and the Sultan of Sokoto, which will maintain the peace of those regions'. More reports poured in from all kinds of 'eye-witnesses' to enhance the military reputation of Rabeh. The Royal Niger Company accordingly revised its plans, and began in 1895 to argue that

> There might be a distinct advantage in seeing the tottering power of the Fulahs overwhelmed by Rabeh, who does not possess a sufficient organization, or religious prestige, to enable him to found a similar authority over such vast regions. The way would then be open, after one or two conflicts, for the firm establishment of British power in those regions.[1]

Apart from the new situation created by Rabeh's activities, the details of which will be given at the appropriate time, the Lugard–Decœur race for Nikki, which the French followed up with the policy of 'effective occupation', tended to push to the background the issue of the extent of the Sokoto empire. It was at this diplomatically awkward time, too, that the Germans undertook to contribute their own views on the character and extent of the Sokoto–Gwandu empire. Two German agents, Lieut. von Carnap and Dr Gruner, made much of the treaties which they claimed had been concluded between themselves and Gurma and Gwandu respectively.[2]

The German intervention produced two important results, in spite of the fact that the Germans were subsequently not seriously concerned about the Anglo–French negotiations resumed in 1896. The German view that Gwandu's political influence over Gurma and Kebbi was either nebulous or non-existent coincided with the French contention. The Royal Niger Company was, in the circumstances, forced to reassess more realistically the claims it formerly made for Gwandu. Secondly, the German suggestion that she might claim Gwandu on the basis of Dr Gruner's treaty made it reasonably expedient

---

[1] Ibid. R.N.C. to Kimberley, no. 90, 20 April 1894. And no. 46, R.N.C. to F.O., 21 August 1895.
[2] *Deutsche Koloniale Zeitung*, 29 June 1895.

for the British government to contemplate the wisdom of surrendering to France not only the region of the Say–Gombe–Argungu triangle but also the northern regions of the Sokoto 'empire', in order to obviate any subsequent controversy with Germany.[1] The new positions adopted by Britain and France in regard to Sokoto and Bornu in the resumed negotiations were briefly as follows: Salisbury would accept an 'equitable' arrangement and give up the Say–Gombe–Argungu triangle, provided the French accepted the Say–Barrua Line, to 'be traced throughout so as not to divide the tribes'. The French accepted the suggestion of possible 'compensations' west of the Niger, but the Foreign Minister, M. Berthelot, insisted that the Say–Barrua Line, admittedly not intended to be a straight line, should deviate to the north along the frontier of Sokoto, but should then curve southward along the southern frontier of Bornu, and then upward to Barrua.[2]

The re-entry of Hanotaux into the negotiations in the spring of 1896 shifted the emphasis from the Say Barrua Line to Borgu, where Hanotaux's heart was set on obtaining not only an adequate hinterland for Dahomey but also on securing for France a point on the navigable Lower Niger. This shift occurred at a time when one of the British boundary commissioners, Everett, with the backing of Joseph Chamberlain, proposed to sacrifice Borgu for Sokoto and Bornu. Goldie's intransigence and the action of the Royal Niger Company against Nupe and Ilorin later in the year escalated the boundary question into a crisis already discussed in the last chapter.[3] The French began in 1897 physically to 'threaten' the Sokoto empire. According to Chamberlain, the portions of the empire most exposed to French aggression included Zaberma, Mauri, Adar, Gobir and Kebbi. The irony of the whole situation was that none of the places mentioned belonged to Sokoto during the last decade of the nineteenth century. In the

[1] F.O.C.P. Confidential 6837, see Inclosure 9 and 11 in no. 41, Hatzfeldt to Salisbury, 19 February 1896.

[2] Ibid., no. 33, Salisbury to Dufferin, 7 February 1896; see also Inclosure in no. 22, Dufferin to Salisbury.

[3] F.O.C.P. Confidential 6894, Intelligence Division to F.O., 31 December 1896.

meantime the French sent armed contingents to Gurma, Say and Dendi, where they noted that 'there is more confusion of tongues, such as is described in the Bible, in these parts than anywhere else'. The position was an uneasy one for Britain, whose energies were concentrated on Borgu. The Sultan of Sokoto could not be counted upon, since he felt very sore over the Niger Company's deposition of the Emirs of Nupe and Ilorin. At one point the Agent-General of the company reported that the French had invaded Sokoto, and he was authorized in a dramatic telegram to go to the 'assistance' of Sokoto. In actual fact, the French never seriously contemplated the occupation of any region within the effective frontiers of Sokoto.[1]

The British commissioners in Paris were quite satisfied with Hanotaux's denial of any French designs against Sokoto.[2] They went further and asked their French colleagues 'whether they did not think we might throw over the Sultan of Sokoto and his rights altogether, and endeavour to settle the question on the grounds of the respective interests of the two countries'. The French naturally thought the commissioners' views very agreeable. In the final phase of the negotiations, the settlement of the northern boundary was largely held up by the Borgu controversy, and as Salisbury observed, the negotiations were calculated to determine the lines on which a compromise might possibly be arrived at between the respective claims of Britain and France in West Africa.[3] The French showed no disposition to dispute British 'rights' to Sokoto except in matters of detail. There were also petty problems to adjust in regard to the shores of Lake Chad. In the last month of 1897 Chamberlain listed the places which the British government were prepared to barter. These included Borgu (outside Bussa), Gurma, the Say–Ilo–Niger triangle, Libtako, Yagha, Asben and the Argungu triangle. The Niger commissioners in

---

[1] Ibid. Confidential 7297, for the views of M. Ballot in no. 141, Monson to Salisbury, 12 April 1898. See also Hanotaux, *Le Partage de l'Afrique*, 1909, pp. 295 f.

[2] Ibid., 7144, nos. 3, 177 and 222, 31 December 1897. Gooch and Temperley, *British Documents*, vol. i, nos. 87 and 101.

[3] F.O. 27/3336, no. 438, Salisbury to Gosselin, 30 December 1897.

Paris assumed that the concessions indicated above meant the dismemberment of the Sokoto empire.

Later, the British commissioners privately congratulated themselves and confessed their conviction that 'every vestige of the authority of Gwandu had long since disappeared' in that region.[1] The only complication admitted by the commissioners was the possibility of French military action in Bornu, a place not covered by any British treaty. In fact, it was reported that at that moment, Gentil from the French Congo was already on the borders of Bornu. It would therefore be politic for Britain to recognize the northern and eastern shores of Lake Chad as falling within the sphere of France, before she occupied Kuka. Salisbury and Chamberlain agreed.[2]

Hanotaux's *Projet de Convention* of 16 May 1898 was at first rejected by Salisbury. The latter's subsequent modifications of the French proposals did not seriously affect the outline of the settlement of the northern boundary, which was already discernible and mutually acceptable. The British government would require that

> The circumference of a circle drawn from the town of Sokoto, with a radius of 100 miles, should be the frontier separating the spheres of influence of the two countries to the north of that town.

The boundary, as tentatively described, struck north from the Mauri Dallul, followed the circumference indicated above, then the northern frontier of the 'province' of Gobir. For the rest, the boundary was defined in terms of latitudes, longitudes and straight lines up to the northern frontier of Bornu. The underlying illusion was that Britain and France had shared out the northern provinces of Sokoto, Britain securing Gobir, and surrendering to France Asben and 'the wandering Maradi tribes'.[3] Article IV of the Anglo–French Convention

---

[1] F.O.C.P. Confidential 7144, no. 31, Monson to Salisbury, 20 January 1898; see Inclosure, Memorandum by the British Commissioners.

[2] Ibid. Confidential 7297, Monson to Salisbury, no. 159, 6 May 1898. Also C.O. to F.O., 12 May 1898 and no. 240, Salisbury to Monson, 16 May 1898.

[3] F.O. 27/3413, no. 197; see Inclosure in Monson to Hanotaux, 5 June 1898. F.O.C.P. Confidential 7297, Inclosure in no. 175 Monson to Salisbury, 16 May 1898. Also no. 111, C.O. to F.O., 18 May 1898.

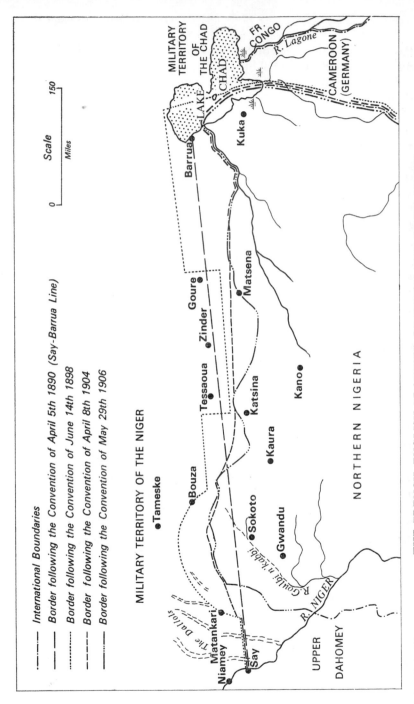

THE FRENCH—ENGLISH FRONTIER BETWEEN THE RIVER NIGER

signed in Paris on 14 June 1898 fully defined the northern boundary.

Very early in this century events in the Central Sudan partly contributed to the French demand for rectifications of the 1898 boundary. Most spectacular of these happenings was the realization of the French dream of uniting their possessions in the Senegal, Algeria, and on the Congo—the meeting place being the Chad. Three expeditions were launched under the leadership of Gentil, Foureau and Voulet. The jubilation occasioned by the success of the missions is admirably summarized as follows:

> *La réunion des trois colonies, si ardemment désirée en 1890, était accomplie dix ans après. C'était la quatrième date historique de l'Afrique équatoriale française.*[1]

In the process of fulfilling her African dream, France realized the literal truth of Lord Salisbury's taunt about the Gallic cock being left nothing to do but scratch the sand. France also provoked a war with Rabeh, the current ruler of Bornu. The route from the Niger to the Chad in the French sphere was a vast desert region without water. A practicable route had to pass through Konni and Maradi and follow the Yobe River to the Chad. It was this kind of route, not a death trap, that France needed. The war with Rabeh was, after one disaster, terminated with the death of Rabeh in the battle of Kouseri (near Fort Lamy) in 1900. The subsequent French pursuit of Rabeh's son into Gujba merely accelerated British and German movements into their portions of Bornu.

In 1900 Britain proclaimed the Protectorate of Northern Nigeria and Lugard was appointed the High Commissioner. British occupation of the new territory did not prove as peaceful as Lugard had anticipated. A conciliatory letter to the Sultan of Sokoto was treated with contumely. From 1900 to 1904 Lugard had to organize military expeditions against one emirate after another—Yola, Zaria, Bauchi, Kano, finally Sokoto. Lugard could now afford to appreciate the 'truc' nature of the Fulani empire.

---

[1] Hanotaux and Martineau, op. cit., vol. iv, pp. 470–3.

> It is stated that [the] government of Foolahs [is] distasteful to population... Gando at war with Argungu.[1]

Reports now poured in from British political officers to the effect that the people of Sokoto lived in constant dread of the Kebbawa and appeared incapable of defending themselves. 'Gando itself would have ceased to exist in a few years' time.' The local British agents were no longer disposed to be soft towards the claims of Sokoto. Col. Lang of the Boundary Survey Commission observed that

> Native Kings will assert their sovereignty over territory lost in war by their forefathers 100 years ago; the Sultan of Sokoto, no doubt, claims all the country now under the King of Kabbi (Kebbi or Argungu) as well as Zaberma, though his predecessors ceased to have any authority in those regions more than fifty years ago.[2]

He would recommend the transfer to France of the Sokoto 'provinces' of Konni and Maradi, which were essential to the French at Zinder. The attempt by the Frenchman Colonel Perez to march to Zinder round the Sokoto arc had ended in disaster, and the French press began to speak of the possibility of abandoning Zinder if a safe route could not be obtained. Lugard at one stage thought that French withdrawal from Zinder would be a good thing for Nigeria. France could not then form a cordon around Northern Nigeria, cutting off all trade from North Africa. Secondly, a strong alien force in occupation of strategic Zinder could always threaten Kano and Katsina.[3]

The local considerations were insignificant against the background of world diplomatic strategy. The relations between Britain and France were already beginning to be transformed into what came to be known as the *Entente Cordiale*. Both Powers accepted the view that

> It is intelligible that on both sides of the Channel an abstract

---

[1] *Annual Report, Northern Nigeria,* 1902.

[2] F.O.C.P. Confidential 7976, no. 20, C.O. to F.O., 5 August 1901 and Inclosure.

[3] C.S.O. 1/19, 3. High Commissioner to C.O., 1 March 1902.

proposal designed to diminish the risk of collision between two great nations must attract the support of all right-thinking people.[1]

The preliminaries to formal Anglo–French negotiations began with private conversations between Lansdowne and Etienne, a leading member of the French Colonial group. They touched upon Anglo–French differences in Morocco, Newfoundland, Siam, New Hebrides, Egypt and Sokoto. The British view of the question of mutual accommodation can be gauged from this summary:

> These six questions, it would appear, may be grouped thus: In Morocco, Siam and Sokoto the French want various things which we have in our power to give. In Newfoundland and Egypt the situation is reversed.[2]

Lansdowne reported that Etienne had dwelt at great length and 'with considerable earnestness' upon the necessity for a rearrangement of the frontier in the region of Sokoto. Etienne expressed the view that the boundary arrangement there had been made in ignorance of local conditions and, in consequence, France was confined to a barren and waterless region which her agents were obliged to traverse on their way to Lake Chad. In the formal negotiations France was expected by Britain to give up her fishing rights in Newfoundland. As Gambia and Egypt were at all costs to be retained by Britain, the neighbourhood of Sokoto was the region left for barter, 'but on a modest scale', as Lansdowne indicated to the British Ambassador to France, Monson.

Once again the French recalled the data on the local political situation collected by Monteil in 1893. They insinuated that the 1898 boundary arrangement ignored the political divisions of the region involved and the conditions of vassalage

---

[1] F.O. 27/3620, no. 251, Monson to Lansdowne, 22 May 1903; also Newton, *Lord Lansdowne*, London, 1929, pp. 267–90 and Grey, *Twenty-Five Years*, Vol. 1, pp. 50–1.

[2] Gooch and Temperley, *British Documents*, no. 359. F.O. Turkey 5302, Cromer to Lansdowne, 17 July 1903. Also F.O. 27/3616, no. 325, Lansdowne to Monson, 2 July 1903.

and independence of the different Sultans. The French also recalled Lord Salisbury's sneer about the soil of the Sahara. In the end, the territorial compensations to France included the regions west and north of Sokoto and also the neighbourhood of Lake Chad. The British government stoutly refused to accept the River Sokoto as the boundary, but France obtained Maradi. The Yobe river was substituted for 'the northern frontier of Bornu' in the remaining portion of the international boundary. These concessions were made, it was reported, on the ground that 'it was inconvenient to divide tribal territory'.[1] The possibility of a further modification envisaged in the 1904 Convention was to depend on the report of boundary delimitation commissioners, Captains O'Shee and Tilho. In the meantime the boundary that was to be investigated was described by Article VIII of the 1904 Convention as follows:

> Starting from the left bank of the Niger (i.e. the median line of the Dallul Mauri), the frontier shall be drawn along this median line to the 'Sokoto arc' up to the point 5 kilom. south of the intersection of this arc with route from Dosso to Matankari, then drawn direct to a point 20 kilometres north of Konni (Birni-N'Konni), then in a direct line to a point 15 kilometres south of Maradi, then follow eastwards the parallel of 13° 20' north latitude until it strikes the left bank of the River Komaduga Waube (Yobe).[2]

Two things were specifically indicated by the British and French governments for the guidance of the delimitation commissioners: the trade routes and 'the present political divisions of the territories so that the tribes belonging to the territories of Tessaoua-Maradi and Zinder shall, as far as possible, be left to France'. The final conference on the boundary was held in London on 29 May 1906. The boundary west of Sokoto was moved further east of the Dallul Mauri. North of Sokoto, Birni-N'Konni was surrendered to France. Lastly, the straight line of latitude 13° 20' disappeared. The

---

[1] Gooch and Temperley, vol. ii, see nos. 383, 389 and 394.
[2] Ibid., no. 417. Also *Accounts and Papers*, 1905 (col. 2383), C111, 241.

boundary was deflected southwards before striking the Yobe River and thus guaranteed the inclusion of Gummel in Zinder territory. As usual there was a provision that the inhabitants of the boundary zone were free within a stipulated time to move to whichever side of the boundary they preferred.[1] The boundary was located on the spot by means of beacons in 1907–8.

The reactions of the ruler of Sokoto and the inhabitants to the Anglo–French boundary arrangements were noted quite early by the British local administrators. The latter continued, quite mistakenly, to cling to the illusion that the concessions to France were made at the expense of the Sokoto empire. This is the explanation for Lugard's lamentation that

> The Emir of Sokoto felt deeply the loss of the territory ceded to France, which had been assured to him by the government when he accepted British protection, but he accepted the decision loyally, though it would probably have been in his power to create much local opposition to the French.[2]

Lugard dismissed the state of Gobir and referred to its ruler mockingly as 'The king of Gobir . . . with an army of 300 or 400 wild horsemen of the desert'. He also forgot his earlier conviction that the Kebbawa of Argungu exercised effective control over the region close to Gwandu and north-east to within twenty miles of Sokoto. The separation of Maradi from the Sokoto empire was technically right, but a problem was bound to arise from the fact that the Maradi could not give up the idea of recovering their ancient capital, Katsina. As Lugard acknowledged in the Annual Report of 1905–6, the Maradi Habe disliked their separation from Katsina. They had no affinities with the desert tribes and would therefore probably wish to migrate into Nigeria.[3] The French creation

---

[1] Hertslet, *Map of Africa*, vol. ii, no. 256, pp. 843–7. Also Tilho, op. cit., vol. i, xxii–xxviii.

[2] *Colonial Reports, Annual, Northern Nigeria*, 1904.

[3] Ibid., 1905–6 and 1907–8. Population statistics for Sokoto Province in 1922 were as follows: Gobirawa, 120,000; Kebbawa, 100,000; Katsinawa, 70,000; Adarawa, 54,000; Zaberma, 4,000; Fulani, 227,000.

of the 'Third Military Territory', involving the political subordination of Maradi to Zinder did not help to mollify the Maradawa. The immigrations of the latter into the neighbourhood of Katsina and Kano during 1907–8 were estimated to have exceeded 20,000.

The French local representatives in Zinder suspected that the Northern Nigerian government deliberately encouraged the immigration of people with their herds from the French territory. They were concerned with this loss of population, and asserted that

> It would be a real calamity for a country where the population is already very thinned, if the principal force we (France) require, strong and active men, continue to go to a foreign country, the harm being still greater owing to the exportation of cattle, the one wealth of the country.[1]

The French therefore attempted to reverse or rather to stop the flow of trade and peoples which had gone on for centuries. Isolated local Cow Fulani groups were offered various inducements to restrain them from periodically migrating southwards. Tuareg nomads who wished to pursue their traditional sojourn in the south during the dry season were required to leave hostages behind. The French also attempted to divert the desert caravans westwards to Dahomey. In the case of the famous salt caravan, they prohibited the export of Bilma salt to Nigeria. In spite of French repressive measures, the Habe, the Tuareg, the Arab continued to ignore the existence of the boundary. They persisted in the yearly trading migrations of their forefathers, and evidence during field work showed that they were determined to go on doing so, customs posts notwithstanding. The basic problem which was bound to arise with locating any kind of boundary in the Central Sudan was in fact accurately diagnosed by Lugard when he warned that

> It is a matter of some difficulty to decide how the conditions of the modern partition of Africa shall be made to apply to these

---

[1] C.S.O. 1/19, 3. See Memorandum by French Commandant . . . in Northern Nigeria to C.O., 2 January 1903.

nomads, and whether they are to be considered as natives of the British protectorate or as French subjects.[1]

The Bornu kingdom presents an intriguing problem in assessing the effects of the northern boundary on this state situated today in the north-eastern corner of Nigeria. The allusions to Bornu during the early phases of the boundary negotiations appeared to have an air of unreality about them. For instance, when in 1893 Dr Kayser of the German Foreign Office produced his memorandum setting out clearly the frontier 'provinces' of Bornu, south of Lake Chad, Rabeh was on the point of crossing the Shari River in Bornu proper. The indigenous dynasty was overthrown and the capital, Kuka, was reduced to ashes. Seven years of Rabeh's rule produced a new state of political affairs. Dikwa, not Kuka, became Rabeh's capital. The independence of Bagirmi, Kanem, and Zinder (or Damagarim) was confirmed beyond any shadow of a doubt. It was only after the overthrow of Rabeh in 1900 that the process of resurrecting indigenous Bornu was begun by Britain, France and Germany. The Bornu which emerged was one truncated through her defeat by Rabeh. The French found Prince Sanda at the village of Berga on the banks of the Yobe River. Sanda, son of the Sultan of Bornu deposed and executed by Rabeh, had lived in Zinder as a mendicant. It was there the French encountered him and reported that he had sought their aid to help him recover the throne of Bornu.[2] This man was proclaimed Sultan by the French at Dikwa but was later superseded by Garbai. The British, and then the Germans, moved in Bornu in 1902. Shehu Garbai was enticed by the British leader of the Bornu 'expedition' into British Bornu. The Germans protested later against the removal of 'a German Sultan . . . to British territory'. The charges and counter-charges exactly reflected the political confusion in Bornu at the opening of the twentieth century. There were now two Sultans, one enthroned in Maiduguri by the British, another installed in Dikwa by the Germans. The two men—

---

[1] *Annual Report, Northern Nigeria*, 1902. See also *Population Census*, 1952, pp. 10–11.

[2] Foureau, op. cit., p. 143.

both members of El Kanemi's dynasty—claimed jurisdiction over the same towns, irrespective of the international boundary. Complaints about the boundary concerned therefore the arbitrary partition of Bornu between two Sultans.[1] The boundary west of Lake Chad hardly affected Bornu because the region north of the Yobe River had effectively passed out of the Bornu political framework.

The chance to rectify the international boundary south of Lake Chad occurred in 1918 when Germany was eliminated from the region. In the Anglo–French Agreement of 1919, Britain recovered Dikwa province but lost to France the former Bornu 'provinces' of Logon, Gulfei and Kusseri which Rabeh had indeed administered as separate districts. Dikwa was not immediately rejoined to British Bornu because it was administered with the rest of the Northern Cameroons as a British Trust Territory. The plebiscites of 1959 and 1961 finally restored to Nigeria the effective frontiers of the former kingdom of Bornu.[2]

---

[1] F.O.C.P. Confidential 7996, see Inclosure in 43, C.O. to F.O., 5 September 1902. *Report on the Cameroons*, 1951.

[2] *Sunday Times*, 23 April 1961.

8

Conclusions

The foregoing chapters have shown conclusively that the international boundaries which today separate Nigeria from her neighbours were the creation of alien diplomats. Within the boundaries are included large ethnic groups speaking innumerable and mutually unintelligible languages and differing from one another in past history, in culture and in many other respects. The idea of unity within Nigeria and the awareness that Nigeria is destined to achieve corporate national existence are concepts of very recent growth which have indeed not taken deep roots. It is natural to expect that the boundaries which demarcate an artificial state should themselves be arbitrary, in the sense that ethnic groups were in many places disrupted. Today there are Buki and Ekoi groups in Nigeria and in the Cameroun Republic. There are Yoruba speaking peoples in Dahomey and in Nigeria. Hausa speaking peoples predominate in the Republic of Niger and in Northern Nigeria. It has been shown that there are two basic historical factors which helped to produce this state of affairs.

In the first place, when the Europeans set out to partition this part of Africa, they were primarily concerned with the acquisition of territories for profitable economic exploitation. Therefore the control of trade routes and the collection of customs duties appeared to the imperialists to be paramount considerations. The Anglo–French arguments for the control of Lagos and Porto Novo, the British determination not to compromise her position on the Lower Niger and the navigable portion of the Benue, the French frustration over their share of the Central Sudan in 1898, all demonstrate the prime importance of the trade motive in the demarcation of the territories which have been discussed. Evidence has also been adduced to show that the requirements of European concord precluded the possibility of European involvement in war over any particular African territory. Thus however bitter the controversies over the disposition of African groups and over the undesirability of splitting ethnic groups, the result was, as a writer put it, that

> *a modus vivendi* was therefore arranged, and the map of Africa was divided up with ruler and pencil. . . . Each Power retained whatever territory it could at the time establish a claim to.[1]

The paramount consideration was the acquisition of territory, with little or no reference to physical, political and ethnological facts. At the same time, the diplomatic negotiations show that wherever possible the boundary negotiators sought and assembled data on existing indigenous states. They invariably began by claiming entire state areas on the basis of treaty relations with those states. The boundary negotiations were complicated partly by disagreements over the limits of indigenous frontiers or the degree of autonomy enjoyed by the states which they enclosed. This consideration brings us to the second factor—the fluidity of African frontiers, in some places, and the lack of coherence of ethnic groups, in others. It cannot be denied that the indigenous states involved in the boundary controversies were not models of stability. Today we speak of the Borgawa and we like to believe that at some time in the past there was a Borgu nation. The facts of the history of that territory during the nineteenth century present a different picture. When the agents of the European Powers could find their way to Bussa, Kaiama, Nikki and Illo and obtain independent treaties as well as conflicting statements in regard to suzerainty, they could only conclude that the Borgu chieftains were independent of one another. No other conclusion would appear to be tenable. Then again, the Hausa speaking groups were found within and without the frontiers

---

[1] Mockler-Ferryman, *British West Africa*, 1898, pp. 4 and 411.

of the Sudan states, and, in their interminable trade expeditions across the Sudan, attached little importance to political
allegiance to any particular state. When at last the Fulani
attempted to stamp a semblance of political unity on that
region, the outcome during the nineteenth century was
political and ethnic chaos. Hausa fought Hausa, Fulani fought
Fulani. Hausa and Fulani fought 'pagans', and the frontiers
which separated the Sudan states were so fluid as to merit the
description of a 'no-man's-land'. Perhaps, too, we can recall
the situation in Yorubaland. Here an empire was in disintegration during the nineteenth century. As a result, civil wars
dominated political relations, and Yoruba groups found
themselves defenceless against the encroachments of Dahomey.
The latter state completely dominated the western frontiers of
Yorubaland, including the 'incorporation' into Dahomey of
the Yoruba state of Ketu.

The lack of cohesiveness of some ethnic groups is best
illustrated by reference to the Ekoi and the Boki. These groups
traversed by the eastern international boundary did not live in
homogeneous groups. Splinter groups had settled where they
wished. Other non-Ekoi and non-Boki groups also moved into
the region to bring about a situation in which ethnic groups
could not even be classified. It has of course become fashionable
to use collective ethnic terms, but one should bear in mind that
the ethnic groups involved here did not evolve comprehensive
communities. Each village group lived a full life unto itself,
but this is not to deny the existence of ritual and other affinities
which did not express themselves in political relations. In the
mountainous regions of the Central Cameroons and the
Wandala there are many groups described as 'pagans'. These
comprised an unparalleled intermingling of peoples whose
precise identity cannot be determined. Their very existence
has often been ignored by the tendency to give the Adamawa
'empire' a comprehensiveness it never had. Lastly, if history is
any guide, the state of affairs in Bornu at the end of the nineteenth century should be a constant warning against being
preoccupied with traditions of past conquest, past glory and
mythical tribal unity. Indigenous Bornu ceased to exist when
it was overrun by Rabeh, and it was indeed the Europeans

themselves who re-incarnated the Bornu which they proceeded to carve up.

Thus, as far as the boundary arrangements for Nigeria are concerned, unqualified suggestions of arbitrariness and subjective criticisms are misleading and dangerous. It was not without truth that Lord Lansdowne observed in 1904 that

> It must be borne in mind that these tribal limits are of the most elastic and uncertain description. A tribe belongs to one petty ruler at one moment and to another petty ruler at another. We cannot, therefore, attribute to such boundaries the sanctity of well-established limits.[1]

No serious student of African boundaries or of the conditions of vassalage which prevailed can honestly dismiss Lansdowne's remarks as merely derogatory. Therefore no objective criticism of the boundaries of Nigeria should leave out of account the realities of political and ethnic conditions which prevailed in the boundary zones at the time the boundaries emerged. If the results of the negotiations are viewed against the background of these conditions, one cannot escape the conclusion that the boundaries represented to a surprising degree the realities which existed at the time.

Perfection is not of course claimed for the international boundaries. The European diplomats worked on insufficient, and sometimes false, data as far as indigenous and political organizations were concerned. In many cases, too, where the data were evident, the exigencies of diplomacy often reduced the boundary negotiations to compromises calculated to satisfy the requirements of European national honour, interests, peace and concord. Of these compromises, ample evidence has been given. This study has therefore attempted to examine the character of indigenous frontiers as well as the complexities of European diplomatic relations in order to tell the full story of the boundary agreements. The result, it is hoped, has been to reveal faults in the boundaries which African diplomats can, without passion and bitterness, rectify

---

[1] Gooch and Temperley, *British Documents*, vol. ii, no. 397, Lansdowne to Cambon, 3 March 1904.

if the need should arise. A writer on Africa adverted to boundary disputes in Europe and rightly concluded that a war could never settle a boundary problem,

> For a frontier is a compromise—it has to be a compromise. When the many tribes of Europe settled down, they did so indiscriminately—they had no thought of modern political conditions.[1]

The Africans obviously did the same. African boundary problems therefore require calm dispassionate consideration of the factors involved, past factors as well as present factors.

As regards the termini on the Atalantic littoral, it can be said that the decisions which potentially marked out the hinterland of Nigeria were 'happy'. The dominant ethnic groups—the Yoruba, the Edo, the Ibo and the Hausa Fulani—were therefore not ultimately disrupted mortally by the boundaries which emerged. This happy situation should not be taken for granted, because up to 1885 there was no reason why the Germans or the French might not have become firmly established on some portion of the coast between Lagos and Calabar. As a matter of fact the Germans did acquire a foothold on Mahin Beach, between Lagos and the Niger Delta. In addition to securing a continuous coastline, the tenacity with which the British sought to vindicate their exclusive control of the Lower Niger and the Benue ultimately proved an advantage to Nigeria. The availability to Britain of the navigable portions of these rivers guaranteed the large solid block of territory which is called Nigeria. The part the Niger has played in the past history of all the major peoples of Nigeria was brought up when members of the Nigerian parliament were consulted on the question of changing the country's name after independence. One member argued vigorously that

> The River Niger has been of such practical importance to the economic and social structure of the country that to change the name now would be tantamount to discarding our heritage and disregard of our country.[2]

---

[1] *Morning Post*, 4 May 1963, p. 5.
[2] *Sunday Times*, 22 February 1959, pp. 8 and 9.

The member should have added that there might have been no country to disregard if British diplomacy had not won unilateral British control of the Lower Niger and Benue, and with them the regions of Nigeria.

The epithet 'happy' cannot exactly be applied to the hinterland boundaries, at any rate not without reservations. The first section of the eastern boundary which separates Nigeria from Western Cameroons is the most difficult to assess. For the same reasons it is the one least open to objection. The old plea of a Calabar political area was recently raised, although not specifically in connection with the desirability of boundary revision. The memorandum submitted by Efik leaders to a Commission of Inquiry on the Minorities of Nigeria claimed the existence of a former Efik empire which embraced the whole of the Cross River basin and was linked 'by some common use of the Efik language, by the Ekpe society, and by a share . . . of a derived culture'.[1] No such empire ever existed, although the British local administrators did their best to use their illusions about an Efik empire in determining the location of the international boundary. The boundary zone was one characterized by ethnic and political fragmentation and by linguistic heterogeneity. Census reports continue to speak of 'a confusing multitude of tribes'.[2] It is therefore quite misleading to speak of the Ekoi or the Boki as if they represented large coherent tribal groups which the boundary split because of the diabolical whims of Europeans. In that zone the major administrative problem is still to persuade small groups which traditionally lived in isolated villages on either side of the boundary to federate into district councils for more efficient, more meaningful local government. The problem of political irredentism is not likely to arise. In the circumstances it is utterly unrealistic to suggest revisions of this section of the international boundaries in order to satisfy tribal sentiments and unity. No one can sanely contemplate

---

[1] Cmnd. 505, *Report on the Commision on Minorities*, 1958, pp. 37, 48.

[2] Ibid., p. 34. *Population Census of the Eastern Region of Nigeria*, 1953, pp. 18–19, dismisses the groups with an enigmatic description of 'Other Nigerians'.

mass population transfers. The more important question concerns the boundary policies of Nigeria and the Cameroun Republic. The boundary has never been properly marked on the ground. There have been instances when the Cameroun police have invaded Nigeria to arrest people who are believed to be nationals of that country but who are indeed Nigerians. The thinly populated Western Cameroons and the over-populated Eastern Region of Nigeria are economically complementary, but the Western Cameroons government fear that if the boundary did not operate as a 'human divide', the Ibo of Nigeria would flood the Cameroons and dominate the economic life of the people. The two governments have therefore recently decided to erect pillars and barbed wire fences along the boundary in order to prevent border incidents. There was no question of boundary revision.

The international boundary between Nigeria and Dahomey technically raises two questions. The mixed communities of Ewe and Yoruba speaking communities at the southern end of the boundary may be ignored because they present no more than a common enough phenomenon of international boundary problems. The views of the Ewe on the Nigerian side of the boundary reveal no wish to leave Nigeria. An Ewe chief from Badagry was until recently a leading member of the former government of Western Nigeria. In fact, most of the inhabitants of Badagry, Porto Novo, Ipokia and other frontier towns are bilingual. The Yoruba and the Egun (Ewe) work harmoniously in local government bodies.[1] Ketu in Dahomey is a different matter. Ketu was traditionally one of 'the corners of Yoruba-land'. Through the fortunes of war Dahomey more or less wrenched Ketu from the Yoruba. Today, however, it contains a substantial number of Yoruba speaking people. There are many Nigerian towns which have their farms in Dahomey, and the Dahomean villages of Ibate and Oke Awo have farms in Nigeria. The Alaketu of Ketu still ignores the existence of the international boundary and, during his coronation ceremonies, tours 'vassal' towns on the Nigerian side. He maintains that

---

[1] See *Population Census of the Western Region of Nigeria*, 1952; Table B, p. 26.

the boundary separates the British and the French, not the Yoruba. The interview with the Alaketu and conversation with youths in Ketu produced diametrically opposed sentiments. A group of young Africans asked in 1959 whether they were Yoruba or Ewe said without hesitation, 'We are neither. We are French.' Of course what was said under colonial rule may not represent the true sentiments of the people. Has the partition of Ketu therefore left a wound? Sentiments of solidarity are being revived among the Yoruba in Nigeria. This feeling of oneness is so far demonstrated in demands for a revision of the regional boundary between Western and Northern Nigeria. The dispute over the regional boundary indeed provides an illuminating situation, not unlike the one posed by Ketu. The details need not be entered into here, but the outline of the dispute and proposed 'solution' provide a useful guide. The Fulani military thrust across the Niger in the early decades of the jihad resulted in the Fulani domination of Ilorin, a territory traditionally occupied by Yoruba speaking people. Nevertheless, the Fulani Emir proudly refers to Ilorin as 'the home of my fathers'. The first internal administrative boundary recognized the domination of the Fulani as a political reality to be reckoned with, and so Ilorin became a part of Northern Nigeria, in spite of the fact that the vast majority of the people were Yoruba. It was later argued that the old conditions of war had passed away and that ethnic and linguistic claims justified a revision of the regional boundary. Lugard's first reaction was reflected in his statement that the existing arrangement had 'received the sanction of time and usage'.[1] Can Lugard's verdict not be applied to the Ketu question?

The examination of the controversy which the Borgu boundary negotiations produced between Britain and France must have made it clear that the final boundary arrangement in this second section of the Nigerian–Dahomian borderland was unequivocally the product of compromise. The argument that Borgu was a political unit was rejected by France. Nor was it held by Britain with much conviction. In retrospect it

---

[1] Cmnd. 505, *Report of the Commission*, p. 75.

cannot be said that the prevailing tradition of a mythical tribal unity provided any background for the emergence of a Borgu community. Nevertheless, the boundary avowedly mutilated the political area embraced by the Nikki dynasty. The confusions which followed the partition have since died down. No amount of inquiry has elicited satisfactory evidence as to the wishes of the frontier towns of Yashikera, Boria and Okuta—places formerly under Nikki princes—which the boundary placed in Nigeria. The Borgawa in Dahomey and in Nigeria have degenerated into almost complete anonymity.[1] Any suggestion of the possibility of an irredentist movement among the Borgawa is a manifest absurdity. In any case, Nigeria and Dahomey have placed no restrictions on the movement of farmers who move across the boundary, although there is evidence that both governments are anxious to demarcate, not to revise, the boundary. The boundary situation has been admirably summed up as follows:

> Continuous contacts between Dahomey and Nigeria have developed through family ties, trade between the territories, and the absence of frontier formalities except for functionaries. Some Dahomeyans even send their children to school [in Nigeria].[2]

Dahomey's heavy imports are still shipped through Lagos.

General conclusions about the sections of the international boundary which traversed the former Adamawa 'empire' and the region south of Lake Chad involve similar problems. Popular criticisms of the boundary completely ignore the existence of 'pagans' who maintained themselves in complete independence. The rulers of Yola are not likely to give up their plea that a large part of the Cameroun Republic should be reunited under Yola.[3] The plebiscites of 1959 and 1961 have settled the question, and the interesting thing is that the portion of the Mandated Territory which amalgamated with Nigeria has not been returned to Yola by the government of Northern Nigeria. It was made into the separate Sardauna

---

[1] See Joyce Carey, *Aissa Saved*, Preparatory Essay, pp. 6 and 11.

[2] *Nigeria Magazine*, no. 70, September 1961, quoted p. 225.

[3] Kirk-Greene, *Adamawa*, pp. 86–87. *Daily Times*, 4 March 1959, see article reproduced from *Le Monde*.

Province. Bornu too has no rational grounds to complain about the boundary which split off Logone and Kusseri. These 'provinces' were never within the effective frontiers of the kingdom of Bornu, and nobody can sanely defend the right of Bornu to her former slave-raiding preserves. The inaccessibility of the areas occupied by innumerable 'pagan' groups, including the Higi and the Fali, and the absence of any feeling of ethnic solidarity, appear to preclude at present the possibility of disputes based on the claim that many of these groups have been split by the international boundary.

As regards the regions effectively embraced in the former empire of Sokoto–Gwandu and also Bornu, the northern international boundary cannot be improved upon. The states mortally affected by the boundary arrangements were states under fugitive dynasties. These included Argungu, Gobir and Maradi. The inhabitants were in any case Hausa and Cow Fulani, and any boundary would have split these groups. No one could have demarcated the Niger Sudan in a way which exactly conformed to the ethnic, linguistic or political conditions which prevailed during the nineteenth century. The emergence of the boundary at first unfortunately reduced contact between the peoples living on either side of it. The establishment of customs posts and the orientation of the economies of the peoples towards the coast rather than to the desert naturally followed the imposition of British and French rule. The French attempted to export groundnuts through Dahomey instead of through the obvious route in Nigeria. Today, however, close amity between Nigeria and the Republic of Niger has tended to restore close contacts between peoples who mostly speak the same Hausa language. The nomadic Fulani take little notice of boundaries, and their cattle are sold all over Nigeria. On both sides of the border, Hausa marriages take place with no respect for national considerations. Trade goes back and forth with little thought for tariffs or customs. History and geography have thrown the two countries irrevocably together.[1] The eastern end of the Nigeria–Niger

---

[1] *Daily Times*, 27 October 1961. *Nigeria Magazine*, no. 67, December 1960, p. 228.

boundary has also begun to symbolize friendship and co-operation. The bulk of the dates consumed in Northern Nigeria, potash, leather works, and embroidered ceremonial paraphernalia cross the River Yobe from the Niger Republic into Nigeria. In 1962 the Bornu Native Authority decided, with the endorsement of the Nigerian Government, to bridge the river at an estimated cost of £23,000, in order to make trade between the neighbouring countries flow more easily. Any visitor to Lagos or any of the regional capitals will not wait long before he is confronted with the highly coloured and decorative poufs and handbags from Zinder which the Hausa peddle everywhere. Economic links have combined with the great bond of a common religion and the use of Hausa as a lingua franca to nullify the effects of the boundary imposed by Europeans on the Central Sudan. Nigeria's only link with the Tchad Republic to the north-east is Lake Chad. This natural barrier has itself been transformed into a symbol of co-opera-tion. A large proportion of Tchad's imports now come from Nigeria, unlike the situation during the colonial era, when the French routed goods for the area through distant Pointe-Noire. Similarly it has been estimated that hundreds of thousands of cattle and sheep go each year from the Tchad Republic to the markets of Northern Nigeria through the Chad, or through the Cameroun Republic.[1] The desire by Nigeria and the Republics of Niger, Tchad and Cameroun to regard Lake Chad as a link rather than as a barrier has taken concrete form in the setting up of a Joint Commission for the development of that body of water.

It can be said that up to the moment no serious boundary question has been raised in Nigeria or by Nigeria's neigh-bours. In general, the international boundaries have not functioned in a manner detrimental to the comings and goings of farmers and simple folk through whose territories the boundaries are supposed to run. If the inhabitants of the boundary zones were consulted on the issue of boundaries, one would probably get a reply admirably expressed as follows: 'Why do people at the capital of our country have to tell us that

---

[1] See Reprint in *Daily Times*, 4 March 1959, p. 5.

we can't visit our cousins a mile or two across the invisible fence ... without permission ? ... We can go among our friends and can buy and sell as we choose on one side of the line. Why can't we be trusted to do the same on the other side?'[1] Apart from the implied kind of innocent intercourse, there are other and reprehensible activities which exploit the international boundaries. At times of taxation or even census, boundary zone villagers tend to move across the boundary to escape their civic duties. The southern end of the Nigeria–Cameroun boundary is an area of large-scale smuggling which continues to flourish in spite of repressive government counter-measures.

The subject of Nigeria's international boundaries cannot be concluded without reference to the possible effects of present-day developments in Nigeria and in Africa. The growth of Nigerian nationalism will undoubtedly tend to undermine whatever unity may exist among the small groups directly affected by the international boundaries. The development of a national network of communication, new economic and social habits are inculcating a new sense of national oneness in Nigerian ethnic groups formerly at odds with one another. In the same way, the diminishing role of chiefdoms in contemporary Nigerian society may finally destroy the traditional foci of tribal allegiances and so neutralize the attractions of common language and culture across boundary zones. In any case, it seems very unlikely that the Government of Nigeria, based as it is on the delicate balance of co-operation among the major ethnic groups, will show undue sensibility to a clamour by any one zonal ethnic group for boundary revision calculated to satisfy tribal solidarity. Thus, in a way, the very complexity in the ethnic and linguistic pattern is perhaps an advantage which the emerging African states have over the more homogeneous European states. The point is that the African states cannot afford to let nationalism become irrational and hysterical.[2] This is not to deny that in a subtle

---

[1] Boggs, *International Boundaries*, 1940, quoted p. 21.

[2] See Reprint from *West Africa* in *Daily Times*, 14 March 1960, p. 5. Namier, *Avenues of History*, 1952, pp. 21–5. Cohen, *British Policy in Changing Africa*, 1959, pp. 46–7.

way the international boundaries are already determining for the population they embrace the language and the ideas which children should study in school, the kind of money which people use, the markets in which they may buy and sell with impunity, the national culture with which the people should be identified, and the territory which the army may be called upon to defend. Nigerians welcome these developments because they know that excessive devotion to territorial units and their past history would mean the revival of the traditions of ancient conquests such as those of the Yoruba, the Bini, dan Fodio, the Kanuri, Yola and the Aro, and little basis would then be left for the continued unity of Nigeria.

Lastly, recent years have witnessed the revival of a movement usually described as Pan-Africanism. It has rightly been claimed that

> The simultaneous effort to create Pan-African political unity and to build effective national societies in Africa creates political paradoxes which, difficult to resolve, may hold the key to Africa's future.[1]

Without going into details about the intellectual perspectives which have inspired the Pan-Africanist movement, it can be said that on the more practical plane three voices represent the trend of political thought. These trends are best illustrated with the words and ideas of the protagonists. President Senghor of Senegal thinks primarily in terms of the unification of the French-speaking African states. His country, he said, 'would extend over artificial frontiers and tribal diversities forming itself by integrating the negro-African values with the impregnating contributions of France'.[2] This ideal would seem to imply a 'cold war' between the English and French speaking states. This point was elaborated upon by M. Keita when he referred to the size of Nigeria and concluded that (French) African unity was the best way to avoid the attraction of the small states towards Nigeria. The ideal of one government for the whole of 'black' Africa was ardently pursued by

---

[1] *Pan-Africanism Reconsidered*, Berkeley and Los Angeles, 1962, p. 81.
[2] See Paris Interview in *Daily Times*, 16 May 1959.

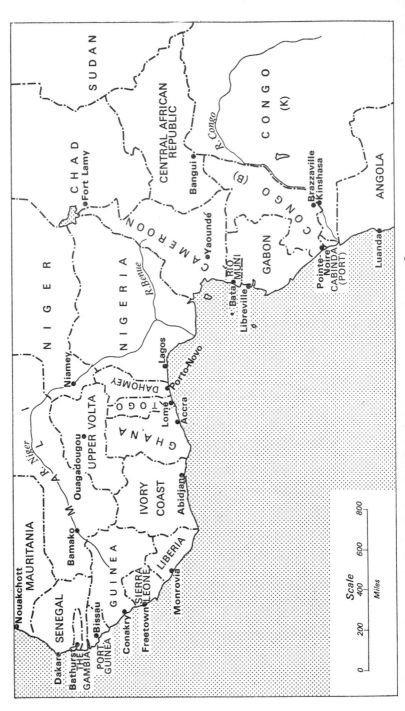

THE STATES OF WEST AFRICA 1967

Dr Nkrumah of Ghana. This ideal was given temporarily concrete form by the union of Ghana, Guinea and Mali. The fate of the union has been anything but encouraging. The more conservative African countries, including Nigeria and Liberia, advocate co-operation instead of outright political union. In his speech to the heads of African states at a conference in Liberia, President Tubman listed the issues which he believed would lay solid foundations for the development of amity among the member states. Among them was the issue of 'working out general principles for the settlement of frontier and border disputes which may arise from the emergence of independent states'.[1] He concluded by emphasizing the need to create a community of economic interest, cultural cross-fertilization as well as free social intercourse and association.

The limited objectives advocated by the conservatives imply a recognition that the international boundaries should become 'a symbol of co-operation, friendship, and mutually profitable trade . . . [and not] one of separation of interests, injustice, fear'.[2] The least statesmanship demands of African leaders is the creation of a vast zone of free trade and free movements in which the lives of the people of the continent will be richer and more secure. Thus only will be eliminated the explosive issue of boundary revision. 'Must Africa renew the proliferation of nations and of national quarrels? It remains to be seen.'[3]

---

[1] *Daily Times*, 15 May 1961, p. 17.
[2] Boggs, op. cit. See Foreword by Bowman.
[3] Davidson, *Old Africa Rediscovered*, p. 268.

SELECT BIBLIOGRAPHY

A. Documentary Sources

1 *British Foreign Office Records*

Confidential Prints, Africa 35 and 38, 1885–1902 (Foreign Office Research Library).

F.O. Series (P.R.O.)
    F.O. 84, Berlin W.A. Conference, France, Germany, 1870–92.
    F.O. 83, 'Africa Various', 1893–9.
    F.O. 27 (France) Africa, 1893–8.
    F.O. 64 (Germany) Africa, 1893–1905.
    F.O. 2, Africa, West Africa, 1893–9.
    F.O. West Africa, 1049, Correspondence, 1916–23.

2 *British Colonial Office Records* (*P.R.O.*)

C.O. 806, Lagos, Dahomey, etc., 1874–91.
C.O. 444, Niger Coast, 1899.
C.O. 445, West African Frontier Force, 1898–1900.
C.O. 446, Nigeria Northern, 1898–1900.

3 *Parliamentary Papers*

1864 XXXVII 287 Col. Ord's Report on the West African Settlements.
1865 Vol. I. Report of Committee on the above, etc.
1885 C. 4284 Africa no. 7 (West African Conference).
    C. 4360   ,,   ,, 2 Further Correspondence.
    C. 4361   ,,   ,, 4 Protocol and General Act.
    C. 4279 The Cameroons.
1886 C. 4739 Africa no. 3.
1889 C. 5905   ,,   ,, 3 (1890) Britain and France.
    C. 6130   ,,   ,, 9 (1890) Britain and France.
1892 C. 6046   ,,   ,, 6 (1890) The Anglo-German Agreement.
    C. 6701   ,,   ,, 7 (1890) The Anglo-German Agreement.
1895 C. 7596   ,,   ,, 1 Report on the Niger Coast Protectorate,
                                                   1891–4.
1899 C. 9375 The Royal Niger Company.
    C. 9046 Reports on the W.A.F.F.
    C. 9334 The Anglo-French Convention (1898).
1903 Cmd. 1433, 45, Correspondence Relating to Kano.

1919 Cmd. 468, 36, Report on the Amalgamation.
1926 Cmd. 2744, Report by the Rt. Hon. W. G. A. Ormsby-Gore.
1958 Cmd. 505, Report of the Commission on Minorities.

4 *National Archives Records*

C.S.O. 1/1, 10–22.
Calprof.

5 *French Official Records*

Documents Diplomatiques Français, 1871-1900, Ière Série, V & VI.

6 *German Official Records*

Die Grosse Politik, Vols. II–IV, VIII, XIV–XVI.

7 *Miscellaneous Documents, Official and Semi-Official Reports,* etc.
(University of Ibadan Library and National Archives Ibadan).

DUGDALE, E. T. S., *German Diplomatic Documents, 1871–1914* (English
Select Translations) London, 1927, Vol. I.
GOOCH and TEMPERLEY, *British Documents on the Origins of the War,*
London, 1927, Vols. 1 and 2 (1898-1904).
Précis of Information concerning the Colony of Lagos, 1888 (War
Office).
Report on the Oil Rivers District, West Coast of Africa, 1888
(JOHNSTON).
Report of Visit to the Niger, Confidential 5913, 1890 (MACDONALD).
Colonial Reports Annual – Northern Nigeria, 1902–1908.
Annual Reports by H.B.M. Government on the British Cameroons,
1925–1956.
HERTSLET, (SIR) F., *The Map of Africa by Treaty,* 3 vols., London,
1909.
F.O. List 1880–1960.
C.O. List 1880–1960.

B. Secondary Sources

1. *General Works*

AJAYI, J. F. A. AND SMITH, R. S.	*Yoruba Warfare in the Nineteenth Century,* Cambridge, 1964.
AJISAFE, A. K.	*History of Abeokuta,* Bungay, 1916, revised, 1924.

ANENE, J. and BROWN, G.   *Africa in the Nineteenth and Twentieth Centuries*, London, 1966.

ARNETT, E. J.   *Gazetteer of Sokoto Province*, London, 1920. *The Rise of the Sokoto Empire*, London, 1929.

AYDELOTTE, W. O.   *Bismarck and British Colonial Policy*, Oxford 1937.

BAILLAUD, G.   *La Politique indigène de l'Angleterre en Afrique occidentale*, Paris, 1912.

BARNES, J. A.   *Politics in a Changing Society*, Oxford, 1954.

BARTH, H.   *Travels and Discoveries in North and Central Africa*, 5 vols., London, 1857.

BEER, G. L.   *African Questions at the Paris Peace Conference*, New York, 1923.

BELLO, MUHAMMAD   'The *Raudthat ul Afkari*' (1823–7), Translation by Palmer in *J.A.S.*, 1916. *Infanku'l Maisuri* (Translated and paraphrased by Arnett).

BENTON, P. A.   *The Sultanate of Bornu*, London, 1913.

BINGER, L. G.   *Du Niger au Golfe de Guinée par le pays de Kong et le Mossi*, 2 vols., Paris, 1892.

BIOBAKU, S. O.   *The Egba and Their Neighbours, 1842–1872*, Oxford, 1957.

BOGGS, S. W.   *International Boundaries, A Study of Boundary Functions*, New York, 1940.

BOVILL, E. W.   *Caravans of the Old Sahara*, Oxford, 1933. *The Golden Trade of the Moors*, Oxford 1958.

BRUEL, G.   *L'Occupation du Bassin du Tchad*, Moulins, 1902.

BUCHANAN, A.   *Exploration of Air: Out of the World North of Nigeria*, London, 1921.

BUCHANAN, K. M. and PUGH, J. C.   *Land and People in Nigeria*, London, 1955.

BURDO, A.   *A Voyage up the Niger and Benue*, London, 1880.

BURTON, R. F.   *A Mission to Gelele, King of Dahomey*, 2 vols., London, 1864.

	Abeokuta and the Cameroons Mountains, 2 vols., London, 1863.
CALVERT, A. F.	*The Cameroons*, London, 1917.
CECIL, LADY GWENDOLEN	*Life of Robert, Marquis of Salisbury*, 4 vols., London, 1932.
CHADWICK, H. M.	*The Nationalities of Europe and the Growth of National Ideologies*, Cambridge 1945.
CHEVALIER, A.	*Mission Chari–Lac Tchad 1902–4*, Paris, 1907.
CHURCH, A.	*East Africa, A New Dominion*, London, 1929.
CLAPPERTON, H.	*Journal of a Second Expedition . . .*, London, 1829.
COHEN, (SIR) A.	*British Policy in Changing Africa*, London, 1959.
COLEMAN, J. S.	*Nigeria—Background to Nationalism*, California, 1958.
COOK, A. N.	*British Enterprise in Nigeria*, Oxford, 1943.
COUPLAND, R.	*East Africa and its Invaders*, Oxford, 1938.
CREWE (MARQUESS)	*Lord Rosebery*, 2 vols., London, 1931.
CROWE, S. E.	*The Berlin West African Conference, 1884–5*, London, 1942.
DALZEL, A.	*The History of Dahomey*, London, 1793.
DARCY, J.	*France et Angleterre: Cent Années de Rivalité Coloniale*, Paris, 1904.
DAVIDSON, B.	*Old Africa Rediscovered*, London, 1959.
DELAFOSSE, M.	*The Negroes of Africa*, Washington D.C., 1931.
DENHAM and CLAPPERTON	*Narrative of Travels . . .*, 2 vols., London, 1928.
DUBOIS et TERRIER	*Un Siècle d'Expansion Coloniale*, Paris, 1902.
DUFF, E. C.	*Gazetteer of Kontagora Province*, London, 1920.
EAST, W. G. and MOODY, A. E.	*The Changing World*, London, 1956.
ELLIS, A. B.	*The Ewe-speaking Peoples of the Slave Coast of Africa*, London, 1890.
	The Yoruba-speaking Peoples of the Slave Coast of Africa, London, 1894.

EVANS, I. L.   *The British in Tropical Africa*, Cambridge, 1929.

FITZMAURICE, E.   *Life of Lord Granville*, 2 vols., London, 1905.

FLINT, J. E.   *Sir George Goldie and the Making of Nigeria*, London, 1960.

FORBES, F. E.   *Dahomey and the Dahomians*, London, 1851.

FORDE, D.   *Efik Traders of Old Calabar*, Oxford, 1956.

FORTES, M. and
EVANS-PRITCHARD, E.   *African Political Systems*, Oxford, 1940.

FREMANTLE, J. M. (ed.)   *Gazetteer of Muri Province*, London, 1922.

FROBENIUS, L.   *The Voice of Africa*, 2 vols., London, 1913.

GAMMIE, A.   *Cruickshank of Calabar*, London, 1938.

GARVIN, J. L.   *The Life of Joseph Chamberlain*, Vol. III, London, 1934.

GENTIL, E.   *La Chute de l'Empire de Rabah*, Paris, 1902.

GLOVER (LADY)   *Life of Sir John H. Glover*, London, 1897.

GOLDIE, (REV.) H.   *Calabar and Its Mission*, Edinburgh, 1890 and a new edition by Dean J. T. (1901).
Memoir of King Eyo VII of Old Calabar, Old Calabar, 1894.

GOOCH, G. P.   *Nationalism*, London, 1920.
History of Modern Europe (1878–1919), London, 1924.
Franco–German Relations (1871–1914), London, 1925.
History of Our Times (1885–1913), 10th edn., London, 1937.

GORGES, E. H.   *The Great War in West Africa*, London, 1930.

GRANT, A. J. and
TEMPERLEY, H.   *Europe in the Nineteenth Century*, 3rd edn., London, 1931.

GREENBERG, J. H.   *Studies in African Linguistic Classification*, New Haven, 1955.

GREY (VISCOUNT)   *Twenty-Five Years 1892–1916*, 2 vols., London, 1925.

GROVES, C. P.   *The Planting of Christianity in Africa*, 4 vols., London, 1948.

HAMBLY, W. D.   *Culture Areas of Nigeria*, Chicago, 1935.

HANOTAUX, G. and MARTINEAU, A.	*Histoire des Colonies Françaises*, 4 vols., Paris, 1939.
HANOTAUX, G.	*Le Partage de l'Afrique: Fachoda*, Paris, 1909.
HARGREAVES, J. D.	*Prelude to the Partition of West Africa*, London, 1963.
HARRIS, J. A.	*Dawn in Darkest Africa*, London, 1912.
HARTSHORNE, L.	*A Study of the Boundary Problems of Europe*, Cambridge 1938.
HÉRISSÉ, A. LE	*Ancien Royaume du Dahomey*, Paris, 1911.
HERMON-HODGE, H. B.	*Gazetteer of Ilorin Province*, London, 1939.
HERSKOVITS, M. J.	*Dahomey, an Ancient West African Kingdom*, 2 vols., New York, 1938.
HINDERER, A.	*Seventeen Years in the Yoruba Country*, 1872.
HOBSON, J. A.	*Imperialism, a Study*, 3rd edn., London, 1938.
HOGBEN, S. J.	*The Muhammadan Emirates of Nigeria*, London, 1930.
HOLDICH, (SIR) T. H.	*Political Frontiers and Boundary Making*, London, 1916.
HOPEN, C. E.	*The Pastoral Fulbe Family in Gwandu*, Oxford, 1958.
HUTCHINSON, T. J.	*Impressions of Western Africa*, London, 1858.
JOHNSON, (REV.) S.	*The History of the Yorubas*, London and Lagos, reprint 1957.
JOHNSTON, A.	*The Life and Letters of Sir H. H. Johnston*, London, 1929
JOHNSTON, H. H.	*A History of the Colonisation of Africa by Alien Races*, Cambridge, 1913.
	The Story of My Life, London, 1923.
	A Comparative Study of the Bantu and Semi-Bantu, Oxford, 1919.
JONES, S. B.	*Boundary Making*, Washington, 1945.
KELTIE, J. S.	*The Partition of Africa*, London, 1893.
KIDD, B.	*The Control of the Tropics*, London, 1898.
KIRK-GREENE, A. H. M.	*Adamawa*, Oxford, 1958.
KUCZYNSKI, R. R.	*The Cameroons and Togoland, a Demographic Study*, Oxford, 1939.

LANDER, R.   *Records of Captain Clapperton's Last Expedition to Africa*, Vol. I, Colburn, 1830.

LANDER, R. and J.   *Narrative of an Expedition . . .*, 2 vols, New York, 1843.

LANGER, W. L.   *The Diplomacy of Imperialism (1890–1902)*, New York, 1935.

LEBON, A.   *La Politique de la France en Afrique, 1896–98*, Paris, 1901.

LEWIN, P. E.   *The Germans and Africa*, London, 1915.

LIVINGSTONE, W. P.   *Mary Slessor of Calabar*, 7th edn., London, 1916.

     The White Queen of Okoyong, London, 1916.

LUCAS, C. P.   *The Partition and Colonisation of Africa*, London, 1922.

     Historical Geography of the British Colonies (Vol. III), London, 1894.

LUGARD (LADY)   *A Tropical Dependency*, London, 1905.

MacFARLAN, D. M.   *Calabar*, London, 1946.

MacKAY, J. H.   *Bornu Survey*, (typescript), 1951.

MACLEOD, O.   *Chiefs and Cities of Central Africa*, London, 1912.

MacMICHAEL, H. A.   *A History of the Arabs in the Sudan*, 2 vols., London, 1912.

McPHEE, A.   *The Economic Revolution in British West Africa*, London, 1926.

MEEK, C. K.   *The Northern Tribes of Nigeria*, 2 vols., London and Oxford, 1925.

     A Sudanese Kingdom, London, 1931.

     Tribal Studies in Northern Nigeria, 2 vols., London, 1931.

MIGEOD, C. O.   *Gazetteer of Yola Province* (n.d.).

MIGEOD, F. W. H.   *Through Nigeria to Lake Chad*, London, 1924.

     Through British Cameroons, London, 1925.

MOCKLER-FERRYMAN, A. F.   *British West Africa*, London, 1898.

     Up the Niger, London, 1892.

MONTEIL, P. L.   *De Saint-Louis à Tripoli par le Lac Tchad*, Paris, 1895.

MOREL, E. D.   *Affairs of West Africa*, London, 1902.
Nigeria, its Peoples and its Problems, London, 1911.

MURDOCK, G. P.   *Africa, its Peoples and their Culture History*, New York, 1959.

NAMIER, L. B.   *Avenues of History*, London, 1952.

NEWBURY, C. W.   *The Western Slave Coast and Its Rulers*, Oxford, 1961.

NEWTON, (LORD)   *Lord Lansdowne*, London, 1929.

NORRIS, R.   *Memoirs of the Reign of Bossa Ahadee, King of Dahomey*, London, 1789.

OLIVER, R.   *Sir Harry Johnston and the Scramble for Africa*, London, 1957.

ORR, C. W. J.   *The Making of Nigeria*, London, 1911.

PALMER, H. R.   *Sudanese Memoirs*, 3 vols., Lagos, 1928.
Bornu, Sahara and Sudan, London, 1936.
Gazetteer of Bornu Province (revised J. B. Welman) Lagos, 1929.

PARRINDER, E. G.   *The Story of Ketu: an Ancient Yoruba Kingdom*, Ibadan, 1956.

PARTRIDGE, C.   *Cross River Natives*, London, 1905.

PASSARGE (DR)   *Adamawa*, Berlin, 1895.

PERHAM, M.   *Native Administration in Nigeria*, Oxford, 1937.
Lugard, Part I: The Years of Adventure, 1858–1898, London, 1956.

RICH, N. and FISHER, M. H.   *The Holstein Papers*, Cambridge, 1957.

ROBERTS, S. H.   *History of French Colonial Policy, 1870–1925*, 2 vols., London, 1925.

ROBINSON, C. H.   *Nigeria: Our Latest Protectorate*, London, 1900.
Hausaland, London, 1896.

ROBINSON, K. E.   *Political Development in French West Africa*, Oxford, 1955.

RODD, F. R.   *People of the Veil*, London, 1926.

RUDIN, H. R.   *Germans in the Cameroons (1884–1914)*, London, 1938.

SELIGMAN, C.   *The Races of Africa*, London, 1957.

SEMPLE, E.	*Influences of Geographic Environment*, London, 1914.
SKERTCHLY, J. A.	*Dahomey as it is*, London, 1874.
TALBOT, P. A.	*In the Shadow of the Bush*, London, 1912. *Life in Southern Nigeria*, London, 1923. *The Peoples of Southern Nigeria*, 4 vols., Oxford, 1926.
TAYLOR, A. J. P.	*Germany's First Bid for Colonies*, London, 1938.
TEMPLE, C. L.	*Native Rulers and Their Rulers*, Cape Town, 1918.
TEMPLE, O.	*Notes on the Tribes etc. of the Northern Provinces of Nigeria*, London, 1922.
THOMSON, J. B.	*Joseph Thomson, African Explorer*, London, 1896.
THE TIMES	*The History of the Times*, Vol. 3, *The Twentieth Century Test*, London, 1947.
TILBY, A. W.	*Britain in the Tropics, 1527–1910*, London, 1912.
TILHO, J.	*Documents Scientifiques de la Mission Tilho, 1910–11*, Paris, 1914.
TOWNSEND, M. E.	*The Rise and Fall of Germany's Colonial Empire, 1884–1918*, New York, 1930.
VANDELEUR, S.	*Campaigning on the Upper Nile and Niger*, London, 1898.
VISCHER, H.	*Across the Sahara from Tripoli to Bornu*, London, 1910.
WADDELL, H. M.	*Twenty-Nine Years in the West Indies and Central Africa*, London, 1863.
WATERLOT, E. G.	*Les Bas-Reliefs des Bâtiments Royaux d'Abomey*, Paris, 1926.
WELLESLEY, D. V.	*Sir George Goldie, Founder of Nigeria*, London, 1934.
WESTERMANN, D. and BRYAN, M. A.	*Languages of West Africa*, London, 1952.
WILLCOCKS, (SIR) J.	*From Kabul to Kamusi*, London, 1904.
ZINTGRAFF, E.	*Nord-Kamerun*, Berlin, 1895.

2. *Surveys and Reports*

FORDE, DARYLL (ed.) *Ethnographic Surveys (of Africa)*
    Part III *The Ibo and Ibibio Speaking Peoples of Southern Nigeria*, London, 1950.
    Part IV *The Yoruba Speaking Peoples of South-Western Nigeria*, London, 1951.
    Part IX *The Peoples of the Central Cameroons*, London, 1954.
    Part X *The Peoples of the Niger–Benue Confluence*, London, 1955.
    Part XI *The Coastal Bantu of the Cameroons*, London, 1956.
Report of the Position, Status, and Influence of Chiefs and Natural Rulers in the Eastern Region of Nigeria (G. I. JONES), 1956.
Church Missionary Society Reports (Salisbury House, London).
Victoria, Southern Cameroons, 1858–1958 (by The Basel Mission Book Depot).

3. *Journals*

Etudes Camerounaises, 57, 1956.
Etudes Dahoméennes IX, 1953 and XIII, 1956. (Le Problème 'Popo').
Etudes Soudanaises 3, 1955.
Institute of Historical Research (London) Bulletin XV, November, 1937, 'The British Attitude to German Colonisation, 1880–5' (M. ADAMS).
The African Society (Journal)
    1908 'From the Niger to the Nile' (BOYD)
    1910 'Historical Notes on the Yola Fulani' (BOYLE)
    1912 'Notes on the Kororofawa and Jukon' (PALMER)
    1916 'Western Sudan History by Bello' (trans. PALMER)
    'Notes on Some Asben Records' (PALMER)
    1923–4, No. 23 'Notes on the "Bororo Fulbe"' (BRACKENBURY)
    1932, XXXI and 1934, XXXIII: 'The Tuareg of the Sahara' (PALMER)
The Royal Anthropological Society (Journal)
    1888–9 'British West Africa and the Trade of the Interior' (JOHNSTON)
    1894–5 'Colonial Expansion' (FLORA SHAW)
    1895–6 'The Extension of British Influence and Trade' (LUGARD)
    1896–7 'The Colony of Lagos' (CARTER)

Select Bibliography

The Royal Geographical Society (Journal and Proceedings)

1879 Vol. I 'Explorations Inland from Mt Cameroons' (COMBER)

1882 Vol. IV 'The Cameroons District, West Africa' (GRENFELL)

1888 Vol. X 'The Bantu Borderland in West Africa' (JOHNSTON)

1888 Vol. XLVI 'Journey to Lake Chad and Neighbouring Regions' (NACHTIGAL)

1890 (Proceedings) Vol. 12 'Notes on the Yoruba . . .' (MOLONEY)

1891 (Proceedings) Vol. 13 'African Boundaries' (HOLDICH)

'Exploration of the Benue' (MACDONALD)

'The Yoruba Country' (MILLISON)

1894 Vol. III 'The Benue and the Anglo–German Treaty of 1893' (RAVENSTEIN)

1895 Vol. V 'The Anglo–German Expedition to Adamawa' (PASSARGE)

1895 Vol. VI 'An Expedition to Borgu' (LUGARD)

1896 Vol. VIII 'The Hausa Territories' (ROBINSON)

'Notes on a Journey through the Sokoto Empire and Borgu' (WALLACE)

1898 Vol. XIV 'The Anglo–French Boundaries in West Africa' (RAVENSTEIN)

1899 Vol. XIV 'The Regions of the Benue' (MOSELEY)

1901 Vol. XVII 'From Algeria to the French Congo' (FOUREAU)

1904 Vol. XXIV 'The Anglo–French Niger–Chad Boundary Commission' (ELLIOTT)

'The Fulani Emirates of Nigeria' (BURDON)

1905 Vol. XXVI 'The Anglo–German Boundary Expedition in Nigeria' (JACKSON)

1906 Vol. XXVIII 'The Geography of International Boundaries' (HILL)

1910 Vol. XXXVI 'The Land of the Ekoi' (TALBOT)

'The Yola–Cross River Boundary Commission' (WHITLOCK)

'The French Mission to Lake Chad' (TILHO)

1914 Vol. XLIII 'The Geographical Results of the Nigerian–Cameroons Boundary Demarcation Commission' (NUGENT)

1915 Vol. XLV 'The Types of Political Frontiers in Europe' (LYDE)

1916 Vol. XLVII 'Geographical Problems in Boundary Making' (HOLDICH)

1935 Vol. LXXXV 'Some Nigerian Population Problems' (NIVEN)
The Nigerian Geographical Journal
1959 Vol. 2, No. 2 'The Evolution of Nigeria's Boundaries' (PRESCOTT)
Royal Niger Company (Report of Proceedings) July, 1891, 1892, 1893, 1894.

4 *Reviews, Magazines and Newspapers* (British Museum, Colindale, and University of Ibadan Library, Ibadan).

Africa, VI, 1933 'The Census of Nigeria 1931' (PERHAM); XVII, 1947 'Yoruba Speaking Peoples in Dahomey' (PARRINDER); XXIV, 1954
American Historical Association (*Annual Report*, Vol. II)
American Political Science Review, XLVIII, 2, June 1904 (KNAPLUND)
Deutsches Kolonialblatt, 1893, 1895 (Articles by UECHTRITZ)
International Affairs XXXI, 3, 1955 (HARGREAVES)
Journal Officiel, 1892
L'Afrique Française (The Monthly Journal of the Committee on French Africa)
Payne's Lagos and West African Almanack and Diary, 1894
Politique Coloniale, January–September 1895
The Cologne Gazette, July 1898
Le Figaro, Le Siècle and *Le Temps* (1889–1900)
The Journal of Modern History, Vol. XXXI, No. 1, March 1959
The London Gazette, June 1885, October 1887, June 1895
The Daily Times (Lagos), 1959–60
The Times (London), August 1890–June 1898
West Africa, 1922, 1937, 1954 and 1956
Universitas II, 3, 1956 (WILKS).

C. Local Evidence

The sources under this category include oral tradition and personal interviews with local political leaders, secretaries of Local Government Councils in the northern, western and eastern boundary zones, and political officers who have had to deal with the problem of trading and migrations across the international boundaries.

Index

Index

Index

Erima, Sabi, 229
Ethiopia, 2
Europe, European Powers, *see* Britain, France, etc.
European Powers, negotiations between, *see* Boundary Negotiations
Everett, 221
Ewe, and Yoruba, ethnic considerations, 141–5, 158; mixing with Yoruba, 46, 158; relations with Dahomey, 162–4; satisfaction with western boundary, 291; territory, 9–10, 42
Eyamba, 48, 61, 64
Ezio, 167

Fada Ngurma, 214
Fadipe, 144
Fali, 97, 98, 102, 103, 131, 136, 294
Fellata, *see* Fulani
Ferry, Jules, 35
Filani, *see* Fulani
Flatters, Colonel, and scheme for railway from Mediterranean coast, 38
Flegel, 17, 70, 111, 113
Fodio, Abdullahi dan, 246, 248, 252
Fodio, Usuman (Othman) dan, 10, 105, 238, 244, 248
Fon, 141
Foncha, John, 91
Forbes, Commander, 170
Foureau, 277
Fra (Frah), 158, 159, 168
France, activities in Bornu, 223, 230; activities in Sudan, **1890**, 38; activities in western boundary region, 174–84; agreement with Nikki, 214; attempts at 'French Adamawa', 112, 122–3; attempts on Niger, 222; attempts to retain population in colonial territories, 282; claims over Borgu, 207; competing for control of Nigerian coastline, 29–31; conquest of Dahomey, 22; debate on colonial estimates **1897**, 221–2; encirclement of Gambia and Sierra Leone, 35; entrenchment in Borgu and along Niger, 215; in struggle for control of Niger, 23, 35, 37–8; negotiations, with Britain, etc., *see* Boundary Negotiations; postwar aims in Adamawa, 135; Protectorate of Porto Novo, 30, 168, 173; relations with coastal states, 44; request for corridor between Dahomey and Niger, 211; request for corridor from Nikki to Niger, 226; submissions to Berlin West African Conference, 40; 'threat' to Sokoto empire, 273; union of Sénégal, Algeria and Congo possessions, **1900**, 277; war with Dahomey, **1892–94**, 188, 210
Free Trade, and territorial acquisition, 23
Freetown, 27
Frey, Colonel, 38
Frontiers, indigenous, affected by northern boundary, 294; and eastern boundary, 87–8; between Yorubaland and Dahomey, 165, 176, 189; determination of, Bornu, 258; disruption, effect on international boundary, Bornu, 261; effect of inland eastern boundary on, 131, 136; factors affecting, 8; importance in relation to failure of Berlin West African Conference, 41; indeterminacy, 6, 19, 286–8, (Borgu), 219–222, (Dahomey), 162, 167, (Egba), 154, (Fulani empire), 252, 256, (Ketu), 185, 187, (northern boundary zone) 266, (Oyo empire), 149, (western boundary zone), 146, 182; influence on European-imposed boundaries,

320